THE

WORD

ON

FINANCES

THE
WORD
ON
FINANCES

LARRY
BURKETT

MOODY PRESS
CHICAGO

Originally published in a different format as *What the Bible Says About Money* (Brentwood, Tenn.: Wolgemuth & Hyatt, 1989).

ISBN: 0-8024-9238-X

3 5 7 9 10 8 6 4 2

Printed in the United States of America

To the many men and women around the country who teach and counsel on a nonprofit basis so that others may know God's principles of finances

CONTENTS

Part 2: Scripture Index

INTRODUCTION

The Word on Finances was never meant to be a book. It actually began in 1971 as my personal study into what God's Word has to say about finances.

After a Monday morning men's Bible study, at which I mentioned that the Bible had more than a hundred references on the subject of money, I was challenged by a participant who said, "I just don't think money is that important to God." Being a pragmatist about nearly everything, I simply went home, took out a brand new Bible, and began my own study on what the Bible says about money.

As I read through the Bible in my study time, I yellow-lined every passage that dealt specifically with finances. I discovered that there are more than 1,000 references to money in the Bible—second only to the subject of love.

I had my secretary type out all the verses I had yellow-lined, thus creating a sequential reference. Then I studied each reference carefully and sorted them by topic, i.e., borrowing, lending, saving, investing, stealing, cheating, and so on. Once these were retyped, I had an index for the biblical principles of finances.

Over the years I have used this "index" or reference thousands of times in writing. It is always on my desk when I am working on some new project about family finances from a biblical perspective. (The information was formerly published under the title *What the Bible Says About Money.*)

The Word on Finances is this same reference guide, updated, and made available to you. I trust you will find it as beneficial and enlightening as I have. The Lord Himself said that if we are not found faithful in the use of money (mammon) we will not be found faithful in other things; so, money really *is* that important to God.

My many thanks to my editor, Adeline Griffith, for her tireless efforts in bringing this project to its finished state.

Also, my unending praise for the tens of thousands of Christians who have committed themselves to being good stewards of God's resources as a result of that early effort. Even one changed life would make this, or any other project, a worthwhile venture.

LARRY BURKETT

PART ONE

TOPICAL
SCRIPTURES

SECTION ONE
ATTITUDES, RIGHT

Our relationship with God is determined in great part by our attitudes. Having right attitudes doesn't just mean learning to live on a budget and tithing to the Lord. Right attitudes include total commitment to God, listening to the counsel of other people (including husbands or wives), dealing fairly and honestly with other people, being humble and thankful, and forgiving others (in terms of debts that are owed). The right attitudes God will honor are spiritual values being reflected through finances.

COMMITMENT

God calls each of us to a radical lifestyle—total commitment to Him. You can determine a great deal about spiritual commitment by what Christians treasure. God's Word says that our treasures will be wherever our hearts are. All that truly matters is what we can do for the kingdom of God. Certainly, the things we accumulate are not important. They are simply tools for us to use in accomplishing God's work.

Sometimes commitment breaks down when a sacrifice is required. We must make a choice about our commitment and there are only two choices. We cannot serve God and mammon.

Delight yourself in the Lord; and He will give you the desires of your heart. **Commit your way to the Lord, trust also in Him,** and He will do it. And He will bring forth your righteousness as the light, and your judgment as the noonday.

Psalm 37:4–6

Trust in the Lord with all your heart, and do not lean on your own understanding. In all your ways **acknowledge Him,** and He will make your paths straight.

Proverbs 3:5–6

Seek first His kingdom and His righteousness; and all these things shall be added to you. Therefore do not be anxious for tomorrow; for tomorrow will care for itself. Each day has enough trouble of its own.

Matthew 6:33–34

Peter answered and said to Him, "Behold, we have left everything and followed You; what then will there be for us?" And Jesus said to them, . . . "And **everyone who has left houses or brothers or sisters or father or mother or**

children or farms for My name's sake, shall receive many times as much, and shall inherit eternal life."

Matthew 19:27–29

"He who is **faithful in a very little thing is faithful also in much;** and he who is unrighteous in a very little thing is unrighteous also in much. . . . No servant can serve two masters; for either he will hate the one, and love the other, or else he will hold to one, and despise the other. You cannot serve God and mammon."

Luke 16:10, 13

I count all things to be loss in view of the surpassing value of knowing Christ Jesus my Lord . . . and count them but rubbish in order **that I may gain Christ.**

Philippians 3:8

Consider it all joy, my brethren, when you encounter various trials, knowing that the testing of your faith produces endurance. And let endurance have its perfect result, that you may be perfect and complete, lacking in nothing. . . . But **prove yourselves doers of the word, and not merely hearers** who delude themselves.

James 1:2–4, 22

As obedient children, **do not be conformed to the former lusts** which were yours in your ignorance, but like the Holy One who called you, be holy yourselves also in all your behavior.

1 Peter 1:14–15

The world is passing away, and also its lusts; but **the one who does the will of God abides forever.**

1 John 2:17

Whatever we ask we receive from Him, because we keep His commandments and **do the things that are pleasing in His sight.**

1 John 3:22

18

CONTENTMENT

In the area of finances, contentment does not mean complacency. Complacency means that I have a problem and I suffer through it with a good attitude; but contentment means I know that I'm in the center of God's will. I change the things I can. The things I can't change I am willing to accept and be content with because I know the One who is in control. The secret of a happy life is learning how to deal with both the good times and the bad and, like the apostle Paul, knowing how to be content with either.

He said, "**Naked I came from my mother's womb, and naked I shall return there.** The Lord gave and the Lord has taken away. Blessed be the name of the Lord."

Job 1:21

He said to her, "You speak as one of the foolish women speaks. **Shall we indeed accept good from God and not accept adversity?**" In all this Job did not sin with his lips.

Job 2:10

Better is the little of the righteous than the abundance of many wicked.

Psalm 37:16

The Lord is my portion; I have promised to keep Thy words.

Psalm 119:57

Better is a little with the fear of the Lord, than great treasure and turmoil with it.

Proverbs 15:16

A sated man loathes honey, but to a famished man any bitter thing is sweet.

Proverbs 27:7

Two things I asked of Thee, do not refuse me before I die: keep deception and lies far from me, **give me neither poverty nor riches;** feed me with the food that is my portion, lest I be full and deny Thee and say, "Who is the Lord?" Or lest I be in want and steal, and profane the name of my God.

Proverbs 30:7–9

The sleep of the working man is pleasant, whether he eats little or much. But the full stomach of the rich does not allow him to sleep.

Ecclesiastes 5:12

Jesus said to him, "**The foxes have holes,** and the birds of the air have nests; but the Son of Man has nowhere to lay His head."

Matthew 8:20

Some soldiers were questioning him, saying, "And what about us, what shall we do?" And he said to them, "**Do not take money from anyone by force,** or accuse anyone falsely, and be content with your wages."

Luke 3:14

"**I have coveted no one's silver or gold or clothes.** You your-selves know that these hands ministered to my own needs and to the men who were with me. In everything I showed you that by working hard in this manner you must help the weak and remember the words of the Lord Jesus, that He Himself said, 'It is more blessed to give than to receive.'"

Acts 20:33–35

Not that I speak from want; for I have learned to be con-tent in whatever circumstances I am. I know how to get along with humble means, and I also know how to live in prosperity; in any and every circumstance I have learned the secret of being filled and going hungry, both of having abundance and suffering need. I can do all things through Him who strengthens me. Nevertheless, you have done well to share with me in my affliction.

Philippians 4:11–14

Set your mind on the things above, not on the things that are on earth.
Colossians 3:2

In everything give thanks; for **this is God's will for you** in Christ Jesus.
1 Thessalonians 5:18

Not addicted to wine or pugnacious, but gentle, uncontentious, **free from the love of money.**
1 Timothy 3:3

Godliness actually is a means of great gain, when accompanied by contentment. For we have brought nothing into the world, so we cannot take anything out of it either. And if we have food and covering, **with these we shall be content.**
1 Timothy 6:6–8

Let your character be free from the love of money, being content with what you have; for He Himself has said, "**I will never desert you, nor will I ever forsake you.**"
Hebrews 13:5

Shepherd the flock of God among you, exercising oversight not under compulsion, but voluntarily, according to the will of God; and not for sordid gain, but with eagerness.
1 Peter 5:2

Now for this very reason also, applying all diligence, in your faith supply moral excellence, and in your moral excellence, knowledge; **and in your knowledge,** self-control, and in your self-control, perseverance, and in your perseverance, godliness.

2 Peter 1:5–6

COUNSEL OF OTHERS

Balance is what God teaches us—the balance between verses that say it is a wise person who seeks the counsel of many others and verses that warn if we listen to too many people we will go astray. Somewhere in between is the balance. God wants us to be open, listen to people with the same value systems, but not follow their direction for our lives too closely; rather, use it cautiously—as counsel in finding God's direction.

How blessed is the man who does not walk in the counsel of the wicked, nor stand in the path of sinners, nor sit in the seat of the scoffers! But his delight is in the law of the Lord, and in His law he meditates day and night.

Psalm 1:1–2

A wise man will hear and increase in learning, **and a man of understanding will acquire wise counsel.**

Proverbs 1:5

Give instruction to a wise man, and he will be still wiser, teach a righteous man, and he will increase his learning.

Proverbs 9:9

Where there is no guidance, the people fall, but in abundance of counselors there is victory.

Proverbs 11:14

Whoever loves discipline loves knowledge, but he who hates reproof is stupid.

Proverbs 12:1

The way of a fool is right in his own eyes, but a wise man is he who listens to counsel.

Proverbs 12:15

He who speaks the truth tells what is right, but a false witness, deceit.
Proverbs 12:17

Anxiety in the heart of a man weighs it down, but a good word makes it glad.
Proverbs 12:25

Through presumption comes nothing but strife, but with **those who receive counsel is wisdom.**
Proverbs 13:10

Poverty and shame will come to him who neglects discipline, but he who regards reproof will be honored.
Proverbs 13:18

He who walks with wise men will be wise, but the companion of fools will suffer harm.
Proverbs 13:20

The naive believes everything, but the prudent man considers his steps.
Proverbs 14:15

Without consultation, plans are frustrated, but with many counselors they succeed.
Proverbs 15:22

Listen to counsel and accept discipline, that you may be wise the rest of your days.
Proverbs 19:20

Prepare plans by consultation, and make war by wise guidance.
Proverbs 20:18

By wise guidance you will wage war, and in abundance of counselors there is victory.
Proverbs 24:6

Oil and perfume make the heart glad, so **a man's counsel is sweet** to his friend. **Do not forsake your own friend** or your father's friend, and do not go to your brother's house in the day of your calamity; better is a neighbor who is near than a brother far away.

Proverbs 27:9–10

A poor, yet wise lad is better than an old and foolish king who no longer knows how to receive instruction.

Ecclesiastes 4:13

"**If your brother sins, go and reprove him in private;** if he listens to you, you have won your brother. But if he does not listen to you, take one or two more with you, so that by the mouth of two or three witnesses every fact may be confirmed. And if he refuses to listen to them, tell it to the church; and if he refuses to listen even to the church, let him be to you as a Gentile and a tax-gatherer."

Matthew 18:15–17

So then each one of us shall give account of himself to God.

Romans 14:12

FAIRNESS

The first step in establishing the principle of fairness is to recognize that all people are important, regardless of their position. God is not concerned about what others think is fair, only what He thinks is fair. From God's perspective, fairness is determined by your attitude toward other people and the way you treat them. Do you treat others the way you would want them to treat you if the situations were reversed?

Therefore **he treated Abram well for her sake;** and gave him sheep and oxen and donkeys and male and female servants and female donkeys and camels.

Genesis 12:16

"That which was torn of beasts I did not bring to you; **I bore the loss of it myself.** You required it of my hand whether stolen by day or stolen by night."

Genesis 31:39

Esau took his wives and his sons and his daughters and all his household, and his livestock and all his cattle and all his goods which he had acquired in the land of Canaan, **and went to another land away from his brother Jacob. For their property had become too great for them to live together,** and the land where they sojourned could not sustain them because of their livestock.

Genesis 36:6–7

Nor shall you be partial to a poor man in his dispute."

Exodus 23:3

"**Nor shall you glean your vineyard,** nor shall you gather the fallen fruit of your vineyard; you shall leave them for the needy and for the stranger. I am the Lord your God."

Leviticus 19:10

"**You shall not show partiality in judgment;** you shall hear the small and the great alike. You shall not fear man, for the judgment is God's. And the case that is too hard for you, you shall bring to me, and I will hear it."

Deuteronomy 1:17

"**You shall not distort justice;** you shall not be partial, and you shall not take a bribe, for a bribe blinds the eyes of the wise and perverts the words of the righteous."

Deuteronomy 16:19

"**You shall not see your countryman's ox or his sheep straying away, and pay no attention to them;** you shall certainly bring them back to your countryman. And if your countryman is not near you, or if you do not know him, then you shall bring it home to your house, and it shall remain with you until your countryman looks for it; then you shall restore it to him."

Deuteronomy 22:1–2

"**You shall not see your countryman's donkey or his ox fallen down on the way, and pay no attention to them;** you shall certainly help him to raise them up."

Deuteronomy 22:4

"**You shall not pervert the justice due an alien** or an orphan, nor take a widow's garment in pledge."

Deuteronomy 24:17

The fear of the Lord is clean, enduring forever; the judgments of the Lord are true; they are righteous altogether. They are more desirable than gold, yes, than much fine gold.

Psalm 19:9–10

I know that **the Lord will maintain the cause of the afflicted,** and justice for the poor.

Psalm 140:12

The Lord protects the strangers; **he supports the fatherless and the widow;** but He thwarts the way of the wicked.

Psalm 146:9

Then you will discern righteousness and justice and equity and every good course.

Proverbs 2:9

What is desirable in a man is his kindness, and it is better to be a poor man than a liar.

Proverbs 19:22

"**Do not mistreat** or do violence to the stranger, **the orphan, or the widow;** and do not shed innocent blood in this place."

Jeremiah 22:3

"Therefore, O king, may my advice be pleasing to you: **break away now from your sins** by doing righteousness, and from your iniquities **by showing mercy to the poor,** in case there may be a prolonging of your prosperity."

Daniel 4:27

Thus has the Lord of hosts said, "Dispense true justice, and practice kindness and compassion each to his brother; and **do not oppress the widow or the orphan,** the stranger or the poor; and do not devise evil in your hearts against one another."

Zechariah 7:9–10

"For this reason **the kingdom of heaven may be compared to a certain king who wished to settle accounts with his slaves.** And when he had begun to settle them, there was brought to him one who owed him ten thousand talents. But since he did not have the means to repay, his lord commanded him to be sold, along with his wife and children and all that he had, and repayment to be made. The slave therefore falling down, prostrated himself before him, saying, 'Have patience with me, and I will repay you everything.' And the lord of that slave felt compassion and released him and forgave him the debt. But that slave went out and found one of his fellow slaves who owed him a hundred denarii; and he seized him and began to choke him, saying, 'Pay back what you owe.' So his fellow slave fell down and began to entreat him, saying, 'Have patience with me and I will repay you.' He was unwilling however, but went and threw him in prison until he should pay back what was owed. So when his fellow slaves saw what had happened, they were deeply grieved and came and reported to their lord all that had happened. Then summoning him, his lord said to him, 'You wicked slave, I forgave you all that debt because you entreated me. Should you not also have had mercy on your fellow slave, even as I had mercy on you?' And his lord, moved with anger, handed him over to the torturers until he should repay all that was owed him. So shall My heavenly Father also do to you, if each of you does not forgive his brother from your heart."

Matthew 18:23–35

He was saying to them, "Take care what you listen to. **By your standard of measure it shall be measured to you;** and more shall be given you besides."

Mark 4:24

FORGIVENESS

The biblical principle of financial forgiveness is a clear one. It means that you put aside a wrong suffered, never to be remembered again, even if someone has deceived you or cheated you financially. How far does forgiveness extend? As far as the Lord is concerned, it stretches without end. In our society, we all will have an opportunity to exercise forgiveness.

Do not rejoice when your enemy falls, and do not let your heart be glad when he stumbles; lest the Lord see it and be displeased, and He turn away His anger from him.

Proverbs 24:17–18

If your enemy is hungry, give him food to eat; and if he is thirsty, give him water to drink; for you will heap burning coals on his head, and the Lord will reward you.

Proverbs 25:21–22

He who conceals his transgressions will not prosper, but he who confesses and forsakes them will find compassion.

Proverbs 28:13

"**If you do not forgive men,** then your Father will not forgive your transgressions."

Matthew 6:15

"For this reason **the kingdom of heaven may be compared to a certain king who wished to settle accounts with his slaves.** And when he had begun to settle them, there was brought to him one who owed him ten thousand talents. But since he did not have the means to repay, his lord commanded him to be sold, along with his wife and children and all that he had, and repayment to be made. The slave therefore falling down, prostrated himself before him, saying, 'Have patience with me, and I will repay you everything.' And the lord of that slave felt compassion and released him and forgave him the debt. But that slave went out and found one of his fellow slaves who owed him a hundred denarii; and he seized him and began to choke him, saying, 'Pay back what you owe.' So his fellow slave fell down and began to entreat him, saying, 'Have patience with me and I will repay you.' He was unwilling however, but went and threw him in prison until he should pay back what was owed. So when his fellow slaves saw what had happened, they were deeply grieved and came and reported to their lord all that had happened. Then summoning him, his lord said to him, 'You wicked slave, I forgave you all that debt because you entreated me. Should you not also have had mercy on your fellow slave, even as I had mercy on you?' And his lord, moved with anger, handed him over to the torturers until he should repay all that was owed him. So shall My heavenly Father also do to you, if each of you does not forgive his brother from his heart."

Matthew 18:23–35

"Whenever you stand praying, **forgive,** if you have anything against anyone; **so that your Father** also who is in heaven **may forgive you** your transgressions."

Mark 11:25

"A certain moneylender had two debtors: one owed five hundred denarii, and the other fifty. When they were unable to repay, he graciously forgave them both. Which of them therefore will love him more?"

Luke 7:41–42

"Be on your guard! If your brother sins, rebuke him; and **if he repents, forgive him.**"

Luke 17:3

"Therefore, let it be known to you, brethren, that **through Him forgiveness of sins is proclaimed** to you."

Acts 13:38

HONESTY

Our usefulness to God is directly proportional to our honesty. We should never allow ourselves to be trapped into anything that is unethical, immoral, or dishonest, no matter how inviting it seems. According to God's Word, honesty means telling the whole truth, regardless of how much it costs. It means revealing the whole truth, even when it isn't necessary. There are no small lies—only lies; there are no small thefts—only thefts.

"**Such shall be my wages.** So my honesty will answer for me later, when you come concerning my wages. Every one that is not speckled and spotted among the goats and black among the lambs, if found with me, will be considered stolen."

Genesis 30:32–33

"Furthermore, you shall select out of all the people able men who fear God, men of truth, **those who hate dishonest gain;** and you shall place these over them, as leaders of thousands, of hundreds, of fifties and of tens."

Exodus 18:21

"**You shall not swear falsely** by My name, so as to profane the name of your God; I am the Lord."

Leviticus 19:12

You shall do no wrong in judgment, in measurement of weight, or capacity. **You shall have just balances, just weights,** a just ephah, and a just hin: I am the Lord your God, who brought you out from the land of Egypt."

Leviticus 19:35–36

"**You shall surely set a king** over you whom the Lord your God chooses, one from among your countrymen you shall set as king over yourselves; you may not put a foreigner over yourselves who is not your countryman. Moreover, **he**

shall not multiply horses for himself, nor shall he cause the people to return to Egypt to multiply horses, since the Lord has said to you, 'You shall never again return that way.' Neither shall he multiply wives for himself, lest his heart turn away; nor shall he greatly increase silver and gold for himself."

Deuteronomy 17:15–17

"Here I am; bear witness against me before the Lord and His anointed. Whose ox have I taken, or whose donkey have I taken, or **whom have I defrauded? Whom have I oppressed,** or from whose hand have I taken a bribe to blind my eyes with it? I will restore it to you."

1 Samuel 12:3

The Lord said to Satan, "**Have you considered My servant Job?** For there is no one like him on the earth, a blameless and upright man fearing God and turning away from evil. And he still holds fast his integrity, although you incited Me against him, to ruin him without cause."

Job 2:3

Do not let kindness and truth leave you; bind them around your neck, write them on the tablet of your heart. So you will find favor and good repute in the sight of God and man.

Proverbs 3:3–4

He who walks in integrity walks securely, but he who perverts his ways will be found out.

Proverbs 10:9

The mouth of the righteous flows with wisdom, but the perverted tongue will be cut out. **The lips of the righteous bring forth what is acceptable,** but the mouth of the wicked, what is perverted.

Proverbs 10:31–32

The integrity of the upright will guide them, but the false-ness of the treacherous will destroy them.

Proverbs 11:3

The thoughts of the righteous are just, but the counsels of the wicked are deceitful.

Proverbs 12:5

He who speaks truth tells what is right, but a false witness, deceit.

Proverbs 12:17

He who walks in his uprightness fears the Lord, but he who is crooked in his ways despises Him.

Proverbs 14:2

A just balance and scales belong to the Lord; all the weights of the bag are His concern.

Proverbs 16:11

Better is a poor man who walks in his integrity than he who is perverse in speech and is a fool.

Proverbs 19:1

Differing weights and differing measures, **both of them are abominable to the Lord.**

Proverbs 20:10

A wicked man shows a bold face, but as for the upright, he makes his way sure.

Proverbs 21:29

A good name is more desired than great riches, favor is better than silver and gold.

Proverbs 22:1

Better is the poor who walks in his integrity, than he who is crooked though he be rich.

Proverbs 28:6

When the righteous triumph, there is great glory, but **when the wicked rise, men hide themselves. He who conceals his transgressions will not prosper,** but he who confesses and forsakes them will find compassion.

Proverbs 28:12–13

He who walks righteously, and speaks with sincerity, **he who rejects unjust gain,** and shakes his hands so that they hold no bribe; he who stops his ears from hearing about bloodshed, and shuts his eyes from looking upon evil.

Isaiah 33:15

You shall have just balances, a just ephah, and a just bath. The ephah and the bath shall be the same quantity, so that the bath may contain a tenth of a homer, and the ephah a tenth of a homer; their standard shall be according to the homer. And the shekel shall be twenty gerahs; twenty shekels, twenty-five shekels, and fifteen shekels shall be your maneh."

Ezekiel 45:10–12

"The good man out of his good treasure brings forth what is good; and the evil man out of his evil treasure brings forth what is evil."

Matthew 12:35

"You know the commandments, 'Do not murder, Do not commit adultery, Do not steal, Do not bear false witness, **Do not defraud,** Honor your father and mother.'"

Mark 10:19

Some tax-gatherers also came to be baptized, and they said to him, "Teacher, what shall we do?" And he said to them, **"Collect no more than what you have been ordered to."**

Luke 3:12–13

"You shall not commit adultery, You shall not murder, You shall not steal, You shall not covet," and if there is any other commandment, it is summed up in this saying, "You shall love your neighbor as yourself."

Romans 13:9

We are not like many, peddling the word of God, but as from sincerity, but as from God, we speak in Christ in the sight of God.

2 Corinthians 2:17

Deacons likewise must be **men of dignity,** not double-tongued, or addicted to much wine or **fond of sordid gain.**

1 Timothy 3:8

The overseer must be above reproach as God's steward, not self-willed, not quick-tempered, not addicted to wine, not pugnacious, not fond of sordid gain.

Titus 1:7

Not pilfering, but showing all good faith that they may adorn the doctrine of God our Savior in every respect.

Titus 2:10

HUMILITY

E ven though Christ is the most exalted being in the eternal kingdom of God, He assumed the lowliest, most humbling position possible during His lifetime. God wants us to question the condition of our hearts. Do we really consider ourselves higher than someone else simply because we may have the ability to earn more money or have more advantages? We might not have even earned the money but, instead, inherited it. Either way, having humility means we can accept God's blessings without feeling superior to any other individual.

"My people who are called by My name humble themselves and pray, and seek My face and turn from their wicked ways, then I will hear from heaven, will forgive their sin, and will heal their land."

2 Chronicles 7:14

The humble will inherit the land, and will delight themselves in abundant prosperity.

Psalm 37:11

O Lord, **my heart is not proud,** nor my eyes haughty; nor do I involve myself in great matters, or in things too difficult for me. Surely I have composed and quieted my soul; like a weaned child rests against his mother, my soul is like a weaned child within me.

Psalm 131:1–2

Better is he who is lightly esteemed and has a servant, than he who honors himself and lacks bread.

Proverbs 12:9

The fear of the Lord is the instruction for wisdom, and **before honor comes humility.**

Proverbs 15:33

Better is a little with righteousness than great income with injustice.

Proverbs 16:8

The reward of humility and the fear of the Lord **are riches,** honor and life.

Proverbs 22:4

A man's pride will bring him low, but a humble spirit will obtain honor.

Proverbs 29:23

The pride of man will be humbled, and the **loftiness of men will be abased,** and the Lord alone will be exalted in that day.

Isaiah 2:17

"To this one **I will look, to him who is humble** and contrite of spirit, and who trembles at My word."

Isaiah 66:2

What does the Lord require of you but to do justice, to love kindness, and to **walk humbly** with your God?

Micah 6:8

"**Make friends quickly with your opponent at law** while you are with him on the way, in order that your opponent may not deliver you to the judge, and the judge to the officer, and you be thrown into prison. Truly I say to you, you shall not come out of there, until you have paid up the last cent."

Matthew 5:25–26

"You have heard that it was said, 'An eye for an eye, and a tooth for a tooth.' But I say to you, do not resist him who is evil; but whoever slaps you on your right cheek, turn to him the other also. And **if anyone wants to sue you, and take your shirt, let him have your coat also.**"

Matthew 5:38–40

"You have heard that it was said, 'You shall love your neighbor, and hate your enemy.' But I say to you, love your enemies, and pray for those who persecute you in order that you may be sons of your Father who is in heaven; for He causes His sun to rise on the evil and the good, and sends rain on the righteous and the unrighteous. **For if you love those who love you, what reward have you?** Do not even the tax-gatherers do the same?"

Matthew 5:43–46

"Beware of practicing your righteousness before men to be noticed by them; otherwise you have no reward with your Father who is in heaven."

Matthew 6:1

"**Whoever then humbles himself** as this child, he is the greatest in the kingdom of heaven."

Matthew 18:4

Jesus called them to Himself, and said, "You know that the rulers of the Gentiles lord it over them, and their great men exercise authority over them. It is not so among you, but whoever wishes to become great among you shall be your servant, and whoever wishes to be first among you shall be your slave."

Matthew 20:25–27

"**Whoever exalts himself shall be humbled; and whoever humbles himself shall be exalted.**"

Matthew 23:12

He called the twelve and said to them, "**If anyone wants to be first, he shall be last of all,** and servant of all."

Mark 9:35

"**Everyone who exalts himself shall be humbled,** and he who humbles himself shall be exalted."

Luke 14:11

"**Two men went up into the temple to pray,** one a Pharisee, and the other a tax-gatherer. The Pharisee stood and was praying thus to himself, 'God, I thank Thee that I am not like other people; swindlers, unjust, adulterers, or even like this tax-gatherer. I fast twice a week; I pay tithes of all that I get.' But the tax-gatherer, standing some distance away, was even unwilling to lift up his eyes to heaven, but was beating his breast, saying, 'God, be merciful to me, the sinner!' I tell you, this man went down to his house justified rather than the other; for everyone who exalts himself shall be humbled, but he who humbles himself shall be exalted."

Luke 18:10–14

Be of the same mind toward one another; **do not be haughty in mind, but associate with the lowly.** Do not be wise in your own estimation. Never pay back evil for evil to anyone. Respect what is right in the sight of all men.

Romans 12:16–17

Do nothing from selfishness or empty conceit, but with humility of mind let each of you regard one another as more important than himself.

Philippians 2:3

Humble yourselves, therefore, under the mighty hand of God, **that He may exalt you** at the proper time.

1 Peter 5:6

"**I know your tribulation and your poverty** (but you are rich), and the blasphemy by those who say they are Jews and are not, but are a synagogue of Satan."

Revelation 2:9

OBEDIENCE

Since finances is one of the most often discussed topics in the New Testament, it would seem obvious that God would use that area to test our obedience to Him. We must come to the point that God's approval is more important than the world's riches. Being obedient means being willing to do what God's Word says, regardless of the cost. Then, and only then, will the full measure of God's peace and power be experienced.

Moses gave the ransom money to Aaron and to his sons, at the command of the Lord, just as the Lord had commanded Moses.

Numbers 3:51

"I will indeed honor you richly, and I will do whatever you say to me. Please come then, curse this people for me." And Balaam answered and said to the servants of Balak, "Though Balak were to give me his house full of silver and gold, I could not do anything, either small or great, contrary to the command of the Lord my God."

Numbers 22:17–18

"Though Balak were to give me his house full of silver and gold, I could not do anything contrary to the command of the Lord, either good or bad, of my own accord. What the Lord speaks, that I will speak."

Numbers 24:13

"You shall observe to do just as the Lord your God has commanded you; **you shall not turn aside to the right or to the left."**

Deuteronomy 5:32

"The Lord shall make you the head and not the tail, and you only shall be above, and you shall not be underneath, if you will listen to the commandments of the Lord your God, which I charge you today, to observe them carefully."

Deuteronomy 28:13

"The word is very near you, in your mouth and in your heart, that you may observe it. See, I have set before you today **life and prosperity, and death and adversity.**"

Deuteronomy 30:14–15

"If it is disagreeable in your sight to serve the Lord, **choose for yourselves today whom you will serve:** whether the gods which your fathers served which were beyond the River, or the gods of the Amorites in whose land you are living; but as for me and my house, we will serve the Lord."

Joshua 24:15

"**I will raise up for Myself a faithful priest** who will do according to what is in my heart and in My soul; and I will build him an enduring house, and he will walk before My anointed always. And it shall come about that everyone who is left in your house shall come and bow down to him for a piece of silver or a loaf of bread, and say, 'Please assign me to one of the priest's offices so that I may eat a piece of bread.'"

1 Samuel 2:35–36

"**Please, give back to them this very day their fields,** their vineyards, their olive groves, and their houses, also the hundredth part of the money and of the grain, the new wine, and the oil that you are exacting from them." Then they said, "We will give it back and will require nothing from them; we will do exactly as you say." So I called the priests and took an oath from them that they would do according to this promise. I also shook out the front of my garment and said, "Thus may God shake out every man from his house and from his possessions who does not fulfill this promise; even thus may he be shaken out and emptied." And all the assembly said, "Amen!" And they praised the Lord. Then the people did according to this promise.

Nehemiah 5:11–13

My eyes shall be upon the faithful of the land, that they may dwell with me; he who walks in a blameless way is the one who will minister to me.

Psalm 101:6

My son, **if sinners entice you, do not consent.**

Proverbs 1:10

Righteousness exalts a nation, but sin is a disgrace to any people.

Proverbs 14:34

"If you consent and obey, you will eat the best of the land; but **if you refuse and rebel,** you will be devoured by the sword."

Isaiah 1:19

"**No one can serve two masters;** for either he will hate the one and love the other, or he will hold to one and despise the other. You cannot serve God and mammon."

Matthew 6:24

"So then, **you will know them by their fruits.**"

Matthew 7:20

Another of the disciples said to Him, "Lord, permit me first to go and bury my father." But Jesus said to him, "Follow Me; and **allow the dead to bury their own dead.**"

Matthew 8:21–22

He presented another parable to them, saying, "The kingdom of heaven may be compared to **a man who sowed good seed in his field.**"

Matthew 13:24

Jesus said to His disciples, "If anyone wishes to come after Me, **let him deny himself, and take up his cross, and follow Me.**"

Matthew 16:24

Peter answered and said to Him, "**Behold, we have left everything** and followed You; what then will there be for us?"

Matthew 19:27

"Everyone who has left houses or brothers or sisters or father or mother or children or farms for My name's sake, shall receive many times as much, and shall inherit eternal life."

Matthew 19:29

"**Blessed is that slave whom his master finds so doing** when he comes. Truly I say to you, that he will put him in charge of all his possessions."

Matthew 24:46–47

When they had brought their boats to land, they left everything and followed Him.

Luke 5:11

He left everything behind, and rose and began to follow Him.

Luke 5:28

"Take care how you listen; **for whoever has, to him shall more be given;** and whoever does not have, even what he thinks he has shall be taken away from him."

Luke 8:18

He was saying to them all, "If anyone wishes to come after Me, let him deny himself, and **take up his cross daily,** and follow Me."

Luke 9:23

Another also said, "I will follow You, Lord; but first **permit me to say good-bye to those at home."** But Jesus said to him, "No one, after putting his hand to the plow and looking back, is fit for the kingdom of God."

Luke 9:61–62

"**He who is faithful in a very little thing** is faithful also in much; and he who is unrighteous in a very little thing is unrighteous also in much."

Luke 16:10

"On that day, let not the one who is on the housetop and whose goods are in the house go down to take them away; and likewise **let not the one who is in the field turn back."**

Luke 17:31

He said to him again a second time, "Simon, son of John, do you love Me?" He said to him, "Yes, Lord; You know that I love You." He said to him, "Shepherd My sheep." He said to him the third time, "Simon, son of John, do you love Me?" Peter was grieved because He said to him the third time, "Do you love Me?" And he said to him, "Lord, You know all things; You know that I love You." Jesus said to him, "Tend My sheep."

John 21:16–17

Peter and the apostles answered and said, "We must obey God rather than men."

Acts 5:29

Many of **those who practiced magic brought their books together and began burning them** in the sight of all; and they counted up the price of them and found it fifty thousand pieces of silver.

Acts 19:19

Thanks be to God that though you were slaves of sin, you **became obedient from the heart.**

Romans 6:17

By faith Moses, when he had grown up, refused to be called the son of Pharaoh's daughter; choosing rather to endure ill-treatment with the people of God, than to enjoy the passing pleasures of sin; **considering the reproach of Christ greater riches than the treasures of Egypt;** for he was looking to the reward.

Hebrews 11:24–26

Prove yourselves doers of the word, and not merely hearers who delude themselves.

James 1:22

As obedient children, **do not be conformed to the former lusts** which were yours in your ignorance, but like the Holy One who called you, be holy yourselves also in all your behavior.

1 Peter 1:14–15

PAYING VOWS

A vow can be defined as "an earnest promise to pledge that binds one to perform in a certain manner." Repeatedly in the Bible the term is used to refer to a promise or pledge, and the emphasis is that such promises are binding. Few scriptural principles are clearer than that of keeping our vows—literally keeping our word both to God and to others. When we give our word to do something, we are obligated to do it. When we obligate ourselves financially, we must pay.

They said, "We see plainly that the Lord has been with you; so we said, 'Let there now be an oath between us, even between you and us, and **let us make a covenant with you.**'"

Genesis 26:28

Again, the Lord spoke to Moses, saying, "Speak to the sons of Israel, and say to them, '**When a man makes a difficult vow,** he shall be valued according to your valuation of persons belonging to the Lord. If your valuation is of the male from twenty years even to sixty years old, then your valuation shall be fifty shekels of silver, after the shekel of the sanctuary. Or if it is a female, then your valuation shall be thirty shekels. And if it be from five years even to twenty years old then your valuation for the male shall be twenty shekels, and for the female ten shekels. But if they are from a month even up to five years old, then your valuation shall be five shekels of silver for the male, and for the female your valuation shall be three shekels of silver. And if they are from sixty years old and upward, if it is a male, then your valuation shall be fifteen shekels, and for the female ten shekels. But if he is poorer than your valuation, then he shall be placed before the priest, and the priest shall value him; according to the means of the one who vowed, the priest shall value him. Now if it is an animal of the kind which men can present as an offering to the Lord, any such that one gives to the Lord shall be holy.'"

Leviticus 27:1–9

"**If a man makes a vow to the Lord,** or takes an oath to bind himself with a binding obligation, he shall not violate his word; he shall do according to all that proceeds out of his mouth."

Numbers 30:2

"**When you make a vow to the Lord your God,** you shall not delay to pay it, for it would be sin in you, and the Lord your God will surely require it of you."

Deuteronomy 23:21

"**You shall be careful to perform what goes out from your lips,** just as you have voluntarily vowed to the Lord your God, what you have promised."

Deuteronomy 23:23

From Thee comes my praise in the great assembly; **I shall pay my vows before those who fear Him.**

Psalm 22:25

"**Offer to God a sacrifice of thanksgiving,** and **pay your vows to the Most High;** and call upon Me in the day of trouble; I shall rescue you, and you will honor Me."

Psalm 50:14–15

When you make a vow to God, do not be late in paying it, for He takes no delight in fools. Pay what you vow!

Ecclesiastes 5:4

It is better that you should not vow than that you should vow and not pay.

Ecclesiastes 5:5

Where a covenant is, there must of necessity be the death of the one who made it. For **a covenant is valid only when men are dead,** for it is never in force while the one who made it lives.

Hebrews 9:16–17

POSITIVE ATTITUDES

According to God's Word, having a positive attitude simply means that we trust God, we are thankful for whatever He provides, and we seek His help in knowing how to use what we have.

Not only should we be positive about our own finances, but we should be able to praise God when He benefits someone else, even though we may not have as much. If we can praise God when someone else is prospering, we have a positive attitude toward finances.

"Choose for yourselves today whom you will serve . . . but as for me and my house, **we will serve the Lord.**"

Joshua 24:15

All the ways of a man are clean in his own sight, but **the Lord weighs the motives.**

Proverbs 16:2

To **do righteousness and justice** is desired by the Lord rather than sacrifice.

Proverbs 21:3

"He said to them, "What man shall there be among you, who shall have one sheep, and if it falls into a pit on the Sabbath, will he not take hold of it, and lift it out? Of how much more value then is a man than a sheep! **So then, it is lawful to do good on the Sabbath.**"

Matthew 12:11–12

"**Whoever is ashamed of Me and My words,** of him will the Son of Man be ashamed when He comes in His glory, and the glory of the Father and of the holy angels."

Luke 9:26

When they had finished breakfast, Jesus said to Simon Peter, "Simon, son of John, do you love Me more than these?" He said to Him, "Yes, Lord; You know that I love You." He said to him, "Tend My lambs." He said to him again a second time, "Simon, son of John, do you love Me?" He said to Him, "Yes, Lord; You know that I love You." He said to him, "Shepherd My sheep." He said to him the third time, "Simon, son of John, do you love Me?" Peter was grieved because He said to him the third time, "Do you love Me?" And he said to Him, "Lord, You know all things; You know that I love You." Jesus said to him, "Tend My sheep."

John 21:15–17

I am not ashamed of the gospel, for it is the power of God for salvation to everyone who believes, to the Jew first and also to the Greek.

Romans 1:16

We know that **God causes all things to work together for good** to those who love God, to those who are called according to His purpose.

Romans 8:28

I can do all things through Him who strengthens me.
Philippians 4:13

Do not love the world, nor the things in the world. If anyone loves the world, the love of the Father is not in him. For all that is in the world, the lust of the flesh and the lust of the eyes and the boastful pride of life, is not from the Father, but is from the world.

1 John 2:15–16

STEWARDSHIP

The key to understanding God's will in finances is to have the proper understanding of stewardship. A steward is one who manages another's property. We are merely stewards of God's property while we are on earth. He can choose to entrust us with as much or as little as He desires, but in no case will we ever take ownership.

Quite often the demonstration of our stewardship is not how much we give but how we react when there is not much to give. We cannot experience peace in the area of finances until we have surrendered total control of this area to God and have accepted the role of steward.

There is one who **scatters, yet increases** all the more, and there is one who withholds what is justly due, but it results only in want.

Proverbs 11:24

He who is gracious to a poor man lends to the Lord, and He will repay him for his good deed.

Proverbs 19:17

"Do not lay up for yourselves treasures upon earth, where moth and rust destroy, and where thieves break in and steal. But **lay up for yourselves treasures in heaven,** where neither moth nor rust destroys, and where thieves do not break in or steal; for where your treasure is, there will your heart be also. No one can serve two masters; for either he will hate the one and love the other, or he will hold to one and despise the other. You cannot serve God and mammon. But **seek first His kingdom and His righteousness;** and all these things shall be added to you.

Matthew 6:19–21, 24, 33

"His master said to him, 'Well done, good and faithful slave; you **were faithful with a few things,** I will put you in charge of many things, enter into the joy of your master.'"

Matthew 25:21

"Then He will answer them, saying, 'Truly I say to you, to the extent that you did not do it to one of the least of these, you did not do it to Me.'"

Matthew 25:45

"Give, and it will be given to you; good measure, pressed down, shaken together, running over, they will pour into your lap. For **by your standard of measure it will be measured to you in return.**"

Luke 6:38

"Do not be anxious for your life, as to what you shall eat; nor for your body, as to what you shall put on. For life is more than food, and the body more than clothing. And do not seek what you shall eat, and what you shall drink, and do not keep worrying. For all these things the nations of the world eagerly seek; but your Father knows you need these things. But **seek for His kingdom, and these things shall be added** to you. Sell your possessions, and give to charity. For **where your treasure is, there will your heart be also.**"

Luke 12:22–23, 29–31, 33–34

Let a man regard us in this manner, as servants of Christ, and **stewards of the mysteries of God.** . . . It is required of stewards that one be **found trustworthy.**

1 Corinthians 4:1–2

Instruct them to do good, to be rich in good works, to be **generous and ready to share,** storing up for themselves the treasure of a good foundation for the future, so that they may take hold of that which is life indeed.

1 Timothy 6:18–19

THANKFULNESS

Are we grateful for what we have, rather than resentful for what we don't have? When we look around, there's always someone else who has more. It's easy to ask, "Why did he (or she) get that instead of me?" Satan tries to get us to be discontented by comparing ourselves to others. The way to counteract that is to praise God for what we have and not let what others have affect us. Thankfulness is not based on an accumulation of assets; it is a positive attitude toward life.

———————

I have rejoiced in the way of Thy testimonies, as much as in all riches.

Psalm 119:14

The law of Thy mouth is better to me than thousands of gold and silver pieces.

Psalm 119:72

Therefore, I love Thy commandments above gold, yes, above fine gold.

Psalm 119:127

I rejoice at Thy word, as one who finds great spoil.

Psalm 119:162

The poor man utters supplications, but the rich man answers roughly.

Proverbs 18:23

"What woman, **if she has ten silver coins and loses one coin,** does not light a lamp and sweep the house and search carefully until she finds it? And when she has found it, she calls together her friends and neighbors, saying, 'Rejoice with me, for I have found the coin which I had lost!'"

Luke 15:8–9

As sorrowful yet always rejoicing, **as poor yet making many rich,** as having nothing yet possessing all things.

2 Corinthians 6:10

Be anxious for nothing, but in everything by **prayer and supplication with thanksgiving** let your requests be made known to God.

Philippians 4:6

In everything give thanks; for this is God's will for you in Christ Jesus.

1 Thessalonians 5:18

Godliness actually is a means of great gain, when accompanied by contentment. For we have brought nothing into the world, so we cannot take anything out of it either. And if we have food and covering, with these we shall be content.

1 Timothy 6:6–8

Consider it all joy, my brethren, when you encounter various trials, knowing that the testing of your faith produces endurance. And let endurance have its perfect result, that you may be perfect and complete, lacking in nothing.

James 1:2–4

TRUST

Are we willing to put God totally in control of our finances? Will we give away the last dime or dollar we have, even if it looks like we'll do without as a result of giving? If we really trust God with everything we have, He will satisfy all our needs as He promised. God gives small things at first because we are only capable of trusting Him for small things. But the more we exercise our faith, and our trust in Him grows, the more He will supply.

"[Deliver money] to the carpenters and the builders and the masons and for buying timber and hewn stone to repair the house. Only no accounting shall be made with them for the money delivered into their hands, for they deal faithfully."

2 Kings 22:6–7

He hired also 100,000 valiant warriors out of Israel for one hundred talents of silver. But a man of God came to him saying, "O king, do not let the army of Israel go with you, for the Lord is not with Israel nor with any of the sons of Ephraim. But if you do go, do it, be strong for the battle; yet God will bring you down before the enemy, for God has power to help and to bring down." And Amaziah said to the man of God, "But **what shall we do for the hundred talents which I have given to the troops of Israel?**" And the man of God answered, "The Lord has much more to give you than this."

2 Chronicles 25:6–9

"You will know that your tent is secure, for **you will visit your abode and fear no loss.**"

Job 5:24

"**I have treasured the words of His mouth more than my necessary food.**"

Job 23:12

Many are the sorrows of the wicked; but he who trusts in the Lord, lovingkindness shall surround him.

Psalm 32:10

Rest in the Lord and wait patiently for Him; **do not fret because of him who prospers in his way,** because of the man who carries out wicked schemes. Cease from anger, and forsake wrath; do not fret, it leads only to evildoing. For evildoers will be cut off, but those who wait for the Lord, they will inherit the land.

Psalm 37:7–9

Praise the Lord! **How blessed is the man who fears the Lord,** who greatly delights in His commandments.

Psalm 112:1

Trust in the Lord with all your heart, and do not lean on your own understanding. In all your ways acknowledge Him, and He will make your paths straight.

Proverbs 3:5–6

The fear of the Lord prolongs life, but the years of the wicked will be shortened.

Proverbs 10:27

An arrogant man stirs up strife, but he who trusts in the Lord will prosper.

Proverbs 28:25

I know that **it will be well for those who fear God,** who fear Him openly.

Ecclesiastes 8:12

The conclusion when all has been heard is: **fear God and keep His commandments,** because this applies to every person.

Ecclesiastes 12:13

"The **Lord is my portion**," says my soul, "Therefore I have
hope in Him."

Lamentations 3:24

"He has told you, O man, what is good; and **what does the
Lord require of you but to do justice,** to love kindness, and
to walk humbly with your God?"

Micah 6:8

"For this reason I say to you, **do not be anxious for your
life,** as to what you shall eat, or what you shall drink; nor
for your body, as to what you shall put on. Is not life more
than food, and the body than clothing? Look at the birds of
the air, that they do not sow, neither do they reap, nor
gather into barns, and yet your heavenly Father feeds them.
Are you not worth much more than they? And which of you
by being anxious can add a single cubit to his life's span?
And why are you anxious about clothing? Observe how the
lilies of the field grow; they do not toil nor do they spin, yet
I say to you that even Solomon in all his glory did not
clothe himself like one of these. But if God so arrays the
grass of the field, which is alive today and tomorrow is
thrown into the furnace, will He not much more do so for
you, O men of little faith? **Do not be anxious then,** saying
'What shall we eat?' or 'What shall we drink?' or 'With
what shall we clothe ourselves?' For all these things the
Gentiles eagerly seek; for your heavenly Father knows that
you need all these things. But **seek first His kingdom** and
His righteousness; and all these things shall be added to you.
Therefore do not be anxious for tomorrow; for tomorrow will
care for itself. Each day has enough trouble of its own."

Matthew 6:25–34

"What man is there among you, when his son shall ask him
for a loaf, will give him a stone? Or if he shall ask for a fish,
he will not give him a snake, will he? If you then, being
evil, know how to give good gifts to your children, **how
much more shall your Father who is in heaven give** what is
good to those who ask Him!"

Matthew 7:9–11

"**Are not two sparrows sold for a cent?** And yet not one of them will fall to the ground apart from your Father. But the very hairs of your head are all numbered."

Matthew 10:29–30

"**He who loves father or mother more than Me is not worthy of Me;** and he who loves son or daughter more than Me is not worthy of Me."

Matthew 10:37

Jesus answered and said to them, "Truly I say to you, **if you have faith, and do not doubt,** you shall not only do what was done to the fig tree, but even if you say to this mountain, 'Be taken up and cast into the sea,' it shall happen. And all things you ask in prayer, believing, you shall receive."

Matthew 21:21–22

He instructed them that **they should take nothing for their journey,** except a mere staff; no bread, no bag, no money in their belt.

Mark 6:8

"Therefore I say to you, all things for which you pray and ask, **believe that you have received them,** and they shall be granted you."

Mark 11:24

He said to them, "**Take nothing for your journey, neither a staff, nor a bag, nor bread, nor money; and do not even have two tunics apiece.**"

Luke 9:3

"**Carry no purse,** no bag, no shoes; and greet no one on the way."

Luke 10:4

"Which of you by being anxious can add a single cubit to his life's span?"

Luke 12:25

"**Do not seek what you shall eat,** and what you shall drink, and do not keep worrying. For all these things the nations of the world eagerly seek; but your Father knows that you need these things. But **seek for His kingdom,** and these things shall be added to you. For **where your treasure is,** there will your heart be also."

Luke 12:29–31, 34

"So therefore, no one of you can be My disciple who does not **give up all his own possessions.**"

Luke 14:33

Peter said, "**Behold, we have left our own homes,** and followed You." And He said to them, "Truly I say to you, there is no one who has left house or wife or brothers or parents or children, for the sake of the kingdom of God, who shall not receive many times as much at this time and in the age to come, eternal life."

Luke 18:28–30

He said to them, "When I sent you out without purse and bag and sandals, **you did not lack anything, did you?**" And they said, "No, nothing." And He said to them, "But now, let him who has a purse take it along, likewise also a bag, and let him who has no sword sell his robe and buy one."

Luke 22:35–36

"**Do not work for the food which perishes,** but for the food which endures to eternal life, which the Son of Man shall give to you, for on Him the Father, even God, has set His seal."

John 6:27

"**He who loves his life loses it;** and he who hates his life in this world shall keep it to life eternal. If anyone serves Me, let him follow Me; and where I am, there shall My servant also be; if anyone serves Me, the Father will honor him."

John 12:25–26

This man was listening to Paul as he spoke, who, when he had fixed his gaze upon him, and **had seen that he had faith** to be made well, said with a loud voice, "Stand upright on your feet." And he leaped up and began to walk.

Acts 14:9–10

Do you not know that when you present yourselves to someone as slaves for obedience, you are slaves of the one whom you obey, either of sin resulting in death, or of **obedience resulting in righteousness?**

Romans 6:16

Be anxious for nothing, but in everything by prayer and supplication with thanksgiving let your requests be made known to God.

Philippians 4:6

Set your mind on the things above, not on the things that are on earth. For you have died and your life is hidden with Christ in God.

Colossians 3:2–3

All Scripture is inspired by God and profitable for teaching, for reproof, for correction, for training in righteousness; that the man of God may be adequate, equipped for every good work.

2 Timothy 3:16–17

[Rejoice] that **the proof of your faith, being more precious than gold** which is perishable, even though tested by fire, may be found to result in praise and glory and honor at the revelation of Jesus Christ.

1 Peter 1:7

Casting all your anxiety on Him, because He cares for you.

1 Peter 5:7

WISDOM

When we have problems, the first thing we should ask for is wisdom—not money, not power, but wisdom. That's the key that will unlock all the doors. God's Word says that if we trust Him He will grant wisdom to us liberally and without reproach. How can we seek God's wisdom in our finances? God's Word promises that if we ask anything according to His will, and believe we will receive it, it will be given to us. That includes wisdom, which is fundamental in the area of finances if we are going to make sound financial decisions.

"Nevertheless I did not believe the reports, until I came and my eyes had seen it. And behold, the half was not told me. **You exceed in wisdom and prosperity the report which I heard.**"

1 Kings 10:7

The fear of the Lord is the beginning of knowledge; fools despise wisdom and instruction.

Proverbs 1:7

How blessed is the man who finds wisdom, and the man who gains understanding. **For its profit is better than the profit of silver,** and its gain than fine gold. She is more precious than jewels; and nothing you desire compares with her. Long life is in her right hand; in her left hand are riches and honor. Her ways are pleasant ways, and all her paths are peace. She is a tree of life to those who take hold of her, and happy are all who hold her fast. The Lord by wisdom founded the earth; by understanding He established the heavens.

Proverbs 3:13–19

The naive inherit folly, but the prudent are crowned with knowledge.

Proverbs 14:18

The king's favor is toward a servant who acts wisely, but his anger is toward him who acts shamefully.

Proverbs 14:35

A wise son makes a father glad, but a foolish man despises his mother.

Proverbs 15:20

How **much better it is to get wisdom than gold!** And to get understanding is to be chosen above silver.

Proverbs 16:16

The mind of the **prudent acquires knowledge,** and the ear of the wise seeks knowledge.

Proverbs 18:15

There is gold, and an abundance of jewels; but the lips of **knowledge are a more precious thing.**

Proverbs 20:15

By wisdom a house is built, and by understanding it is established; and by knowledge the rooms are filled with all precious and pleasant riches.

Proverbs 24:3–4

A man who loves wisdom makes his father glad, but he who keeps company with harlots wastes his wealth.

Proverbs 29:3

Two things I asked of Thee, do not refuse me before I die: keep deception and lies far from me, **give me neither poverty nor riches;** feed me with the food that is my portion, lest I be full and deny Thee and say, "Who is the Lord?" Or lest I be in want and steal, and profane the name of my God.

Proverbs 30:7–9

A poor, yet wise lad is better than an old and foolish king who no longer knows how to receive instruction.

Ecclesiastes 4:13

What advantage does the wise man have over the fool? What advantage does the poor man have, knowing how to walk before the living?

Ecclesiastes 6:8

Wisdom is protection just as money is protection. But the advantage of knowledge is that wisdom preserves the lives of its possessors.

Ecclesiastes 7:12

There was found in it **a poor wise man and he delivered the city by his wisdom.** Yet no one remembered that poor man. So I said, **"Wisdom is better than strength."** But the wisdom of the poor man is despised and his words are not heeded.

Ecclesiastes 9:15–16

The wisdom from above is first pure, then peaceable, gentle, reasonable, full of mercy and good fruits, **unwavering, without hypocrisy.**

James 3:17

I heard the voice of many angels . . . and the living creatures and the elders saying with a loud voice, "Worthy is the Lamb that was slain to receive power and riches and wisdom and might and honor and glory and blessing."

Revelation 5:11–12

SECTION TWO
ATTITUDES, WRONG

The financial principles given throughout God's Word aren't there to test if we're strong enough to live by them—they're given because God knows they are what is best for us. God doesn't say that money or material things are problems; he says they are symptoms of real problems. God constantly warns us to guard our hearts against greed, covetousness, ego, pride, and other wrong attitudes, because these are the tools Satan uses to control and manipulate us. When you see people who are willing to cheat, to cut corners, even to steal, that is evidence of the wrong spiritual attitudes being reflected in their finances.

The possession or absence of material things is not an issue with serving the Lord—the attitude about them is.

BAD COUNSEL

Good admonishes us to seek counsel and not to rely solely on our own resources. Many Christians become frustrated because they lack the necessary knowledge and then give up. God has supplied people with the ability to counsel in the area of finances. The Proverbs deal with both good and bad counsel. There's great good in many counselors, but it's better not to depend wholly on their counsel. Primarily we look to God to discover His plan for our lives.

It's only secondarily that we depend on the counsel of other people. Select your counselors on the basis of their ability and a common value system—for the Christian, that means those who acknowledge Jesus Christ as Savior and Lord.

He who walks with wise men will be wise, but the companion of fools will suffer harm.

Proverbs 13:20

Leave the presence of a fool, or you will not discern words of knowledge.

Proverbs 14:7

Do not associate with a man given to anger; or go with a hot-tempered man, lest you learn his ways, and find a snare for yourself.

Proverbs 22:24–25

Do not be deceived: "**Bad company corrupts good morals.**"

1 Corinthians 15:33

We command you, brethren, in the name of the Lord Jesus Christ, that you keep aloof from every brother who leads an unruly life and not according to the tradition which you received from us.

2 Thessalonians 3:6

BRIBE

There are multiple verses in God's Word telling about the use of bribes to pervert justice. Bribery can come in the form of money, flattering words, inappropriate gifts—even raises and promotions. If we pay someone to give a dishonest report, either about another person or an investment, we are paying someone to cheat for us. God cannot honor anyone who cheats and He detests bribes. We should maintain integrity at all times.

"**You shall not take a bribe,** for a bribe blinds the clear-sighted and subverts the cause of the just."

Exodus 23:8

So the elders of Moab and the elders of Midian departed with the **fees for divination** in their hand; and they came to Balaam and repeated Balak's words to him.

Numbers 22:7

"Moreover, **you shall not take ransom for the life of a murderer** who is guilty of death, but he shall surely be put to death. And you shall not take ransom for him who has fled to his city of refuge, that he may return to live in the land before the death of the priest."

Number 35:31–32

"The Lord your God is the God of gods and the Lord of lords, the great, the mighty, and the awesome God **who does not show partiality,** nor take a bribe."

Deuteronomy 10:17

"**You shall not distort justice;** you shall not be partial, and you shall not take a bribe, for a bribe blinds the eyes of the wise and perverts the words of the righteous. Justice, and

only justice, you shall pursue, that you may live and possess the land which the Lord your God is giving you."
Deuteronomy 16:19–20

"'**Cursed is he who accepts a bribe** to strike down an innocent person.' And all the people shall say, 'Amen.'"
Deuteronomy 27:25

They gave him seventy pieces of silver from the house of Baal-berith with which **Abimelech hired worthless and reckless fellows,** and they followed him.
Judges 9:4

The lords of the Philistines came up to her, and said to her, "**Entice him, and see where his great strength lies** and how we may overpower him that we may bind him to afflict him. Then we **will each give you eleven hundred pieces of silver.**"
Judges 16:5

When Delilah saw that he had told her all that was in his heart, she sent and called the lords of the Philistines, saying, "Come up once more, for he has told me all that is in his heart." Then the lords of the Philistines came up to her, and brought the money in their hands.
Judges 16:18

His sons, however, did not walk in his ways, but turned aside after dishonest gain and took bribes and perverted justice.
1 Samuel 8:3

The men of Israel said, "Have you seen this man who is coming up? Surely he is coming up to defy Israel. And it will be that **the king will enrich the man who kills him** with great riches and will give him his daughter and make his father's house free in Israel."
1 Samuel 17:25

Joab said to the man who had told him, "Now behold, you saw him! Why then did you not strike him there to the ground? And I would have given you ten pieces of silver and a belt." And the man said to Joab, "**Even if I should receive a thousand pieces of silver in my hand, I would not put out my hand against the king's son;** for in our hearing the king charged you and Abishai and Ittai, saying, 'Protect for me the young man Absalom!'"

2 Samuel 18:11–12

The king said to the man of God, "Come home with me and refresh yourself, and I will give you a reward." But the man of God said to the king, "**If you were to give me half your house I would not go out with you,** nor would I eat bread or drink water in this place."

1 Kings 13:7–8

Ahaz took the silver and gold that was found in the house of the Lord and in the treasuries of the king's house, and **sent a present to the king of Assyria.**

2 Kings 16:8

Asa brought out silver and gold from the treasuries of the house of the Lord and the king's house, and **sent them to Ben-hadad king of Aram,** who lived in Damascus, saying, "Let there be a treaty between you and me, as between my father and your father. Behold, I have sent you silver and gold; go, break your treaty with Baasha king of Israel so that he will withdraw from me."

2 Chronicles 16:2–3

"Let the fear of the Lord be upon you; be very careful what you do, **for the Lord our God will have no part in unrighteousness, or partiality,** or the taking of a bribe."

2 Chronicles 19:7

Ahaz took a portion out of the house of the Lord and out of the palace of the king and of the princes, and **gave it to the king of Assyria;** but it did not help him.

2 Chronicles 28:21

"If it is pleasing to the king, let it be decreed that they be destroyed, and **I will pay ten thousand talents of silver** into the hands of those who carry on the king's business, to put into the king's treasuries."

Esther 3:9

Then Haman recounted to them the glory of his riches, and the number of his sons, and every instance where the king had magnified him, and how he had promoted him above the princes and servants of the king.

Esther 5:11

"Have I said, 'Give me something,' or, '**Offer a bribe for me from your wealth.**'"

Job 6:22

He does not put out his money at interest, nor does he take a bribe against the innocent. He who does these things will never be shaken.

Psalm 15:5

In whose hands is a wicked scheme, and whose right hand is full of bribes.

Psalm 26:10

A bribe is a charm in the sight of its owner; wherever he turns, he prospers.

Proverbs 17:8

A wicked man received a bribe from the bosom to pervert the ways of justice.

Proverbs 17:23

A gift in secret subdues anger, and a bribe in the bosom, strong wrath.

Proverbs 21:14

The king gives stability to the land by justice, but a man who takes bribes overthrows it.

Proverbs 29:4

Oppression makes a wise man mad, and a bribe corrupts the heart.

Ecclesiastes 7:7

"Your rulers are rebels, and companions of thieves; everyone loves a bribe, and chases after rewards. They do not defend the orphan, nor does the widow's plea come before them."

Isaiah 1:23

Woe to those . . . who justify the wicked for a bribe, and take away the rights of the ones who are in the right!

Isaiah 5:22–23

"Men give gifts to all harlots, but **you give your gifts to all your lovers to bribe** them to come to you from every direction for your harlotries. Thus you are different from those women in your harlotries, in that no one plays the harlot as you do, because you give money and no money is given you; thus you are different."

Ezekiel 16:33–34

"In you **they have taken bribes to shed blood;** you have taken **interest and profits,** and you have injured your neighbors for gain by oppression, and you have forgotten Me," declares the Lord God. "Behold, then, I smite My hand at your dishonest gain which you have acquired and at the bloodshed which is among you."

Ezekiel 22:12–13

"I know your transgressions are many and your sins are great, **you who distress the righteous and accept bribes,** and turn aside the poor in the gate."

Amos 5:12

Her **leaders pronounce judgment for a bribe,** her priests instruct for a price, and her prophets divine for money. Yet they lean on the Lord saying, "Is not the Lord in our midst? Calamity will not come upon us."

Micah 3:11

"Concerning evil, both hands do it well. The prince asks, also **the judge, for a bribe,** and a great man speaks the desire of his soul; so they weave it together."

Micah 7:3

When they had assembled with the elders and counseled together, **they gave a large sum of money to the soldiers,** and said, "You are to say, 'His disciples came by night and stole Him away while we were asleep.' And if this should come to the governor's ears, we will win him over and keep you out of trouble." And they took the money and did as they had been instructed; and this story was widely spread among the Jews, and is to this day.

Matthew 28:12–15

Judas Iscariot, who was one of the twelve, went off to the chief priests, in order to betray Him to them. And they were glad when **they heard this, and promised to give him money.** And he began seeking how to betray Him at an opportune time.

Mark 14:10–11

He was also saying to the disciples, "**There was a certain rich man who had a steward,** and this steward was reported to him as squandering his possessions. And he called him and said to him, 'What is this I hear about you? Give an account of your stewardship, for you can no longer be steward.' And the steward said to himself, 'What shall I do, since my master is taking the stewardship away from me? I am not strong enough to dig; I am ashamed to beg. I know what I shall do, so that when I am removed from the stewardship, they will receive me into their homes.' And he summoned each one of his master's debtors, and he began saying to the first, 'How much do you owe my master?' And he said, 'A hundred measures of oil.' And he said to him, 'Take your bill, and sit down quickly and write fifty.' Then he said to another, 'And how much do you owe?' And he said, 'A hundred measures of wheat.' He said to him, 'Take your bill, and write eighty.' And his master praised the unrighteous steward because he had acted shrewdly;

for the sons of this age are more shrewd in relation to their own kind than the sons of light. And I say to you, make friends for yourselves by means of the mammon of unrighteousness; that when it fails, they may receive you into the eternal dwellings."

Luke 16:1–9

He went away and discussed with the chief priests and officers how he might betray Him to them. And **they were glad, and agreed to give him money.**

Luke 22:4–5

When **Simon** saw that the Spirit was bestowed through the laying on of the apostles' hands, he **offered them money, saying, "Give this authority to me as well,** so that everyone on whom I lay my hands may receive the Holy Spirit." But Peter said to him, "May your silver perish with you, because you thought you could obtain the gift of God with money! You have no part or portion in this matter, for your heart is not right before God."

Acts 8:18–21

At the same time too, **he was hoping that money would be given him by Paul;** therefore he also used to send for him quite often and converse with him.

Acts 24:26

COVETOUSNESS

God is not opposed to His children having wealth. He is opposed to their being covetous: inordinately desiring what belongs to someone else. Financial bondage exists if a Christian looks at what others have and desires it. Covetousness, often accompanied by selfishness, greed, and even ruthlessness, should not characterize the life of a Christian. Don't set your goals based on what others have because, in the long run, you can be covetous and still not have anything.

"You **shall not covet your neighbor's house;** you shall not covet your neighbor's wife or his male servant or his female servant or his ox or his donkey or anything that belongs to your neighbor."

Exodus 20:17

Actually, I wrote to you **not to associate with any so-called brother** if he should be an immoral person, or **covetous,** or an idolater, or a reviler, or a drunkard, or a swindler—not even to eat with such a one.

1 Corinthians 5:11

Thieves, nor the covetous, nor drunkards, nor revilers, nor swindlers, shall inherit the kingdom of God.

1 Corinthians 6:10

This you know with certainty, that no immoral or impure person or **covetous man,** who is an idolater, **has an inheritance** in the kingdom of Christ and God.

Ephesians 5:5

DECEPTION

Trickery, fraud, double-dealing, lying, cheating, and subterfuge are all the practices of one who deliberately deceives. The most devastating loss associated with deceit is the dulling of spiritual awareness. Guilt associated with a known deception will cause the Christian to withdraw from God's presence. Once withdrawn, subsequent deceptions become easier, less conviction is felt, and life is full of defeat and frustration.

Deception destroys trust and leads to hypocrisy and a critical spirit. No one is immune to the temptation to deceive, particularly when money is concerned. God's Word gives us guidelines for making decisions in spite of our normal reactions.

How blessed is the man to whom the Lord does not impute iniquity, and in whose spirit there is no deceit!

Psalm 32:2

Keep your tongue from evil, and your lips from speaking deceit.

Psalm 34:13

The words of his mouth are wickedness and deceit; he has ceased to be wise and to do good.

Psalm 36:3

He who walks in a blameless way is the one who will minister to me. He who practices deceit shall not dwell within my house; he who speaks falsehood shall not maintain his position before me.

Psalm 101:6–7

Deliver my soul, O Lord, from lying lips, from a deceitful tongue.

Psalm 120:2

Put away from you a deceitful mouth, and put devious lips far from you.

Proverbs 4:24

The perverse in heart are an abomination to the Lord, but **the blameless in their walk are His delight.** Assuredly, the evil man will not go unpunished.

Proverbs 11:20–21

Deceit is in the heart of those who devise evil, but counselors of peace have joy.

Proverbs 12:20

He who **conceals his transgressions** will not prosper, but he who confesses and forsakes them will find compassion.

Proverbs 28:13

He who hates unjust gain will prolong his days. . . . He who is crooked will fall at once.

Proverbs 28:16, 18

Keep deception and lies far from me.

Proverbs 30:8

"The **heart is more deceitful than all else** and is desperately sick; who can understand it?"

Jeremiah 17:9

"The **deceitfulness of riches** choke the word, and it becomes unfruitful.

Matthew 13:22

See to it that no one takes you captive through philosophy and **empty deception,** according to the tradition of men, according to the elementary principles of the world, rather than according to Christ. For **in Him all the fullness of Deity dwells in bodily form, and in Him you have been made complete,** and He is the head over all rule and authority.

Colossians 2:8–10

DISHONESTY

To be dishonest means that you've gone outside the structure of God's Word in making financial decisions: you've cheated another person and, in reality, you've cheated God. You've also cheated yourself. No matter how successful dishonest people seem to be, they will pay for their dishonesty in many ways. Never allow yourself to be trapped into anything that is unethical, immoral, or dishonest, no matter how inviting it seems. Following the worldly path results in the loss of God's full blessings.

He said, "Your brother **came deceitfully, and has taken away your blessing.**" Then he said, "Is he not rightly named Jacob, for he has supplanted me these two times? He took away my birthright, and behold, now he has taken away my blessing." And he said, "Have you not reserved a blessing for me?"

Genesis 27:35–36

So it came about in the morning that, behold, it was Leah! And he said to Laban, "What is this you have done to me? Was it not for Rachel that I served with you? **Why then have you deceived me?**"

Genesis 29:25

"Yet **your father has cheated me and changed my wages ten times;** however, God did not allow him to hurt me. Then the angel of God said to me in the dream, 'Jacob,' and I said, 'Here I am.' And he said, 'Lift up, now, your eyes and see that all the male goats which are mating are striped, speckled, and mottled; for I have seen all that Laban has been doing to you.'"

Genesis 31:7, 11–12

When Laban had gone to shear his flock, then **Rachel stole the household idols that were her father's.** And Jacob de-

78

ceived Laban the Aramean, by not telling him that he was fleeing.

Genesis 31:19–20

"You shall not steal."

Exodus 20:15

"**You shall not steal,** nor deal falsely, nor lie to one another."

Leviticus 19:11

"**You shall not have in your bag differing weights,** a large and a small. You shall not have in your house differing measures, a large and a small. You shall have a full and just weight; you shall have a full and just measure, that your days may be prolonged in the land which the Lord your God gives you."

Deuteronomy 25:13–15

"'**Cursed is he who moves his neighbor's boundary mark.**' And all the people shall say, 'Amen.' '**Cursed is he who misleads a blind person on the road.**' And the people shall say, 'Amen.' '**Cursed is he who distorts the justice due an alien,** orphan, and widow.' And all the people shall say, 'Amen.'"

Deuteronomy 27:17–19

"Israel has sinned, and they have also transgressed My covenant which I commanded them. And they have even taken some of the things under the ban and have both stolen and deceived. Moreover, they have also put them among their own things."

Joshua 7:11

He went in and stood before his master. And Elisha said to him, "Where have you been, Gehazi?" And he said, "Your servant went nowhere." Then he said to him, "Did not my heart go with you, when the man turned from his chariot to meet you? Is it a time to receive money and to receive clothes and olive groves and vineyards and sheep and oxen and male and female servants? Therefore, the leprosy of

Naaman shall cleave to you and to your descendants forever.'' So he went out from his presence a leper as white as snow.

2 Kings 5:25–27

"The schemer is eager for their wealth."

Job 5:5

"He returns what he has attained and cannot swallow it; **as to the riches of his trading, he cannot even enjoy them.** For he has oppressed and forsaken the poor; he has seized a house which he has not built. Because he knew no quiet within him he does not retain anything he desires.

Job 20:18–20

He who practices deceit shall not dwell within my house; he who speaks falsehood shall not maintain his position before me.

Psalm 101:7

Incline my heart to Thy testimonies, **and not to dishonest gain.**

Psalm 119:36

I hate those who are double-minded, but I love Thy law.

Psalm 119:113

Deliver my soul, O Lord, from lying lips, **from a deceitful tongue.**

Psalm 120:2

To **deliver you from the way of evil,** from the man who speaks perverse things.

Proverbs 2:12

Whose paths are crooked, and who are devious in their ways.

Proverbs 2:15

The crooked man is an abomination to the Lord; but He is intimate with the upright.

Proverbs 3:32

Put away from you a deceitful mouth, and put devious lips far from you.

Proverbs 4:24

A worthless person, a wicked man, **is the one who walks with a false mouth,** who winks with his eyes, who signals with his feet, who points with his fingers.

Proverbs 6:12–13

There are six things which the Lord hates, yes, seven which are an abomination to Him: haughty eyes, a lying tongue, and hands that shed innocent blood, a heart that devises wicked plans, feet that run rapidly to evil, a false witness who utters lies, and one who spreads strife among brothers.

Proverbs 6:16–19

Ill-gotten gains do not profit, but righteousness delivers from death.

Proverbs 10:2

He who winks the eye causes trouble, and a babbling fool will be thrown down.

Proverbs 10:10

The mouth of the righteous flows with wisdom, but the perverted tongue will be cut out.

Proverbs 10:31

A false balance is an abomination to the Lord, but a just weight is His delight.

Proverbs 11:1

The perverse in heart are an abomination to the Lord, but the blameless in their walk are His delight.

Proverbs 11:20

Lying lips are an abomination to the Lord, but those who deal faithfully are His delight.

Proverbs 12:22

Wealth obtained by fraud dwindles, but the one who gathers by labor increases it.

Proverbs 13:11

He who profits illicitly troubles his own house, but he who hates bribes will live.

Proverbs 15:27

He who winks his eyes does so to devise perverse things; he who compresses his lips brings evil to pass.

Proverbs 16:30

The words of a whisperer are like dainty morsels, and they go down into the innermost parts of the body.

Proverbs 18:8

A false witness will not go unpunished, and he who tells lies will perish.

Proverbs 19:9

Differing weights and differing measures, both of them are abominable to the Lord.

Proverbs 20:10

"Bad, bad," says the buyer; but when he goes his way, then he boasts.

Proverbs 20:14

Bread obtained by falsehood is sweet to a man, but afterward his mouth will be filled with gravel.

Proverbs 20:17

Differing weights are an abomination to the Lord, and a false scale is not good.

Proverbs 20:23

The getting of treasure by a lying tongue is a fleeting vapor, the pursuit of death.

Proverbs 21:6

A wicked man shows a bold face, but as for the upright, he makes his way sure.

Proverbs 21:29

Do not move the ancient boundary which your fathers have set.

Proverbs 22:28

He who plans to do evil, men will call him a schemer.

Proverbs 24:8

Like a madman who throws firebrands, arrows and death, so is the man **who deceives his neighbor,** and says, "Was I not joking?"

Proverbs 26:18–19

A lying tongue hates those it crushes, and a flattering mouth works ruin.

Proverbs 26:28

Better is the poor who walks in his integrity, than he who is crooked though he be rich.

Proverbs 28:6

He who turns away his ear from listening to the law, even his prayer is an abomination.

Proverbs 28:9

When the righteous triumph, there is great glory, but **when the wicked rise, men hide themselves. He who conceals his transgressions will not prosper,** but he who confesses and forsakes them will find compassion.

Proverbs 28:12–13

"**No one sues righteously and no one pleads honestly.** They trust in confusion, and speak lies; they conceive mischief, and bring forth iniquity."

Isaiah 59:4

"I will give their wives to others, their fields to new owners; because from the least even to the greatest **everyone is greedy for gain;** from the prophet even to the priest everyone practices deceit."

Jeremiah 8:10

"Let everyone be on guard against his neighbor, and do not trust any brother; because **every brother deals craftily,** and every neighbor goes about as a slanderer."

Jeremiah 9:4

"**The heart is more deceitful** than all else and is desperately sick; who can understand it?"

Jeremiah 17:9

"Your eyes and your heart are **intent only upon your own dishonest gain,** and on shedding innocent blood and on practicing oppression and extortion."

Jeremiah 22:17

"By the multitude of your iniquities, in **the unrighteousness of your trade,** you profaned your sanctuaries. Therefore I have brought fire from the midst of you; it has consumed you, and I have turned you to ashes on the earth in the eyes of all who see you."

Ezekiel 28:18

"In a time of tranquility he will enter the richest parts of the realm, and he will accomplish what his fathers never did, nor his ancestors; he will distribute plunder, booty, and possessions among them, and **he will devise his schemes against strongholds,** but only for a time."

Daniel 11:24

"He will return to his land with much plunder; but his heart will be set against the holy covenant, and he will take action and then return to his own land."

Daniel 11:28

A merchant, in whose hands are false balances, he loves to oppress. And Ephraim said, "Surely I have become rich, I have found wealth for myself; **in all my labors they will find in me no iniquity,** which would be sin."

Hosea 12:7–8

"When will the new moon be over, so that we may buy grain, and the sabbath, that we may open the wheat market, to make the bushel smaller and the shekel bigger, and to **cheat with dishonest scales,** so as to **buy the helpless for money** and the needy for a pair of sandals, and that we may sell the refuse of the wheat?"

Amos 8:5–6

"If thieves came to you, if robbers by night—O how you will be ruined!—**would they not steal only until they had enough?** If grape gatherers came to you, would they not leave some gleanings?"

Obadiah 1:5

"Just as you drank on My holy mountain, all the nations will drink continually. They will drink and swallow, and become as if they had never existed."

Obadiah 1:16

"**The women of my people you evict,** each one from her pleasant house. From her children you take My splendor forever."

Micah 2:9

"Is there yet a man in the wicked house, along with treasures of wickedness, and a short measure that is cursed? **Can I justify wicked scales** and a bag of deceptive weights? For the rich men of the city are full of violence,

her residents speak lies, and their tongue is deceitful in
their mouth."
Micah 6:10–12

"Woe to him who gets evil gain for his house to put his
nest on high to be delivered from the hand of calamity!"
Habakkuk 2:9

"Woe to him who says to a piece of wood, 'Awake!' to a
dumb stone, 'Arise!' and that is your teacher? Behold, it is
overlaid with gold and silver."
Habakkuk 2:19

**"The good man out of his good treasure brings forth what
is good;** and the evil man out of his evil treasure brings
forth what is evil."
Matthew 12:35

"Out of the heart come evil thoughts, murders, adulteries,
fornications, thefts, false witness, slanders."
Matthew 15:19

He was also saying to the disciples, **"There was a certain
rich man who had a steward,** and this steward was reported to him as squandering his possessions. And he called
him and said to him, 'What is this I hear about you? Give
an account of your stewardship, for you can no longer be
steward.' And the steward said to himself, 'What shall I do,
since my master is taking the stewardship away from me?
I am not strong enough to dig; I am ashamed to beg. I
know what I shall do, so that when I am removed from the
stewardship, they will receive me into their homes.' And
he summoned each one of his master's debtors, and he began saying to the first, 'How much do you owe my master?'
And he said, 'A hundred measures of oil.' And he said to
him, 'Take your bill, and sit down quickly and write fifty.'
Then he said to another, 'And how much do you owe?' And
he said, 'A hundred measures of wheat.' He said to him,
'Take your bill, and write eighty.' And his master praised
the unrighteous steward because he had acted shrewdly;

for the sons of this age are more shrewd in relation to their own kind than the sons of light. And I say to you, make friends for yourselves by means of the mammon of unrighteousness; that when it fails, they may receive you into the eternal dwellings."

Luke 16:1–9

A certain man named Ananias, with his wife Sapphira, sold a piece of property, and kept back some of the price for himself, with his wife's full knowledge, and bringing a portion of it, he laid it at the apostles' feet. But Peter said, "Ananias, why has Satan filled your heart to lie to the Holy Spirit, and to keep back some of the price of the land? While it remained unsold, did it not remain your own? And after it was sold, was it not under your control? Why is it that you have conceived this deed in your heart? You have not lied to men, but to God." And as he heard these words, Ananias fell down and breathed his last; and great fear came upon all who heard of it. And the young men arose and covered him up, and after carrying him out, they buried him. Now there elapsed an interval of about three hours, and his wife came in, not knowing what had happened. And Peter responded to her, "Tell me whether you sold the land for such and such a price?" And she said, "Yes, that was the price." Then Peter said to her, "Why is it that you have agreed together to put the Spirit of the Lord to the test? Behold, the feet of those who have buried your husband are at the door, and they shall carry you out as well." And she fell immediately at his feet, and breathed her last; and the young men came in and found her dead, and they carried her out and buried her beside her husband.

Acts 5:1–10

You, therefore, who teach another, do you not teach yourself? You who preach that one should not steal, do you steal?

Romans 2:21

Nor thieves, nor the covetous, nor drunkards, nor revilers, nor swindlers, shall inherit the kingdom of God.

1 Corinthians 6:10

As a result, **we are no longer to be children,** tossed here and there by waves, and carried about by every wind of doctrine, by the trickery of men, by craftiness in deceitful scheming.

Ephesians 4:14

Let him who steals steal no longer; but rather let him labor, performing with his own hands what is good, in order that he may have something to share with him who has need.

Ephesians 4:28

These are matters which have, to be sure, the appearance of wisdom in self-made religion and self-abasement and severe treatment of the body, but are of no value against fleshly indulgence.

Colossians 2:23

Deacons likewise must be **men of dignity,** not double-tongued, or addicted to much wine or **fond of sordid gain.**

1 Timothy 3:8

By no means let any of you suffer as a murderer, or thief, or evildoer, or a troublesome meddler.

1 Peter 4:15

Forsaking the right way they have gone astray, **having followed the way of Balaam, the son of Beor,** who loved the wages of unrighteousness.

2 Peter 2:15

DISOBEDIENCE

If we are disobedient to God's written Word, which never changes, we will be disobedient to God's Holy Spirit as well, Who is even more difficult to discern. Disobedience means ignoring the counsel of God. In the area of finances, this can spell disaster. If we don't accept the counsel that God has already given us in His Word, then we will not accept His verbal counsel either. That's why so few Christians hear God speak to them.

The people quarreled with Moses and said, "Give us water that we may drink." And Moses said to them, "Why do you quarrel with me? **Why do you test the Lord?**" But the people thirsted there for water, and they grumbled against Moses and said, "Why, now, have you brought us up from Egypt, to kill us and our children and our livestock with thirst?"

Exodus 17:2–3

"You shall eat . . . a whole month, until it comes out of your nostrils and becomes loathsome to you; because **you have rejected the Lord** who is among you and have wept before Him, saying, 'Why did we ever leave Egypt?'"

Numbers 11:19–20

"Like the nations that the Lord makes to perish before you, so you **shall perish; because you would not listen to the voice of the Lord** your God."

Deuteronomy 8:20

Joshua said to the sons of Israel, "How long will you put off entering to take possession of the land which the Lord, the God of your fathers, has given to you?"

Joshua 18:3

She said, "I will surely go with you; nevertheless, the honor shall not be yours on the journey that you are about to take, for **the Lord will sell Sisera into the hands of a woman.**" Then Deborah arose and went with Barak to Kedesh.

Judges 4:9

Gideon made it into an ephod, and placed it in his city, Ophrah, and all Israel played the harlot with it there, so that it became a snare to Gideon and his household.

Judges 8:27

He said to his mother, "The eleven hundred pieces of silver which were taken from you, about which you uttered a curse in my hearing, behold, the silver is with me; I took it." And his mother said, "Blessed be my son by the Lord." He then returned the eleven hundred pieces of silver to his mother, and his mother said, "**I wholly dedicate the silver from my hand to the Lord for my son to make a graven image and a molten image;** now therefore, I will return them to you." So when he returned the silver to his mother, his mother took two hundred pieces of silver and gave them to the silversmith who made them into a graven image and a molten image, and they were in the house of Micah.

Judges 17:2–4

"**The people took some of the spoil,** sheep and oxen, the choicest of the things devoted to destruction, to sacrifice to the Lord your God at Gilgal."

1 Samuel 15:21

So **the king consulted, and made two golden calves,** and he said to them, "It is too much for you to go up to Jerusalem; behold your gods, O Israel, that brought you up from the land of Egypt."

1 Kings 12:28

This came about, because the sons of Israel had sinned against the Lord their God, who had brought them up from the land of Egypt from under the hand of Pharaoh, king of Egypt, and they had feared other gods and walked in the customs of the nations whom the Lord had driven out before the sons of Israel, and in the customs of the kings of Israel which they had introduced. And the sons of Israel did things secretly which were not right, against the Lord their God. Moreover, they built for themselves high places in all their towns, from watchtower to fortified city.

2 Kings 17:7–9

They made their sons and their daughters pass through the fire, and practiced divination and enchantments, and **sold themselves to do evil in the sight of the Lord,** provoking Him.

2 Kings 17:17

"Now you intend to resist the kingdom of the Lord through the sons of David, being a great multitude and having with you the golden calves which Jeroboam made for gods for you."

2 Chronicles 13:8

"**The eyes of the Lord** move to and fro throughout the earth that He may strongly support those whose heart is completely His. You have acted foolishly in this. Indeed, from now on you will surely have wars."

2 Chronicles 16:9

Whoever would not come within three days, according to the counsel of the leaders and the elders, **all his possessions should be forfeited** and he himself excluded from the assembly of the exiles.

Ezra 10:8

"'Who is the Almighty, that we should serve Him, and what would we gain if we entreat Him?' Behold, **their prosperity is not in their hand;** the counsel of the wicked is far from me."

Job 21:15–16

If I regard wickedness in my heart, the Lord will not hear.
Psalm 66:18

Disobedience

Stern discipline is for him who forsakes the way; he **who hates reproof will die.**

Proverbs 15:10

"You have not brought to me the sheep of your burnt offerings; nor have you honored Me with your sacrifices. I have not burdened you with offerings, nor wearied you with incense. You have bought Me no sweet cane with money, neither have you filled Me with the fat of your sacrifices; rather you have burdened Me with your sins, you have wearied Me with your iniquities."

Isaiah 43:23–24

"I spoke to you in your prosperity; but you said, 'I will not listen!' This has been your practice from your youth, that you have not obeyed My voice."

Jeremiah 22:21

"If therefore **you have not been faithful in the use of unrighteous mammon,** who will entrust the true riches to you? And if you have not been faithful in the use of that which is another's, who will give you that which is your own?"

Luke 16:11–12

The rest of mankind, who were not killed by these plagues, **did not repent of the works of their hands,** so as not to worship **demons, and the idols of gold and of silver and of brass and of stone and of wood, which can neither see nor hear nor walk.**

Revelation 9:20

EGO

The most common cause of discouragement has finances at its roots. We grade people by their finances in America. We put subtle pressures on each other to achieve success as a testimony to the Lord. But the greatest threat to our service to God is being sidetracked into a preoccupation about success.

On the other hand, we can excel at whatever we do without egotism—allowing ourselves to be elevated beyond where God wants us to be. According to God's Word we must have a servant's attitude—not a superior attitude—toward others. That's certainly true in finances. Is position or financial accomplishment encouraging an egotistical attitude?

He displayed the riches of his royal glory and the splendor of his great majesty for many days, 180 days.

Esther 1:4

It is vain for you to rise up early, to retire late, to eat the bread of painful labors; for He gives to His beloved even in his sleep.

Psalm 127:2

Do not boast about tomorrow, for you do not know what a day may bring forth.

Proverbs 27:1

The rich man is wise in his own eyes, but the poor who has understanding sees through him.

Proverbs 28:11

An arrogant man stirs up strife, but he who trusts in the Lord will prosper.

Proverbs 28:25

He said, "What have they seen in your house?" So Hezekiah answered, "They have seen all that is in my house;
**there is nothing among my treasures that I have not shown
them.**"

Isaiah 39:4

Thus says the Lord, "Let not a wise man boast of his wisdom, and let not the mighty man boast of his might, **let not
a rich man boast of his riches.**"

Jeremiah 9:23

When therefore you give alms, do not sound a trumpet before you, as the hypocrites do in the synagogues and in the
streets, that they may be honored by men. Truly I say to
you, they have their reward in full. But when you give
alms, do not let your left hand know what your right hand
is doing that your alms may be in secret; and your Father
who sees in secret will repay you."

Matthew 6:2–4

"**Whoever exalts himself shall be humbled; and whoever
humbles himself shall be exalted.**"

Matthew 23:12

"**Everyone who exalts himself shall be humbled,** and he
who humbles himself shall be exalted."

Luke 14:11

You are already filled, **you have already become rich,** you
have become kings without us; and I would indeed that
you had become kings so that we also might reign with
you.

1 Corinthians 4:8

Instruct those who are rich in this present world not to be
conceited or to fix their hope on the uncertainty of riches,
but on God, who richly supplies us with all things to enjoy.

1 Timothy 6:17

ENVY

E nvy is the desire to achieve based on observation of other people's successes. When we envy, we look at what someone else has and lust over it or become resentful or angry. In God's Word the sin of envy is always grouped together with malice, deceit, strife, hatefulness, greed, and wickedness. These have no place in the lives of Christians.

———————

So **Esau bore a grudge against Jacob** because of the blessing with which his father had blessed him; and Esau said to himself, "The days of mourning for my father are near; then I will kill my brother Jacob."

Genesis 27:41

Jacob heard the words of Laban's sons saying, "**Jacob has taken away all that was our father's,** and from what belonged to our father he has made all this wealth."

Genesis 31:1

Do not fret because of evildoers, **be not envious toward wrongdoers.**

Psalm 37:1

As for me, my feet came close to stumbling; my steps had almost slipped. **For I was envious of the arrogant,** as I saw the prosperity of the wicked.

Psalm 73:2–3

Do not let your heart envy sinners, but live in the fear of the Lord always.

Proverbs 23:17

Do not be envious of evil men, nor desire to be with them.

Proverbs 24:1

Do not fret because of evildoers, or be envious of the wicked; for there will be no future for the evil man; the lamp of the wicked will be put out.

Proverbs 24:19–20

I have seen that **every labor and every skill** which is done is the result of rivalry between a man and his neighbor. This too **is vanity** and striving after wind.

Ecclesiastes 4:4

"The kingdom of heaven is like a landowner who went out early in the morning to hire laborers for his vineyard. And when he had agreed with the laborers for a denarius for the day, he sent them into his vineyard. And he went out about the third hour and saw others standing idle in the market place; and to those he said, 'You too go into the vineyard, and whatever is right I will give you.' And so they went. Again he went out about the sixth and the ninth hour, and did the same thing. And about the eleventh hour he went out, and found others standing; and he said to them, 'Why have you been standing here idle all day long?' They said to him, 'Because no one hired us.' He said to them, 'You too go into the vineyard.' And when evening had come, the owner of the vineyard said to his foreman, 'Call the laborers and pay them their wages, beginning with the last group to the first.' And when those hired about the eleventh hour came, each one received a denarius. And when those hired first came, they thought that they would receive more; and they also received each one a denarius. And when they received it, they grumbled at the landowner, saying, 'These last men have worked only one hour, and you have made them equal to us who have borne the burden and the scorching heat of the day.' But he answered and said to one of them, 'Friend, I am doing you no wrong; did you not agree with me for a denarius? Take what is yours and go your way, but I wish to give to this last man the same as to you. Is it not lawful for me to do what I wish with what is my own? **Or is your eye envious**

because I am generous?' Thus the last shall be first, and
the first last."

Matthew 20:1–16

"What did you go out to see? A man dressed in soft clothing? Behold, those who are splendidly clothed and live in
luxury are found in royal palaces."

Luke 7:25

"The patriarchs **became jealous of Joseph and sold him
into Egypt.** And yet God **was with him.**"

Acts 7:9

What is your source of quarrels and conflicts among you?
Is it not the source of your pleasures that wage war in your
members? **You lust and do not have;** so you commit murder. And you are envious and cannot obtain; so you fight
and quarrel. You do not have because you do not ask. **You
ask and do not receive, because you ask with wrong motives,** so that you may spend it on your pleasures.

James 4:1–3

Therefore, **putting aside all malice** and all guile and hypocrisy **and envy** and all slander.

1 Peter 2:1

FEAR

Our anxieties and worries usually are not related to the lack of things but rather to the loss of things. One of Satan's favorite tools is the question, "What if?" Dedicated Christians get trapped in fear—the "What if" of retirement, disability, unemployment, extended illness, economic collapse. God wants us to consider these things and even plan for them—within reason. But a Christian must consciously reject the attitude of fear.

Fear is the antithesis of trust; therefore, if we live in fear of the future, financially, we suffer from the problem of not putting our trust in God. That doesn't mean that we shouldn't plan for the future, but if we live in fear it means that we have taken on a responsibility that belongs to God. If other people see us living lives of fear, we lose our witness.

When Joseph's brothers saw that their father was dead, they said, "What if Joseph should bear a grudge against us and **pay us back in full** for all the wrong which we did to him!"

Genesis 50:15

The Lord is my light and my salvation; whom shall I fear? **The Lord is the defense of my life;** whom shall I dread?

Psalm 27:1

Behold, the **eye of the Lord is on those who fear** Him, on those who hope for His lovingkindness.

Psalm 33:18

How **blessed is the man who fears the Lord,** who greatly delights in His commandments. His descendants will be mighty on earth.

Psalm 112:1–2

The fear of the Lord is the **beginning of knowledge;** fools despise wisdom and instruction.

Proverbs 1:7

Anxiety in the heart of a man weighs it down, but a good word makes it glad.

Proverbs 12:25

In the fear of the Lord there is strong confidence, and **his children will have refuge.**

Proverbs 14:26

Better is a little with fear of the Lord, than great treasure and turmoil with it.

Proverbs 15:16

Do not be excessively wicked, and do not be a fool. . . . It is good that you grasp one thing, and also not let go of the other; for **the one who fears God comes forth** with both of them.

Ecclesiastes 7:17–18

"I am the Lord your God who upholds your right hand, who says to you, 'Do not fear, **I will help you.**'"

Isaiah 41:13

"Peace I leave with you; My peace I give to you; not as the world gives, do I give to you. Let not **your heart be troubled, nor let it be fearful.**"

John 14:27

There is no fear in love; but **perfect love casts out fear,** because fear involves punishment, and the one who fears is not perfected in love.

1 John 4:18

FUTILITY OF RICHES

Poverty is not God's norm, but neither is lavish-ness. It is clear from God's Word that affluence presents the greatest threat to our walk with the Lord: Where your treasure is, there your heart will be. Perhaps in our society nothing reflects more the futility of riches than very wealthy people who, at the end of their lifetimes, look back and decide their entire lives have been spent in true futility.

Howard Hughes was the consummate example of this problem. One of the world's wealthiest men, he ended up starving himself because he feared dying. Truly the futility of riches is a lack of trust in God.

"**Let him not trust in emptiness,** deceiving himself; for emptiness will be his reward."

Job 15:31

"**Pure gold cannot be given in exchange for it,** nor can silver be weighed as its price. It cannot be valued in the gold of Ophir, in precious onyx, or sapphire. Gold or glass cannot equal it, nor can it be exchanged for articles of fine gold. Coral and crystal are not to be mentioned; and the acquisition of wisdom is above that of pearls. The topaz of Ethiopia cannot equal it, nor can it be valued in pure gold."

Job 28:15–19

"Terrors are turned against me, they pursue my honor as the wind, and my **prosperity has passed away like a cloud.**"

Job 30:15

Arise, O Lord, confront him, bring him low; deliver my soul from the wicked with Thy sword, **from men with Thy hand, O Lord, from men of the world, whose portion is in**

this life; and whose belly Thou dost fill with Thy treasure; they are satisfied with children, and leave their abundance to their babes. As for me, I shall behold Thy face in righteousness; I will be satisfied with Thy likeness when I awake.

Psalm 17:13–15

All the prosperous of the earth will eat and worship, all those who go down to the dust will bow before Him, even he who cannot keep his soul alive.

Psalm 22:29

"Surely every man walks about as a phantom; surely they make an uproar for nothing; **he amasses riches, and does not know who will gather them.**"

Psalm 39:6

Even those who trust in their wealth, and boast in the abundance of their riches? No man can by any means redeem his brother, or give to God a ransom for him.

Psalm 49:6–7

He sees that **even wise men die;** the stupid and the senseless alike perish, **and leave their wealth to others.** Their inner thought is, that their houses are forever, and their dwelling places to all generations; they have called their lands after their own names. **But man in his pomp will not endure;** he is like the beasts that perish.

Psalm 49:10–12

Do not be afraid when a man becomes rich, when the glory of his house is increased; For when he dies he will carry nothing away; his glory will not descend after him.

Psalm 49:16–17

"Behold, the man who would not make God his refuge, **but trusted in the abundance of his riches,** and was strong in his evil desire."

Psalm 52:7

Do not trust in oppression, and do not vainly hope in robbery; **if riches increase, do not set your heart upon them.**
Psalm 62:10

Behold, **these are the wicked;** and always at ease, they have increased in wealth.
Psalm 73:12

"**He has taken a bag of money with him,** at full moon he will come home."
Proverbs 7:20

The rich man's wealth is his fortress, the ruin of the poor is their poverty.
Proverbs 10:15

Riches do not profit in the day of wrath, but righteousness delivers from death.
Proverbs 11:4

He who trusts in his riches will fall, but the righteous will flourish like the green leaf.
Proverbs 11:28

There is a way which seems right to a man, but its end is the way of death.
Proverbs 14:12

A rich man's wealth is his strong city, and like a high wall in his own imagination.
Proverbs 18:11

I have seen all the works which have been done under the sun, and behold, **all is vanity** and striving after wind.
Ecclesiastes 1:14

I said to myself, "Come now, **I will test you with pleasure. So enjoy yourself."** And behold, it too was futility.
Ecclesiastes 2:1

I collected for myself silver and gold, and the treasure of kings and provinces. I provided for myself male and female singers and the pleasures of men—many concubines. Then I became great and increased more than all who preceded me in Jerusalem. My wisdom also stood by me. And **all that my eyes desired I did not refuse them.** I did not withhold my heart from any pleasure, for my heart was pleased because of all my labor and this was my reward for all my labor. Thus I considered all my activities which my hands had done and the labor which I had exerted, and behold **all was vanity** and striving after wind and there was no profit under the sun.

Ecclesiastes 2:8–11

I completely despaired of all the fruit of my labor for which I had labored under the sun.

Ecclesiastes 2:20

What does a man get in all his labor and in his striving with which he labors under the sun?

Ecclesiastes 2:22

I looked again at vanity under the sun. There was **a certain man without a dependent,** having neither a son nor a brother, yet there was no end to all his labor. Indeed, **his eyes were not satisfied with riches** and he never asked, "And for whom am I laboring and depriving myself of pleasure?" This too is vanity and it is a grievous task.

Ecclesiastes 4:7–8

As he had come naked from his mother's womb, so will he return as he came. He will take nothing from the fruit of his labor that he can carry in his hand.

Ecclesiastes 5:15

There is an evil which I have seen under the sun and it is prevalent among men—**a man to whom God has given riches** and wealth and honor so that his soul lacks nothing of all that he desires, but **God has not empowered him to**

eat from them, for a foreigner enjoys them. This is a vanity and a severe affliction.

Ecclesiastes 6:1–2

All a man's labor is for his mouth and yet the appetite is not satisfied.

Ecclesiastes 6:7

In the day of prosperity be happy, but **in the day of adversity consider—God has made the one as well as the other** so that man may not discover anything that will be after him.

Ecclesiastes 7:14

So then, I have seen the wicked buried, those who used to go in and out from the holy place, and **they are soon forgotten** in the city where they did thus. This too is futility.

Ecclesiastes 8:10

Men prepare a meal for enjoyment, and wine makes life merry, and **money is the answer to everything.**

Ecclesiastes 10:19

Their land has also been filled with silver and gold, and there **is no end to their treasures.**

Isaiah 2:7

The oracle concerning the beasts of the Negev. Through a land of distress and anguish, from where come lioness and lion, viper and flying serpent, they carry their riches on the backs of young donkeys and their treasures on camels' humps, to a people **who cannot profit them.**

Isaiah 30:6

"Ho! Every one who thirsts, come to the waters; and **you who have no money come, buy and eat.** Come, buy wine and milk without money and without cost. Why do you spend money for what is not bread, and your wages for

what does not satisfy? Listen carefully to Me, and eat what is good, and delight yourself in abundance."

Isaiah 55:1–2

Thus says the Lord, "**Cursed is the man who trusts in mankind** and makes flesh his strength, and whose heart turns away from the Lord. For he will be like a bush in the desert and will not see when prosperity comes, but will live in stony wastes in the wilderness, a land of salt without inhabitant."

Jeremiah 17:5–6

In the days of her affliction and homelessness Jerusalem **remembers all her precious things** that were from the days of old when her people fell into the hand of the adversary, and no one helped her. The adversaries saw her, they mocked at her ruin.

Lamentations 1:7

How dark the gold has become, **how the pure gold has changed!** The sacred stones are poured out at the corner of every street.

Lamentations 4:1

Those who ate delicacies are desolate in the streets; those reared in purple **embrace ash pits.**

Lamentations 4:5

"You also took your beautiful jewels made of My gold and of My silver, which I had given you, and **made for yourself male images** that you might play the harlot with them."

Ezekiel 16:17

"But he will gain control over the hidden treasures of gold and silver, and over all the precious things of Egypt; and Libyans and Ethiopians will follow at his heels."

Daniel 11:43

Woe to those who are at ease in Zion, and to **those who feel secure** in the mountain of Samaria, the distinguished men of the foremost of nations, to whom the house of Israel comes. Go over to Calneh and look, and go from there to Hamath the great, then go down to Gath of the Philistines. Are they better than these kingdoms, or is their territory greater than yours? Do you put off the day of calamity, and would you bring near the seat of violence? Those who recline on beds of ivory and sprawl on their couches, and eat lambs from the flock and calves from the midst of the stall, who improvise to the sound of the harp, and like David have composed songs for themselves, who drink wine from sacrificial bowls while they anoint themselves with the finest of oils, yet they have not grieved over the ruin of Joseph. Therefore, they will now go into exile at the head of the exiles, and **the sprawlers' banqueting will pass away.**

Amos 6:1–7

"**You have increased your traders** more than the stars of heaven—the creeping locust strips and flies away."

Nahum 3:16

"**Do not lay up for yourselves treasures upon earth,** where moth and rust destroy, and where thieves break in and steal. But lay up for yourselves treasures in heaven, where neither moth nor rust destroys, and where thieves do not break in or steal; for where your treasure is, there will your heart be also."

Matthew 6:19–21

"**Others fell among the thorns,** and the thorns came up and choked them out."

Matthew 13:7

"**The one on whom seed was sown among the thorns,** this is the man who hears the word, and the worry of the world, and the deceitfulness of riches choke the word, and it becomes unfruitful."

Matthew 13:22

"What will a man be profited, if he gains the whole world, and forfeits his soul? Or what will a man give in exchange for his soul?"

Matthew 16:26

Jesus said to His disciples, "Truly I say to you, **it is hard for a rich man to enter the kingdom of heaven."**

Matthew 19:23

"What does it profit a man to gain the whole world, and forfeit his soul? For what shall a man give in exchange for his soul?"

Mark 8:36–37

"Woe to you who are rich, for you are receiving your comfort in full."

Luke 6:24

"The seed which fell among the thorns, these are the ones who have heard, and as they go on their way they are choked with worries and riches and pleasures of this life, and bring no fruit to maturity. And the seed in the good soil, these are the ones who have heard the word in an honest and good heart, and hold it fast, and bear fruit with perseverance."

Luke 8:14–15

"What is a man profited if he gains the whole world, and loses or forfeits himself?"

Luke 9:25

"Which of you being anxious can add a single cubit to his life's span?"

Luke 12:25

"There was a certain rich man, and he habitually dressed in purple and fine linen, gaily living in splendor every day. And a certain poor man named Lazarus was laid at his gate, covered with sores, and longing to be fed with the crumbs which were falling from the rich man's table; besides, even the dogs were coming and licking his sores. Now it came about that the poor man died and he was carried away by the angels to Abraham's bosom; and the rich man also died and was buried. And in Hades he lifted up his eyes, being in torment, and saw Abraham far away, and Lazarus in his bosom. And he cried out and said, 'Father Abraham, have mercy on me, and send Lazarus, that he may dip the tip of his finger in water and cool off my tongue; for I am in agony in this flame.' But Abraham said, 'Child, remember that **during your life you received your good things,** and likewise Lazarus bad things; but now he is being comforted here, and you are in agony.'"

Luke 16:19–25

When Jesus heard this, He said to him, "One thing you still lack; **sell all that you possess, and distribute it to the poor,** and you shall have treasure in heaven; and come, follow Me." But when he heard these things, he became very sad; for he was extremely rich. And Jesus looked at him and said, "How hard it is for those who are wealthy to enter the kingdom of God! For it is easier for a camel to go through the eye of a needle, than for a rich man to enter the kingdom of God."

Luke 18:22–25

"He who loves his life loses it; and he who hates his life in this world shall keep it to life eternal."

John 12:25

If from human motives I fought with wild beasts at Ephesus, what does it profit me? **If the dead are not raised, let us eat and drink, for tomorrow we die.**

1 Corinthians 15:32

Those who want to get rich fall into temptation and a snare and many foolish and harmful desires which plunge men into ruin and destruction.

1 Timothy 6:9

Instruct those who are rich in this present world not to be conceited or to fix their hope on the uncertainty of riches, but on God, who richly supplies us with all things to enjoy.
1 Timothy 6:17

Let the rich man glory in his humiliation, because like flowering grass he will pass away. For the sun rises with a scorching wind, and withers the grass; and its flower falls off, and the beauty of its appearance is destroyed; so too **the rich man in the midst of his pursuits will fade away.**
James 1:10–11

Come now, you rich, weep and howl for your miseries which are coming upon you. Your riches have rotted and your garments have become moth-eaten. Your gold and your silver have rusted; and their rust will be a witness against you and will consume your flesh like fire. It is in the last days that you have stored up your treasure! Behold, the pay of the laborers who mowed your fields, and which has been withheld by you, cries out against you; and the outcry of those who did the harvesting has reached the ears of the Lord of Sabaoth. You have lived luxuriously on the earth and led a life of wanton pleasure; you have fattened your hearts in a day of slaughter.
James 5:1–5

[Conduct yourselves] knowing that **you were not redeemed with perishable things** like silver or gold from your futile way of life inherited from your forefathers.
1 Peter 1:18

The woman was clothed in purple and scarlet, and **adorned with gold and precious stones and pearls,** having in her hand a gold cup full of abominations and of unclean things of her immorality.
Revelation 17:4

The merchants of the earth weep and mourn over her, because no one buys their cargoes any more; **cargoes of gold and silver and precious stones** and pearls and fine linen and purple and silk and scarlet, and every kind of citron wood and every article of ivory and every article made from very costly wood and bronze and iron and marble, and cinnamon and spice and incense and perfume and frankincense and wine and olive oil and fine flour and wheat and cattle and sheep, and cargoes of horses and chariots and slaves and human lives.

Revelation 18:11–13

GET-RICH-QUICK

There's a significant difference between being a good steward (investing for future needs) and trying to get rich quick. Today the get-rich-quick-attitude advocates are evident in the state lotteries proliferating around the U.S. There's a desire to make money very quickly with very little applied effort. In reality, the vast majority of wealthy people in America got that way by working at what they do the best and what they love the most, and the by-product of their efforts was wealth.

Contrary to that work ethic is the get-rich-quick attitude, which has several dangerous premises: (1) you get involved with things you don't understand; (2) you make hasty decisions; (3) you suffer significant losses. Trying to get rich quick is another form of gambling. The Proverbs say that a man who hastens to get wealthy quickly will get poor even more quickly.

Rest in the Lord and **wait patiently for Him;** do not fret because of him who prospers in his way, because of the man who carries out wicked schemes.

Psalm 37:7

Trust in the Lord with all your heart, and do not lean on your own understanding.

Proverbs 3:5

It is the blessing of the Lord that makes rich, and He adds no sorrow to it.

Proverbs 10:22

The way of a fool is right in his own eyes, but a wise man is he who listens to counsel.

Proverbs 12:15

111

The plans of the diligent lead surely to advantage, but **everyone who is hasty comes surely to poverty.**

Proverbs 21:5

By wisdom a house is built, and by understanding it is established; and **by knowledge the rooms are filled with all precious and pleasant riches.**

Proverbs 24:3–4

Do not boast about tomorrow, for you do not know what a day may bring forth.

Proverbs 27:1

The prudent man sees evil and hides himself, the **naive proceed and pay the penalty.**

Proverbs 27:12

She considers a field and buys it; from her earnings she plants a vineyard. She makes linen garments and sells them, and supplies belts to the tradesmen. Strength and dignity are her clothing, and **she smiles at the future.**

Proverbs 31:16, 24–25

reed says, "I want more, I want the best, and I'll not be satisfied with anything less." It causes money to become the object of devotion and commitment. Greed can separate families and friendships and breed dishonesty and guilt. Greed is evident in our society in terms of storage—putting money aside that will never be used, primarily because it brings a feeling of security.

Many Christians are going to be ashamed to face the Lord and explain why they hoarded money while others went hungry. Once commitment has been made to a disciplined lifestyle, regardless of the available income, the danger of greed and its by-products is significantly reduced.

"**Why did you steal my gods?**" Then Jacob answered and said to Laban, "Because I was afraid, for I said, 'Lest you would take your daughter from me by force.' The one with whom you find your gods shall not live. . . ." For Jacob did not know that Rachel had stolen them.

Genesis 31:30–32

The rabble who were among them had greedy desires; and also the sons of Israel wept again and said, "Who will give us meat to eat?"

Numbers 11:4

So the name of that place was called Kibroth-hattaavah, because **they buried the people who had been greedy.**

Numbers 11:34

"**The graven images of their gods you are to burn with fire;** you shall not covet the silver or the gold that is on them, nor take it for yourselves, lest you be snared by it, for it is an abomination to the Lord your God."

Deuteronomy 7:25

113

"Only **keep yourselves from the things under the ban, lest you covet them** and take some of the things under the ban, so you would make the camp of Israel accursed and bring trouble on it. But all the silver and gold and articles of bronze and iron are holy to the Lord; they shall go into the treasury of the Lord."

Joshua 6:18–19

The sons of Israel acted unfaithfully in regard to the things under the ban, for Achan, the son of Carmi, the son of Zabdi, the son of Zerah, from the tribe of Judah, took some of the things under the ban, therefore the anger of the Lord burned against the sons of Israel.

Joshua 7:1

"When I saw among the spoil a beautiful mantle from Shinar and two hundred shekels of silver and a bar of gold fifty shekels in weight, then **I coveted them and took them;** and behold, they are concealed in the earth inside my tent with the silver underneath it." So Joshua sent messengers, and they ran to the tent; and behold, it was concealed in his tent with the silver underneath it.

Joshua 7:21–22

There was a man in Maon whose business was in Carmel; and **the man was very rich,** and he had three thousand sheep and a thousand goats. And it came about while he was shearing his sheep in Carmel (now the man's name was Nabal, and his wife's name was Abigail. And the woman was intelligent and beautiful in appearance, but the man was harsh and **evil in his dealings,** and he was a Calebite).

1 Samuel 25:2–3

The Lord sent Nathan to David. And he came to him, and said, "There were two men in one city, the one rich and the other poor. The rich man had a great many flocks and herds. But the poor man had nothing except one little ewe lamb which he bought and nourished; And it grew up together with him and his children. It would eat of his bread and drink of his cup and lie in his bosom, and was like a daughter to him."

2 Samuel 12:1–3

"**Your silver and your gold are mine;** your most beautiful wives and children are also mine."

1 Kings 20:3

The king of Israel called all the elders of the land and said, "Please observe and see how this man is looking for trouble; for he sent to me for my wives and my children and my silver and my gold, and I did not refuse him."

1 Kings 20:7

"It is close beside my house, and **I will give you a better vineyard than it in its place;** if you like, I will give you the price of it in money."

1 Kings 21:2

He went in and stood before his master. And Elisha said to him, "Where have you been, Gehazi?" And he said, "Your servant went nowhere." Then he said to him, "Did not my heart go with you, when the man turned from his chariot to meet you? Is it a time to receive money and to receive clothes and olive groves and vineyards and sheep and oxen and male and female servants? Therefore, the leprosy of Naaman shall cleave to you and to your descendants forever." So he went out from his presence a leper as white as snow.

2 Kings 5:25–27

"**The schemer is eager for their wealth.**"

Job 5:5

The wicked boasts of his heart's desire, and **the greedy man curses and spurns the Lord.**

Psalm 10:3

The righteousness of the upright will deliver them, but the treacherous will be caught by their own greed.

Proverbs 11:6

A gracious woman attains honor, and violent men attain riches.

Proverbs 11:16

The wicked desires the booty of evil men, but the root of the righteous yields fruit.

Proverbs 12:12

Do not let your heart envy sinners, but live in the fear of the Lord always.

Proverbs 23:17

Have you found honey? **Eat only what you need,** lest you have it in excess and vomit it.

Proverbs 25:16

There is a grievous evil which I have seen under the sun; riches being hoarded by their owner to his hurt.

Ecclesiastes 5:13

"**The dogs are greedy,** they are not satisfied. And they are shepherds who have no understanding; they have all turned to their own way, each one to his unjust gain, to the last one."

Isaiah 56:11

"From the least of them even to the greatest of them, **everyone is greedy for gain,** and from the prophet even to the priest everyone deals falsely."

Jeremiah 6:13

"I will give their wives to others, their fields to new owners; because from the least even to the greatest **everyone is greedy for gain;** from the prophet even to the priest everyone practices deceit."

Jeremiah 8:10

The precious sons of Zion, **weighed against fine gold,** how they are regarded as earthen jars, the work of a potter's hands!

Lamentations 4:2

"They come to you as people come, and they sit before you as My people, and hear your words, but they do not do them, for they do the lustful desires expressed by their mouth, **and their heart goes after their gain.**"

Ezekiel 33:31

"Sheba, and Dedan, and the merchants of Tarshish, with all its villages, will say to you, 'Have you come to capture spoil? Have you assembled your company to seize plunder, to carry away silver and gold, to take away cattle and goods, to capture great spoil?'"

Ezekiel 38:13

"**They covet fields and then seize them,** and houses, and take them away. They rob a man and his house, a man and his inheritance."

Micah 2:2

"**The women of my people you evict,** each one from her pleasant house. From her children you take My splendor forever."

Micah 2:9

"**He who loves father or mother more than Me is not worthy of Me;** and he who loves son or daughter more than Me is not worthy of Me."

Matthew 10:37

"Listen to another parable. There was a landowner who planted a vineyard and put a wall around it and dug a wine press in it, and built a tower, and rented it out to vine-growers, and went on a journey. And when the harvest time approached, he sent his slaves to the vine-growers to receive his produce. And the vine-growers took his slaves and beat one, and killed another, stoned a third. Again he

117

sent another group of slaves larger than the first; and they did the same thing to them. But afterward he sent his son to them, saying, 'They will respect my son.' But when the vine-growers saw the son, they said among themselves, 'This is the heir; come, let us kill him, and seize his inheritance.' And they took him, and threw him out of the vineyard, and killed him. Therefore when the owner of the vineyard comes, what will he do to those vine-growers?" They said to Him, "He **will bring those wretches to a wretched end,** and will rent out the vineyard to other vine-growers, who will pay him the proceeds at the proper seasons."

Matthew 21:33–41

"What are you willing to give me to deliver Him up to you?" And **they weighed out to him thirty pieces of silver.**

Matthew 26:15

When Judas, who had betrayed Him, saw that He had been condemned, **he felt remorse and returned the thirty pieces of silver** to the chief priests and elders, saying, "I have sinned by betraying innocent blood." But they said, "What is that to us? See to that yourself!" And he threw the pieces of silver into the sanctuary and departed; and he went away and hanged himself. And the chief priests took the pieces of silver and said, "It is not lawful to put them into the temple treasury, since it is the price of blood." And they counseled together and with the money bought the Potter's Field as a burial place for strangers. For this reason that field has been called the Field of Blood to this day. Then that which was spoken through Jeremiah the prophet was fulfilled, saying, "And they took the thirty pieces of silver, the price of the One whose price had been set by the son of Israel; and they gave them for the Potter's Field, as the Lord directed me."

Matthew 27:3–10

"Others are **the ones on whom seed was sown among the thorns;** these are the ones who have heard the word, and the worries of the world, and the deceitfulness of riches, and the desires for other things enter in and choke the word, and it becomes unfruitful."

Mark 4:18–19

He began to speak to them in parables: "**A man planted a vineyard, and put a wall around it,** and dug a vat under the wine press, and built a tower, and rented it out to vine-growers and went on a journey. And at the harvest time he sent a slave to the vine-growers, in order to receive some of the produce of the vineyard from the vine-growers. And they took him, and beat him, and sent him away empty-handed. And again he sent them another slave, and they wounded him in the head, and treated him shamefully. And he sent another, and that one they killed; and so with many others, beating some, and killing others. He had one more to send, a beloved son; he sent him last of all to them, saying, 'They will respect my son.' But those vine-growers said to one another, 'This is the heir; come, let us kill him, and the inheritance will be ours!' And they took him, and killed him, and threw him out of the vineyard. What will the owner of the vineyard do? He will come and destroy the vine-growers, and will give the vineyard to others."

Mark 12:1–9

Judas Iscariot, who was one of the twelve, went off to the chief priests, in order to betray Him to them. And they were glad when **they heard this, and promised to give him money.** And he began seeking how to betray Him at an opportune time.

Mark 14:10–11

He said to them, "**Beware, and be on your guard against every form of greed;** for not even when one has an abundance does his life consist of his possessions." And He told them a parable, saying, "The land of a certain rich man was very productive. And he began reasoning to himself, saying, 'What shall I do, since I have no place to store my crops?' And he said, 'This is what I will do: **I will tear down my barns and build larger ones,** and there I will store all my grain and my goods. And I will say to my soul,

119

Greed

"Soul, you have many goods laid up for many years to
come; take your ease, eat, drink, and be merry.'" But God
said to him, 'You fool! This very night your soul is required
of you; and **now who will own what you have prepared?'**
So is the man who lays up treasure for himself, and is not
rich toward God."

Luke 12:15–21

The **Pharisees, who were lovers of money,** were listening to
all these things, and they were scoffing at Him.

Luke 16:14

It happened that as we were going to the place of prayer, a
certain slave-girl having a spirit of divination met us, who
was bringing her masters much profit by fortunetelling.

Acts 16:16

**When her masters saw that their hope of profit was gone,
they seized Paul** and Silas and dragged them into the market place before the authorities.

Acts 16:19

A certain man named **Demetrius,** a silversmith, who made
silver shrines of Artemis, was bringing no little business to
the craftsmen; these he gathered together with the workmen of similar trades, and said, "Men, you know that **our
prosperity depends upon this business.** And you see and
hear that not only in Ephesus, but in almost all of Asia,
this Paul has persuaded and turned away a considerable
number of people, saying that gods made with hands are
no gods at all."

Acts 19:24–26

Just as they did not see fit to acknowledge God any longer,
God gave them over to a depraved mind, to do those things
which are not proper, being filled with all unrighteousness, wickedness, **greed,** evil; full of envy, murder, strife,
deceit, malice; they are gossips.

Romans 1:28–29

You who say that one should not commit adultery, do you commit adultery? You who abhor idols, **do you rob temples?**

Romans 2:22

Do not let immorality or any impurity or **greed even be named among you,** as is proper among saints.

Ephesians 5:3

We never came with flattering speech, as you know, **nor with a pretext for greed**—God is witness.

1 Thessalonians 2:5

[There is] constant friction between **men of depraved mind** and deprived of the truth, **who suppose that godliness is a means** of gain. But godliness actually is a means of great gain, when accompanied by contentment. For we have brought nothing into the world, so we cannot take anything out of it either. And if we have food and covering, with these we shall be content.

1 Timothy 6:5–8

There are many rebellious men, empty talkers and deceivers . . . who must be silenced because they are upsetting whole families, **teaching things they should not teach,** for the sake of sordid gain.

Titus 1:10–11

What is your source of quarrels and conflicts among you? Is it not the source of your pleasures that wage war in your members? **You lust and do not have;** so you commit murder. And you are envious and cannot obtain; so you fight and quarrel. You do not have because you do not ask. **You ask and do not receive, because you ask with wrong motives,** so that you may spend it on your pleasures.

James 4:1–3

In their greed they will exploit you with false words; their judgment from long ago is not idle, and their destruction is not asleep.

2 Peter 2:3

They are stains and blemishes, reveling in their deceptions, as the carouse with you, having eyes full of adultery and that never cease from sin; enticing unstable souls, **having a heart trained in greed,** accursed children.

2 Peter 2:13–14

Woe to them! For they have gone the way of Cain, and for pay **they have rushed headlong** into the error of Balaam, and perished in the rebellion of Korah.

Jude 11

"All nations have drunk of the wine of the passion of her immorality, and the kings of the earth have committed acts of immorality with her, and **the merchants of the earth have become rich by the wealth** of her sensuality."

Revelation 18:3

INDULGENCE

It's easy to rationalize an indulgent lifestyle in a society where most people indulge themselves. While we go to sleep disturbed over whether or not to buy a big screen TV, over half the world's children go to bed hungry or cold. One who never is willing to sacrifice, never willing to deny impulses to spend, and constantly seeks to indulge whimsical desires, will always be in bondage and feel frustrated. We all indulge ourselves to some degree. It is not the cost of an item that determines whether or not it's an indulgence. It's the utility of an item.

A friend of mine bought a $50 million airplane. That is a great deal of money. However, it wasn't an indulgence for him because he owned an airline; it was a tool for making a living. But for someone else, a $3,000 bass boat could be very indulgent, especially if it were never used.

He who loves pleasure will become a poor man; he who loves wine and oil will not become rich.

Proverbs 21:17

Like a city that is broken into and without walls is **a man who has no control over his spirit.**

Proverbs 25:28

A sated man loathes honey, but to a famished man any bitter thing is sweet.

Proverbs 27:7

INJUSTICE

God has placed us in a physical world and expects us to live in it. We are placed in this society so He can reveal Himself through us. For this to happen, we must avoid the devices of the accuser and hold to standards of the Lord.

Injustice occurs when we take unfair advantage of another person financially. The spectrum of sins covered in injustice: oppression of the poor or less-advantaged, cheating, robbing, charging excessive rent, making unjust decisions, showing partiality, receiving unjust gain, bribery, underpaying employees, and more.

Will we be doers of the Word and not hearers only? There's a simple principle established in God's Word in James: "You rich, weep and howl for your miseries which are coming upon you."

Judah said to his brothers, "What profit is it for us to kill our brother and cover up his blood? **Come and let us sell him to the Ishmaelites and not lay our hands on him;** for he is our brother, our own flesh." And his brothers listened to him . . . and sold [Joseph] to the Ishmaelites for twenty shekels of silver. Thus they brought Joseph into Egypt.

Genesis 37:26–28

"**You shall do no injustice in judgment;** you shall not be partial to the poor nor defer to the great, but you are to judge your neighbor fairly."

Leviticus 19:15

"**You shall not pervert the justice due an alien,** or an orphan, nor take a widow's garment in pledge."

Deuteronomy 24:17

"A traveler came to the rich man, and he was unwilling to take from his own flock or his own herd, to prepare for the wayfarer who had come to him; **rather he took the poor man's ewe lamb and prepared it for the man who had come to him.**" Then David's anger burned greatly against the man, and he said to Nathan, "As the Lord lives, surely the man who has done this deserves to die. And he must make restitution for the lamb fourfold, because he did this thing and had no compassion."

2 Samuel 12:4–6

The king said to Haman, "The silver is yours, and the people also, to do with them as you please . . . and to **seize their possessions as plunder.**"

Esther 3:11, 13

Mordecai told him all that had happened to him, and **the exact amount of money that Haman had promised to pay** to the king's treasuries for the destruction of the Jews.

Esther 4:7

"**You would even cast lots for the orphans, and barter over your friend.**"

Job 6:27

"**The tents of the destroyers prosper,** and those who provoke God are secure, whom God brings into their power."

Job 12:6

"He returns what he has attained and cannot swallow it; **as to the riches of his trading, he cannot even enjoy them.** For he has oppressed and forsaken the poor; he has seized a house which he has not built. Because he knew no quiet within him he does not retain anything he desires. Nothing remains for him to devour, therefore his prosperity does not endure. In the fullness of his plenty he will be cramped; the hand of everyone who suffers will come against him."

Job 20:18–22

"**They drive away the donkeys of the orphans;** they take the widow's ox for a pledge. **They push the needy aside** from the road; the poor of the land are made to hide themselves altogether."

Job 24:3–4

"**Others snatch the orphan from the breast,** and against the poor they take a pledge. They cause the poor to go about naked without clothing, and they take away the sheaves from the hungry."

Job 24:9–10

"The murderer arises at dawn; **he kills the poor and the needy,** and at night he is as a thief."

Job 24:14

In pride **the wicked hotly pursue the afflicted;** let them be caught in the plots which they have devised.

Psalm 10:2

The fool has said in his heart, "There is no God." They are corrupt, they have committed abominable deeds; there is no one who does good.

Psalm 14:1

How long will you judge unjustly, and show partiality to the wicked? Vindicate the weak and fatherless; do justice to the afflicted and destitute, rescue the weak and needy; deliver them out of the hand of the wicked.

Psalm 82:2–4

He did not remember to show lovingkindness, **but persecuted the afflicted and needy man,** and the despondent in heart, to put them to death.

Psalm 109:16

"**We shall find all kinds of precious wealth,** we shall fill our houses with spoil; throw in your lot with us, we shall all have one purse."

Proverbs 1:13–14

So are the ways of everyone who gains by violence; it takes away the life of its possessors.

Proverbs 1:19

Abundant food is in the fallow ground of the poor, but it is swept away by injustice.

Proverbs 13:23

The poor is hated even by his neighbor, but those who love the rich are many.

Proverbs 14:20

Better is a little with righteousness than great income with injustice.

Proverbs 16:8

He who mocks the poor reproaches his Maker; he who rejoices at calamity will not go unpunished.

Proverbs 17:5

All the brothers of a poor man hate him; how much more do his friends go far from him! He pursues them with words, but they are gone.

Proverbs 19:7

He who oppresses the poor to make much for himself or who gives to the rich, will only come to poverty.

Proverbs 22:16

Do not rob the poor because he is poor, or crush the afflicted at the gate; for the Lord will plead their case, and take the life of those who rob them.

Proverbs 22:22–23

Do not move the ancient boundary, or go into the fields of the fatherless; for their Redeemer is strong; He will plead their case against you.

Proverbs 23:10–11

A poor man who oppresses the lowly is like a driving rain which leaves no food.

Proverbs 28:3

A leader who is a great oppressor lacks understanding, but he who hates unjust gain will prolong his days.

Proverbs 28:16

Let him drink and forget his poverty, and remember his trouble no more.

Proverbs 31:7

If you see oppression of the poor and denial of justice and righteousness in the province, **do not be shocked** at the sight, for one official watches over another official, and there are higher officials over them.

Ecclesiastes 5:8

For oppression makes a wise man mad, and a bribe corrupts the heart.

Ecclesiastes 7:7

Folly is set in many exalted places while rich men sit in humble places.

Ecclesiastes 10:6

"**What do you mean by crushing my people,** and grinding the face of the poor?" declares the Lord God of hosts.

Isaiah 3:15

Woe to those who enact evil statutes, and to those who constantly record unjust decisions, so as to deprive the needy of justice, and rob the poor of My people of their rights, in order that widows may be their spoil, and that they may plunder the orphans.

Isaiah 10:1–2

"**Because of the iniquity of his unjust gain I was angry** and struck him; I hid My face and was angry, and he went on turning away, in the way of his heart."

Isaiah 57:17

"They are fat, they are sleek, they also excel in deeds of wickedness; **they do not plead the cause,** the cause of the orphan, that they may prosper; and they do not defend the rights of the poor."

Jeremiah 5:28

"As a partridge that hatches eggs which it has not laid, so is **he who makes a fortune, but unjustly;** in the midst of his days it will forsake him, and in the end he will be a fool."

Jeremiah 17:11

To deprive a man of justice in the presence of the Most High, to **defraud a man in his lawsuit**—of these things the Lord does not approve.

Lamentations 3:35–36

"There is a conspiracy of **her prophets** in her midst, like a roaring lion tearing the prey. They have devoured lives; **they have taken treasure and precious things;** they have made many widows in the midst of her."

Ezekiel 22:25

"The **people of the land have practiced oppression** and committed robbery, and they have wronged the poor and needy and have oppressed the sojourner without justice."

Ezekiel 22:29

"In his place one will arise who will send an oppressor through the Jewel of his kingdom; yet within a few days he will be shattered, though neither in anger nor in battle."

Daniel 11:20

Thus says the Lord, "For three transgressions of Israel and for four I will not revoke its punishment, **because they sell**

the righteous for money and the needy for a pair of sandals. These who pant after the very dust of the earth on the head of the helpless also turn aside the way of the humble; and a man and his father resort to the same girl in order to profane My holy name."

Amos 2:6–7

Hear this word, you cows of Bashan who are on the mountain of Samaria, who oppress the poor, **who crush the needy,** who say to your husbands, "Bring now, that we may drink!"

Amos 4:1

"Because **you impose heavy rent on the poor** and exact a tribute of grain from them, though you have built houses of well-hewn stone, yet you will not live in them; you have planted pleasant vineyards, yet you will not drink their wine."

Amos 5:11

"Do not enter the gate of My people in the day of their disaster. Yes, you, do not gloat over their calamity in the day of their disaster. And **do not loot their wealth** in the day of their disaster."

Obadiah 1:13

"They covet fields and then seize them, and houses, and take them away. They rob a man and his house, a man and his inheritance."

Micah 2:2

"Thou didst pierce with his own spears the head of his throngs. They stormed in to scatter us; their exultation was like those who **devour the oppressed in secret.**"

Habakkuk 3:14

"Let none of you devise evil in your heart against another, and **do not love perjury;** for all these are what I hate," declares the Lord.

Zechariah 8:17

130

"**Beware of men;** for they will deliver you up to the courts, and scourge you in their synagogues."

Matthew 10:17

"**No one can enter the strong man's house** and plunder his property unless he first binds the strong man, and then he will plunder his house."

Mark 3:27

"**Beware of the scribes,** who like to walk around in long robes, and love respectful greetings in the market places, and chief seats in the synagogues, and places of honor at banquets, who **devour widow's houses,** and for appearance's sake offer long prayers; these will receive greater condemnation."

Luke 20:46–47

My brethren, **do not hold your faith in our glorious Lord Jesus Christ with an attitude of personal favoritism.** For if a man comes into your assembly with a gold ring and dressed in fine clothes, and there also comes in a poor man in dirty clothes, and you pay special attention to the one who is wearing the fine clothes, and say, "You sit here in a good place," and you say to the poor man, "You stand over there, or sit down by my footstool," have you not made distinctions among yourselves, and become judges with evil motives? Listen, my beloved brethren: **did not God choose the poor of this world** to be rich in faith and heirs of the kingdom which He promised to those who love Him? But you have dishonored the poor man. Is it not the rich who oppress you and personally drag you into court? Do they not blaspheme the fair name by which you have been called? If, however, you are fulfilling the royal law, according to the Scripture, "**You shall love your neighbor as yourself,**" you are doing well. But if you show partiality, you are committing sin and are convicted by the law as transgressors. For whoever keeps the whole law and yet stumbles in one point, he has become guilty of all. For He who said, "**Do not commit adultery,**" also said, "**Do not commit murder.**" Now if you do not commit adultery, but

131

do commit murder, you have become a transgressor of the law. So speak and so act, as those who are to be judged by the law of liberty. For judgment will be merciless to one who has shown no mercy; mercy triumphs over judgment. What use is it, my brethren, if a man says he has **faith, but he has no works?** Can that faith save him? **If a brother or sister is without clothing and in need of daily food,** and one of you says to them, "Go in peace, be warmed and be filled," and yet you do not give them what is necessary for their body, what use is that?

James 2:1–16

LOVE OF MONEY

Paul said the love of money is but the beginning, or the root, of many kinds of evil. The lives of those who love money are characterized by greed, hoarding, and abasement. They have accumulated thousands, or even millions, and the loss of even a few dollars is traumatic. Many people love their money so much they will not part with it—to give to God's work or even to their own children.

The love of money is a form of idol worship, just as surely as the worship of pagan images. It is not the money that is the problem; it's the attitude toward it.

Because **all his days his task is painful** and grievous; even at night his mind does not rest. This too is vanity.

Ecclesiastes 2:23

He who loves money will not be satisfied with money, nor he who loves abundance with its income. This too is vanity.

Ecclesiastes 5:10

"Is it time for you yourselves to dwell in your paneled houses while **this house lies desolate?**"

Haggai 1:4

"You look for much, but behold, it comes to little; when you bring it home, I blow it away. Why?" declares the Lord of hosts, "Because of My house which lies desolate, while each of you runs to his own house."

Haggai 1:9

"**No one can serve two masters;** for either he will hate the one and love the other, or he will hold to one and despise the other. You cannot serve God and mammon."

Matthew 6:24

Looking at him, Jesus felt a love for him, and said to him, **"One thing you lack: go and sell all you possess,** and give to the poor, and you shall have treasure in heaven; and come, follow Me." But at these words his face fell, and he went away grieved, for he was one who owned much property. And Jesus, looking around, said to His disciples, "How hard it will be for those who are wealthy to enter the kingdom of God!" And the disciples were amazed at His words. But Jesus answered again and said to them, "Children, how hard it is to enter the kingdom of God! It is easier for a camel to go through the eye of a needle than for a rich man to enter the kingdom of God." And they were even more astonished and said to Him, "Then who can be saved?"

Mark 10:21–26

"What is a man profited if he gains the whole world, and loses or forfeits himself?"

Luke 9:25

He said to another, "Follow Me." But he said, **"Permit me first to go and bury my father."** But He said to him, "Allow the dead to bury their own dead; but as for you, go and proclaim everywhere the kingdom of God."

Luke 9:59–60

"No servant can serve two masters; for either he will hate the one, and love the other, or else he will hold to one, and despise the other. You cannot serve God and mammon." Now the **Pharisees, who were lovers of money,** were listening to all these things, and they were scoffing at Him.

Luke 16:13–14

Those who want to get rich fall into temptation and a snare and many foolish and harmful desires which plunge men into ruin and destruction. For the love of money is a root of all sorts of evil, and some by longing for it have wandered away from the faith, and pierced themselves with many a pang.

1 Timothy 6:9–10

Realize this, that in the last days difficult times will come. For **men will be lovers of self, lovers of money,** boastful, arrogant, revilers, disobedient to parents, ungrateful, unholy.

2 Timothy 3:1–2

PARTIALITY

When we esteem people on the basis of material success, we begin to equate riches with spirituality. Thus, those who are not materially successful are deemed less spiritual. To be sure, God does not hold to that same value system. There are at least 100 Scripture references that demonstrate God's view of our human tendency to elevate people because of their worldly success. We should never allow one person to be elevated over another simply because of position or riches. When we do that, we are no longer available to God.

I was called one afternoon by a friend who worked in Hollywood. He and one of the very recognizable actors were coming through Atlanta and asked if I could meet with them. Certainly I said yes. It was an opportunity of a lifetime. I told myself, "Who knows what kind of an influence you might be able to have over him?" But interestingly enough, less than an hour before, I had gotten a call from a widow I was counseling who regularly asked for counsel she didn't need. I had turned her down and told her I was too busy to meet with her. But when I realized that even though I was too busy to meet with her I wasn't too busy to meet with the movie star who was coming through, I knew I was showing partiality. God does not honor this attitude.

You shall not follow a multitude in doing evil, nor shall you testify in a dispute so as to turn aside after a multitude in order to pervert justice; **nor shall you be partial** to a poor man in his dispute.

Exodus 23:2–3

You **shall not show partiality in judgment;** you shall hear the small and great alike.

Deuteronomy 1:17

The Lord your God is the God of gods and the Lord of lords, the great, the mighty, and the **awesome God who does not show partiality,** nor take a bribe.

Deuteronomy 10:17

You shall not distort justice; you shall not be partial.

Deuteronomy 16:19

"Now then let the fear of the Lord be upon you; be very careful what you do, for **the Lord our God will have no part in unrighteousness, or partiality,** or the taking of a bribe.

2 Chronicles 19:7

How long will you judge unjustly, and show partiality to the wicked? Vindicate the weak and fatherless; do justice to the afflicted and destitute. Rescue the weak and needy; deliver them out of the hand of the wicked.

Psalm 82:2–4

The poor is hated even by his neighbor, but those who love the rich are many.

Proverbs 14:20

Wealth adds many friends, but a poor man is separated from his friend.

Proverbs 19:4

All the brothers of a poor man hate him; how much more do his friends go far from him! He pursues them with words, but they are gone.

Proverbs 19:7

These also are sayings of the wise. **To show partiality in judgment is not good.**

Proverbs 24:23

To show partiality is not good, because for a piece of bread a man will transgress.

Proverbs 28:21

"If you had known what this means, '**I desire compassion, and not a sacrifice,**' you would not have condemned the innocent."

Matthew 12:7

"Why **do you look at the speck that is in your brother's eye,** but do not notice the log that is in your own eye?"

Luke 6:41

"What did you go out to see? A man dressed in soft clothing? Behold, those who are splendidly clothed and live in luxury are found in royal palaces."

Luke 7:25

Let no one act as your judge in regard to food or drink or in respect to a festival or a new moon or a Sabbath day.

Colossians 2:16

If a man comes into your assembly with a gold ring and dressed in fine clothes, and there also comes in a poor man in dirty clothes, and you pay special attention to the one who is wearing the fine clothes, and say, "You sit here in a good place," and you say to the poor man, "You stand over there, or sit down by my footstool," **have you not made distinctions among yourselves,** and become judges with evil motives?

James 2:2–4

PRIDE

Those who are resentful about the success of others, whose feelings are hurt because of the lack of recognition, or who use their jobs as alter egos all suffer from the same spiritual malady—they are in service to men instead of to God. Pride is the major sin in Christendom today. It is deceptive because it's so normal. Many of our wrong attitudes are products of the sin of pride. Often, if we have an abundance, we want everyone else to know it—we desire to be elevated because of material achievements.

God says that the tug of this world and its pleasures will be the greatest threat to our walk with Him: Love not the world, nor the things in the world. God will give us the opportunity to recognize and correct our pride. The best way to deal with this attitude is to consciously put others first.

"When your herds and your flocks multiply, and your silver and gold multiply, and all that you have multiplies, **then your heart becomes proud,** and you forget the Lord your God who brought you out from the land of Egypt, out of the house of slavery."

Deuteronomy 8:13–14

"You may say in your heart, '**My power and the strength of my hand made me this wealth.**'"

Deuteronomy 8:17

Hezekiah listened to them, and showed them all his treasure house, the silver and the gold and the spices and the precious oil and the house of his armor and all that was found in his treasuries. There was nothing in his house, nor in all his dominion, that Hezekiah did not show them.

2 Kings 20:13

Hezekiah gave no return for the benefit he received, because his heart was proud; therefore wrath came on him and on Judah and Jerusalem.

2 Chronicles 32:25

"Yet all of this does not satisfy me every time I see Mordecai the Jew sitting at the king's gate."

Esther 5:13

"Or with princes who had gold, who were filling their houses with silver."

Job 3:15

"**If I have put my confidence in gold,** and called fine gold my trust, if I have gloated because my wealth was great, and because my hand had secured so much."

Job 31:24–25

"For I would have denied God above."

Job 31:28

"**Will your riches keep you from distress,** or all the forces of your strength?"

Job 36:19

His ways prosper at all times; thy judgments are on high, out of his sight; as for all his adversaries, he snorts at them.

Psalm 10:5

Now as for me, **I said in my prosperity, "I will never be moved."**

Psalm 30:6

"I said to the boastful, '**Do not boast,**' and to the wicked, 'Do not lift up the horn.'"

Psalm 75:4

When pride comes, then comes dishonor, but with the humble is wisdom.

Proverbs 11:2

Better is he who is lightly esteemed and has a servant, than he who honors himself and lacks bread.

Proverbs 12:9

The Lord will tear down the house of the proud, but He will establish the boundary of the widow.

Proverbs 15:25

Everyone who is proud in heart is an abomination to the Lord; assuredly, he will not be unpunished.

Proverbs 16:5

Pride goes before destruction, and a haughty spirit before stumbling. **It is better to be of a humble spirit with the lowly,** than to divide the spoil with the proud.

Proverbs 16:18–19

Before destruction **the heart of man is haughty,** but humility goes before honor.

Proverbs 18:12

The poor man utters supplications, but the rich man answers roughly.

Proverbs 18:23

Do not rejoice when your enemy falls, and do not let your heart be glad when he stumbles; lest the Lord see it and be displeased, and He turn away His anger from him.

Proverbs 24:17–18

A man's pride will bring him low, but a humble spirit will obtain honor.

Proverbs 29:23

The pride of man will be humbled, and the loftiness of men will be abased, and **the Lord alone will be exalted** in that day.

Isaiah 2:17

"By your wisdom and understanding you have acquired riches for yourself, and have acquired gold and silver for your treasuries. By your great wisdom, by your trade you have increased your riches, **and your heart is lifted up because of your riches.**"

Ezekiel 28:4–5

"You have exalted yourself against the Lord of heaven; and they have brought the vessels of His house before you, and you and your nobles, your wives and your concubines have been drinking wine from them; and **you have praised the gods of silver and gold,** of bronze, iron, wood, and stone, which do not see, hear or understand. But the God in whose hand are your life-breath and your ways, you have not glorified."

Daniel 5:23

"**Two men went up into the temple to pray,** one a Pharisee, and the other a tax-gatherer. The Pharisee stood and was praying thus to himself, 'God, I thank Thee that I am not like other people: swindlers, unjust, adulterers, or even like this tax-gatherer. I fast twice a week; I pay tithes of all that I get.' But the tax-gatherer, standing some distance away, was even unwilling to lift up his eyes to heaven, but was beating his breast, saying, 'God, be merciful to me, the sinner!' I tell you, this man went down to his house justified rather than the other; for **every one who exalts himself shall be humbled,** but he who humbles himself shall be exalted."

Luke 18:10–14

Instruct those who are rich in this present world not to be conceited or to fix their hope on the uncertainty of riches, but on God, who richly supplies us with all things to enjoy.

1 Timothy 6:17

142

Let not your adornment be merely external—braiding the hair, and wearing gold jewelry, and putting on dresses; but let it be the hidden person of the heart, with the imperishable quality of a gentle and quiet spirit, which is precious in the sight of God.

1 Peter 3:3–4

All that is in the world, the lust of the flesh and the lust of the eyes and the **boastful pride of life,** is not from the Father, but is from the world.

1 John 2:16

"**Because you say, 'I am rich,** and have become wealthy, and have need of nothing,' and you do not know that you are wretched and miserable and poor and blind and naked, I advise you to buy from Me gold refined by fire, that you may become rich, and white garments, that you may clothe yourself; and that the shame of your nakedness may not be revealed; and eye salve to anoint your eyes, that you may see."

Revelation 3:17–18

SUING

Lawsuits are a common occurrence today and have become a first, rather than a last, recourse. Grounds for lawsuits range from emotional distress to faulty products, to personal injuries, to blatant fraud—all for the purpose of personal profit. Does a Christian have a right to sue another person? The apostle Paul said we should not sue another believer; however, just because he didn't tell us not to sue a non-Christian, it doesn't automatically make it right.

What about the right to justifiable legal remedy? How should a believer respond when cheated by another individual or corporation? What if a Christian is sued? Is countersuit justifiable? These are questions that can only be answered in the light of God's Word.

No one sues righteously and no one pleads honestly. They trust in confusion, and speak lies; they conceive mischief, and bring forth iniquity.

Isaiah 59:4

"If anyone wants to sue you, and take your shirt, let him have your coat also."

Matthew 5:40

"Whoever hits you on the cheek, offer him the other also; and whoever takes away your coat, do not withhold your shirt from him either. Give to everyone who asks of you, and **whoever takes away what is yours, do not demand it** back. And just as you want people to treat you, treat them in the same way."

Luke 6:29–31

Someone in the crowd said to Him, "Teacher, tell my brother to divide the family inheritance with me." But He

144

said to him, "**Man, who appointed Me a judge or arbiter over you?**"

Luke 12:13–14

"We must obey God rather than men."

Acts 5:29

Let every person be in subjection to the governing authorities. For there is **no authority except from God,** and those which exist are established by God.

Romans 13:1

Does any of you, when he has a case against his neighbor, **dare to go to law** before the unrighteous, and not before the saints?

1 Corinthians 6:1

Actually, then, it is **already a defeat** for you, that you have lawsuits with one another. Why not rather be wronged? Why not rather be defrauded?

1 Corinthians 6:7

As those who have been chosen of God, holy and beloved, put on a heart of compassion, kindness, humility, gentleness and patience; bearing with one another, and forgiving each other, whoever has a complaint against anyone; **just as the Lord forgave you, so also should you.**

Colossians 3:12–13

SECTION THREE
CREDIT

Perhaps one of the most misunderstood and violated principles in God's Word is credit—borrowing and lending. Many Christians believe that you should never borrow money. In fact they go to God's Word and try to pick individual Scripture verses that would lend themselves to that interpretation. Others operate no differently than the world; not only do they borrow, they borrow in excess.

God does not prohibit using credit; He simply lays down very clear guidelines for how credit should be used. There are three basic principles: (1) credit should never be normal for God's people; (2) credit should never be long-term; (3) never sign surety—take on an obligation to pay without an absolutely certain way to pay.

BORROWING

According to God's Word, borrowing is a biblical principle. It certainly is not being recognized as one in our society—primarily because we've violated every principle of borrowing. According to the law, bankruptcy is an alternative way out. Unfortunately, when you borrow money, if it is a legitimate debt, God expects you to repay it, irrespective of what the law says. When we make a vow, we should not be late in paying it, for God takes no delight in fools.

The church, as an institution, is to be a light of God's truth in a world of darkness. Our world is out of sync with God's Word on borrowing. The evidence is reflected in the evangelical churches that have followed the lead of the secular world regarding debt. God can and will provide what He ordains by providing surpluses to His people at the appointed time. It's not a lack of money that necessitates church borrowing; it's a lack of commitment to giving. The only source of mature wisdom is God's Word, and you will not find a single instance of God manifesting Himself through a loan.

"**If a man borrows anything from his neighbor,** and it is injured or dies while its owner is not with it, he shall make full restitution. If its owner is with it, he shall not make restitution; if it is hired, it came for its hire."

Exodus 22:14–15

"The alien who is among you shall rise above you higher and higher, but you shall go down lower and lower. **He shall lend to you, but you shall not lend to him;** he shall be the head, and you shall be the tail. So all these curses shall come on you and pursue you and overtake you until you are destroyed, because you would not obey the Lord your

149

God by keeping His commandments and His statutes which He commanded you."

Deuteronomy 28:43–45

There were those who said, "We, our sons and our daughters, are many; therefore let us get grain that we may eat and live." And there were others who said, "**We are mortgaging our fields,** our vineyards, and our houses that we might get grain because of the famine." Also there were those who said, "We have borrowed money for the king's tax on our fields and our vineyards. And now our flesh is like the flesh of our brothers, our children like their children. Yet behold, we are forcing our sons and our daughters to be slaves, and some of our daughters are forced into bondage already, and we are helpless because our fields and vineyards belong to others."

Nehemiah 5:2–5

The wicked borrows and does not pay back, but the righteous is gracious and gives.

Psalm 37:21

The rich rules over the poor, and the borrower becomes the lender's slave.

Proverbs 22:7

The people will be like the priest, the servant like his master, the maid like her mistress, the buyer like the seller, the **lender like the borrower,** the creditor like the debtor.

Isaiah 24:2

INTEREST

When money is borrowed, interest is charged for the use of the money. Huge sums of Christians' money go to meet interest payments. That money could be used to further God's kingdom rather than Satan's. Many major denominations spend more on interest payments than on foreign missions.

There is little Scripture dealing with the specifics of paying interest, but there are many verses that admonish us not to charge interest to those to whom we lend money.

"If you lend money to My people, to the poor among you, you are not to act as a creditor to him; you shall not charge him interest."

Exodus 22:25

"You shall not charge interest to your countrymen: interest on money, food, or anything that may be loaned at interest. You may charge interest to a foreigner, but to your countryman you shall not charge interest, so that the Lord your God may bless you in all that you undertake in the land which you are about to enter to possess."

Deuteronomy 23:19–20

He does not put out his money at interest, nor does he take a bribe against the innocent. He who does these things will never be shaken.

Psalm 15:5

Do not be among those who give pledges, among those who become sureties for debts. If you have nothing with which to pay, why should he take your bed from under you?

Proverbs 22:26–27

He who increases his wealth by interest and usury, gathers it for him who is gracious to the poor.

Proverbs 28:8

"**If a man does not oppress anyone,** but restores to the debtor his pledge, does not commit robbery, but gives his bread to the hungry, and covers the naked with clothing, if he **does not lend money on interest** or take increase, if he keeps his hand from iniquity, and executes true justice between man and man, if he walks in My statutes and My ordinances so as to deal faithfully—he is righteous and will surely live," declares the Lord God.

Ezekiel 18:7–9

"[If he] **oppresses the poor and needy,** commits robbery, does not restore a pledge, but lifts up his eyes to the idols, and commits abomination, he **lends money on interest** and takes increase; will he live? He will not live! He has committed all these abominations, he will surely be put to death; his blood will be on his own head."

Ezekiel 18:12–13

"[He does not] oppress anyone, or retain a pledge, or commit robbery, but he gives his bread to the hungry, and covers the naked with clothing, **he keeps his hand from the poor, does not take interest or increase,** but executes My ordinances, and walks in My statutes; he will not die for his father's iniquity, he will surely live. As for his father, because he practiced extortion, robbed his brother, and did what was not good among his people, behold, he will die for his iniquity."

Ezekiel 18:16–18

"You . . . have taken bribes to shed blood; **you have taken interest** and profits, and **you have injured your neighbors for gain** by oppression, and you have forgotten Me," declares the Lord God. "Behold, then, I smite My hand at your dishonest gain which you have acquired."

Ezekiel 22:12–13

LENDING

This is one of the blessings promised by God for being obedient to His ways. In fact, in Deuteronomy, God says that His plan is for us to be lenders rather than borrowers; however, God set down some very interesting principles. He said that when we lend to one another as believers, we should not charge interest. It is to be a testimony—that we are more committed to God than we are to the loss of a little revenue; and it's a witness to the world that we are literally willing to sacrifice to help one another.

Sometimes a loan turns out to be a gift. If you know you are lending to somebody who is never going to be able to pay you back, perhaps it would be better to give to that person and not keep him or her under that bondage. The Lord says if you lend only to those from whom you expect return, that is of no benefit. Even a sinner will do that. You should lend to people, even to those from whom you never expect to be repaid—then forget it.

"**If you lend money to My people,** to the poor among you, you are not to act as a creditor to him; you shall not charge him interest."

Exodus 22:25

"The Lord your God shall bless you as He has promised you, and **you will lend to many nations,** but you will not borrow; and you will rule over many nations, but they will not rule over you."

Deuteronomy 15:6

"**The Lord will open for you His good storehouse,** the heavens, to give rain to your land in its season and to bless

153

all the work of your hand; and you shall lend to many nations, but you shall not borrow."

Deuteronomy 28:12

All day long he is gracious and lends; and his descendants are a blessing.

Psalm 37:26

It is well with the man who is gracious and lends; he will maintain his cause in judgment.

Psalm 112:5

The people will be like the priest, the servant like his master, the maid like her mistress, the buyer like the seller, **the lender like the borrower,** the creditor like the debtor.

Isaiah 24:2

Woe to me, my mother, that you have borne me as a man of strife and a man of contention to all the land! **I have neither lent, nor have men lent money to me,** yet everyone curses me.

Jeremiah 15:10

"**If a man does not oppress anyone,** but restores to the debtor his pledge, does not commit robbery, but gives his bread to the hungry, and covers the naked with clothing, if he **does not lend money on interest or take increase,** if he keeps his hand from iniquity, and executes true justice between man and man."

Ezekiel 18:7–8

"[If he] oppresses the poor and needy, commits robbery, does not restore a pledge, but lifts up his eyes to the idols, and commits abomination, he **lends money on interest and takes increase; will he live? He will not live!** He has committed all these abominations, he will surely be put to death; his blood will be on his own head."

Ezekiel 18:12–13

"[If he does not] oppress anyone, or retain a pledge, or commit robbery, but he gives his bread to the hungry, and covers the naked with clothing, **he keeps his hand from the poor, does not take interest or increase,** but executes My ordinances, and walks in My statutes; he will not die for his father's iniquity, he will surely live."

Ezekiel 18:16–17

"Will not all of these take up a taunt-song against him, even mockery and insinuations against him, and say, '**Woe to him who increases what is not his—for how long—and makes himself rich with loans?**' Will not your creditors rise up suddenly, and those who collect from you awaken? Indeed, you will become plunder for them."

Habakkuk 2:6–7

"Give to him who asks of you, and **do not turn away from him who wants to borrow from you.**"

Matthew 5:42

"**If you lend to those from whom you expect to receive,** what credit is that to you? Even sinners lend to sinners, in order to receive back the same amount. But love your enemies, and do good, and lend, expecting nothing in return; and your reward will be great, and you will be sons of the Most High; for He Himself is kind to ungrateful and evil men."

Luke 6:34–35

PAYING DEBTS

God's Word is sure and certain on this particular subject. When money is borrowed, there's an obligation to pay it back, no matter what. To become debt free, it may be necessary to sacrifice, including eliminating all credit or selling your second car. It may mean repairing the refrigerator or washing machine instead of buying a new one. Do whatever you must to bring your debt burden under control; determine your priorities; and stick to them.

In America today, the federal bankruptcy code says that if you can't pay your debts, and the judge agrees with you, you can write those debts off and you don't owe them anymore. Unfortunately, that is not true according to God's Word; so even if you've claimed bankruptcy, you still have the obligation to pay the money you owe. There is no greater sense of freedom than to owe no financial obligations.

When Judah sent the kid by his friend the Adullamite, to **receive the pledge from the woman's hand,** he did not find her.

Genesis 38:20

"At the end of every seven years you shall grant a remission of debts. And this is the manner of remission: every creditor shall release what he has loaned to his neighbor; he shall not exact it of his neighbor and his brother, because the Lord's remission has been proclaimed. From a foreigner you may exact it, but your hand shall release whatever of yours is with your brother. However, there shall be no poor among you, since the Lord will surely bless you in the land which the Lord your God is giving you as an inheritance to possess, if only you listen obediently to the voice of the Lord your God, to observe carefully all this commandment which I am commanding you today."

Deuteronomy 15:1–5

Moses commanded them, saying, "At the end of every seven years, at the time of the year of remission of debts, at the Feast of Booths."

Deuteronomy 31:10

A certain woman of the wives of the sons of the prophets cried out to Elisha, "Your servant my husband is dead, and you know that your servant feared the Lord; and **the creditor has come to take my two children** to be his slaves."

2 Kings 4:1

She came and told the man of God. And he said, "**Go, sell the oil and pay your debt,** and you and your sons can live on the rest."

2 Kings 4:7

Do not withhold good from those to whom it is due, when it is in your power to do it. Do not say to your neighbor, "Go, and come back, and tomorrow I will give it," when you have it with you.

Proverbs 3:27–28

"**Make friends quickly with your opponent at law** while you are with him on the way, in order that your opponent may not deliver you to the judge, and the judge to the officer, and you be thrown into prison. Truly I say to you, you shall not come out of there, until you have paid up the last cent."

Matthew 5:25–26

"While you are going with your opponent to appear before the magistrate, on your way there **make an effort to settle with him,** in order that he may not drag you before the judge, and the judge turn you over to the constable, and

157

the constable throw you into prison. I say to you, you shall
not get out of there until you have paid the very last cent."

Luke 12:58–59

Owe nothing to anyone except to love one another; for he
who loves his neighbor has fulfilled the law.

Romans 13:8

When you were dead in your transgressions and the uncir-
cumcision of your flesh, He made you alive together with
Him, having forgiven us all our transgressions, having **can-
celed out the certificate of debt** consisting of decrees
against us and which was hostile to us; and He has taken it
out of the way, having nailed it to the cross.

Colossians 2:13–14

If he has wronged you in any way, or owes you anything,
charge that to my account; I, Paul, am writing this with
my own hand, I will repay it (lest I should mention to you
that you owe to me even your own self as well).

Philemon 18–19

SURETY

This is a simple principle—taking on an obligation to pay without a sure and certain way to pay it. Surety means to deposit a pledge in either money, goods, or part payment for a greater obligation. The consequences of violating the principle of surety is that you presume upon the future and upon God's will. If you are already signed as surety and you can get out of it, you should. If you cannot, work at reducing the liability and paying off the debts early.

The only way to have a clear and certain way to pay a debt is to collateralize it. When you borrow money, you and the lender strike an agreement that if ever you can't pay them, they keep your collateral and you are free of any further obligation. But, if when you sign a note you agree with the lender to have a deficiency agreement, that means that if ever you can't pay them, they can keep the collateral, sell it, and whatever the difference is between the collateral value and the note, you pay that balance.

"I myself will be surety for him; you may hold me responsible for him."

Genesis 43:9

"Your servant became surety for the lad to my father, saying, 'If I do not bring him back to you, then let me bear the blame before my father forever.'"

Genesis 44:32

"If you ever take your neighbor's cloak as a pledge, you are to return it to him before the sun sets."

Exodus 22:26

"When you make your neighbor a loan of any sort, you shall not enter his house to take his pledge. You shall remain outside, and the man to whom you make the loan shall bring the pledge out to you. And if he is a poor man, you shall not sleep with his pledge. When the sun goes down you shall surely return the pledge to him, that he may sleep in his cloak and bless you; and it will be righteousness for you before the Lord your God."

Deuteronomy 24:10–13

"You have taken pledges of your brothers without cause, and stripped men naked."

Job 22:6

Let the creditor seize all that he has; and let strangers plunder the product of his labor.

Psalm 109:11

My son, if you have become surety for your neighbor, have given a pledge for a stranger, if you have been snared with the words of your mouth, have been caught with the words of your mouth, **do this then, my son, and deliver yourself;** since you have come into the hand of your neighbor, go, humble yourself, and importune your neighbor. Do not give sleep to your eyes, nor slumber to your eyelids; deliver yourself like a gazelle from the hunter's hand, and like a bird from the hand of the fowler.

Proverbs 6:1–5

He who is surety for a stranger will surely suffer for it, but **he who hates going surety is safe.**

Proverbs 11:15

A man lacking in sense pledges, and becomes surety in the presence of his neighbor.

Proverbs 17:18

Take his garment **when he becomes surety** for a stranger; and for foreigners, hold him in pledge.

Proverbs 20:16

The sacrifice of the wicked is an abomination, how much more when he brings it with evil intent!

Proverbs 21:27

Do not be among those who give pledges, among those who become sureties for debts. If you have nothing with which to pay, why should he take your bed from under you?

Proverbs 22:26–27

Take his garment when he becomes surety for a stranger; and for an adulterous woman hold him in pledge.

Proverbs 27:13

USURY

The vast majority of interest charged regularly in America is probably usurious, meaning it is an exorbitant or abusive rate of interest. Certainly that would be true of most credit cards.

Obviously you can't call your creditors from whom you've borrowed and say, "I'm sorry you've broken God's principle of usury, therefore I don't owe you any more money." What you can do, if you have charged others a usurious rate of interest, is to call them and tell them they don't owe you any more than one percent per month, because that's what God allows, and all the interest they've paid you in excess of that will apply toward their indebtedness. It's at this point you ask yourself: Do I believe God's Word or have I just been saying I believe?

"In case a countryman of yours becomes poor and his means with regard to you falter, then you are to sustain him, like a stranger or a sojourner, that he may live with you. Do not take usurious interest from him, but revere your God, that your countryman may live with you. **You shall not give him your silver at interest**, nor your food for gain."

Leviticus 25:35–37

I consulted with myself, and contended with the nobles and the rulers and said to them, "You are exacting usury, each from his brother!" Therefore, I held a great assembly against them. And I said to them, "We according to our ability have redeemed our Jewish brothers who were sold to the nations; now would you even sell your brothers that they may be sold to us?" Then they were silent and could not find a word to say. Again I said, "The thing which you are doing is not good; should you not walk in the fear of our God because of the reproach of the nations, our ene-

162

mies? And likewise I, **my brothers and my servants, are lending them money and grain. Please, let us leave off this usury.**"

Nehemiah 5:7–10

He who increases his wealth by interest and usury, gathers it for him who is gracious to the poor.

Proverbs 28:8

SECTION FOUR
GIVING AND PROVIDING

G iving should be an outward, material expression of a deep spiritual commitment, an indication of a willing and obedient heart. We should give out of grateful hearts in an attitude of joy. Sacrificial giving is a way to honor God, but it should be the result of a good attitude.

There are wrong motives for giving: fear (that God will punish you if you don't give) and giving to impress others (giving should be done modestly and humbly—we are not to draw attention to ourselves when we give).

Giving according to God's Word is not mandatory; it is always voluntary. James said we should not be merely hearers of the Word, who delude ourselves, but also effectual doers of the Word. So, in great part, our being doers of the Word is solidified through our giving to God and providing for our families.

COUNSEL AND DISCIPLINE FOR CHILDREN

I t's amazing how quickly our children pick up bad habits and how slowly they learn good habits. There's no better indicator of where our children are spiritually than how they handle their finances. God's Word gives wisdom to enable us to raise our children in a godly fashion; and how to use money will always be a part of that training.

Teaching our children to tithe, to live on a budget, even how to balance their checkbooks is a part of the wisdom and counsel of God. They will learn self-discipline in managing money only as they see it exhibited in our lives. We are to discipline our children in the ways of the Lord so that when they are old they will not soon depart from that teaching.

Hear, my son, your father's instruction, and do not forsake your mother's teaching.

Proverbs 1:8

My son, observe the commandment of your father, and do not forsake the teaching of your mother.

Proverbs 6:20

The proverbs of Solomon. **A wise son makes a father glad,** but a foolish son is a grief to his mother.

Proverbs 10:1

A wise son accepts his father's discipline, but a scoffer does not listen to rebuke.

Proverbs 13:1

A fool rejects his father's discipline, but he who regards reproof is prudent.

Proverbs 15:5

A foolish son is a grief to his father, and bitterness to her who bore him.

Proverbs 17:25

Discipline your son while there is hope, and do not desire his death.

Proverbs 19:18

Train up a child in the way he should go, even when he is old he will not depart from it.

Proverbs 22:6

Do not hold back discipline from the child, although you beat him with the rod, he will not die. You shall beat him with the rod, and deliver his soul from Sheol.

Proverbs 23:13–14

Listen to your father who begot you, and do not despise your mother when she is old.

Proverbs 23:22

The rod and reproof give wisdom, but a child who gets his own way brings shame to his mother.

Proverbs 29:15

Correct your son, and he will give you comfort; he will also delight your soul.

Proverbs 29:17

Fathers, do not provoke your children to anger; but bring them up in the discipline and instruction of the Lord.

Ephesians 6:4

He must be one who **manages his own household well, keeping his children under control with all dignity** (but if a man does not know how to manage his own household, how will he take care of the church of God?).

1 Timothy 3:4–5

FIRST FRUITS

A verse in Proverbs says that God has asked for our first fruits: the first and best of all that we receive. That means that we should tithe from our total (gross) income before taxes. Any profit made from the sale of a home ought to be tithed upon, because it is, in fact, part of our first fruits. Other parts of our first fruits would be inheritances, insurance monies, dividends, and interest. These are all parts of our increase.

A farmer first sets aside a portion from the harvest for seed to plant the following year. If he didn't, he wouldn't have another crop. As Christians, our tithes are like seeds. Clearly, if we give to God the first part of everything that comes into our possession, we are honoring Him. It is an attitude of giving. And it is only by honoring the Lord from the first part of all we have that God can take control.

It came about in the course of time that **Cain brought an offering** to the Lord of the fruit of the ground. And Abel, on his part also brought of the firstlings of his flock and of their fat portions. And the Lord had regard for Abel and for his offering.

Genesis 4:3–4

"You shall not delay the offering from your harvest and your vintage. The first-born of your sons you shall give to Me. You shall do the same with your oxen and with your sheep. It shall be with its mother seven days; on the eighth day you shall give it to Me."

Exodus 22:29–30

"**The first offspring from every womb belongs to Me,** and all your male livestock, the first offspring from cattle and sheep."

Exodus 34:19

"**You shall bring the very first of the first fruits** of your soil into the house of the Lord your God. You shall not boil a kid in its mother's milk."

Exodus 34:26

"Speak to the sons of Israel, and say to them, 'When you enter the land which I am going to give to you and reap its harvest, then **you shall bring in the sheaf of the first fruits of your harvest** to the priest. And he shall wave the sheaf before the Lord for you to be accepted; on the day after the sabbath the priest shall wave it.'"

Leviticus 23:10–11

"**All the first-born are Mine;** on the day that I struck down all the first-born in the land of Egypt, I sanctified to Myself all the first-born in Israel, from man to beast. They shall be Mine; I am the Lord."

Numbers 3:13

"Speak to the sons of Israel, and say to them, 'When you enter the land where I bring you, then it shall be, that when you eat of the food of the land, **you shall lift up an offering to the Lord.** Of the first of your dough you shall lift up a cake as an offering; as the offering of the threshing floor, so you shall lift it up. From the first of your dough you shall give to the Lord an offering throughout your generations.'"

Numbers 15:18–21

"All the best of the fresh oil and all the best of the fresh wine and of the grain, **the first fruits of those which they give to the Lord,** I give them to you. The first ripe fruits of all that is in their land, which they bring to the Lord, shall be yours; everyone of your household who is clean may eat it."

Numbers 18:12–13

"**You are not allowed to eat within your gates the tithe of your grain,** or new wine, or oil, or the first-born of your herd or flock, or any of your votive offerings which you vow, or your freewill offerings, or the contributions of your hand."

Deuteronomy 12:17

"You shall give him the first fruits of your grain, your new wine, and your oil, and the first shearing of your sheep."

Deuteronomy 18:4

"You shall take some of **the first of all the produce of the ground** which you shall bring in from your land that the Lord your God gives you, and you shall put it in a basket and go to the place where the Lord your God chooses to establish His name."

Deuteronomy 26:2

"'Now behold, I have brought the first of the produce of the ground which Thou, O Lord hast given me.' And you shall set it down before the Lord your God, and worship before the Lord your God."

Deuteronomy 26:10

They burned the city with fire, and all that was in it. Only the silver and gold and articles of bronze and iron, **they put into the treasury of the house of the Lord.**

Joshua 6:24

We cast lots for the supply of wood among the priests, the Levites, and the people in order that they might bring it to the house of our God, according to our fathers' households, at fixed times annually, to burn on the altar of the Lord our God as it is written in the law; and in order that they might bring the first fruits of our ground and the first fruits of all the fruit of every tree to the house of the Lord annually.

Nehemiah 10:34–35

We will also bring the first of our dough, our contributions, the fruit of every tree, the new wine and the oil to the priests at the chambers of the house of our God, and the tithe of our ground to the Levites, for the Levites are they who receive the tithes in all the rural towns. And the priest, the son of Aaron, shall be with the Levites when the Levites receive tithes, and the Levites shall bring up the tenth of the tithes to the house of our God, to the chambers of the storehouse. For the sons of Israel and **the sons of Levi shall bring the contribution of the grain,** the new wine and the oil, to the chambers; there are the utensils of the sanctuary, the priests who are ministering, the gate-keepers, and the singers. Thus we will not neglect the house of our God.

Nehemiah 10:37–39

On that day men were also appointed over the chambers for the stores, **the contributions, the first fruits, and the tithes,** to gather into them from the fields of the cities the portions required by the law for the priests and Levites; for Judah rejoiced over the priests and Levites who served.

Nehemiah 12:44

Honor the Lord from your wealth, and from the first of all your produce; so your barns will be filled with plenty, and your vats will overflow with new wine.

Proverbs 3:9–10

"**The first of all the first fruits of every kind** and every contribution of every kind, from all your contributions, shall be for the priests; you shall also give to the priest the first of your dough to cause a blessing to rest on your house."

Ezekiel 44:30

Not only this, but also we ourselves, having the first fruits of the Spirit, even we ourselves groan within ourselves, **waiting eagerly for our adoption as sons,** the redemption of our body.

Romans 8:23

He who sows sparingly shall also reap sparingly; and he who sows bountifully **shall also reap bountifully.**

2 Corinthians 9:6

In the exercise of His will He brought us forth by the word of truth, so that we might be, as it were, **the first fruits among His creatures.**

James 1:18

These are the ones who have not been defiled with women, for they have kept themselves chaste. These are the ones who follow the Lamb wherever He goes. These have been purchased **from among men as first fruits to God** and to the Lamb.

Revelation 14:4

GIFTS

After you have given your tithe, what you give to other people or to organizations is considered a gift. And when you give to the maximum, as the widow did in Luke 12, it's called sacrificial giving: You literally have given up something you need because someone else has a greater need. Until we are able to go beyond the tithe and start giving gifts out of a free nature to other people, we will never really experience the provision God has for us.

Some Christians have received a gift of giving. To them, the multiplication of material worth is an extension of their basic ministry within the Body of Christ.

———

"Also every contribution pertaining to all the holy gifts of the sons of Israel, which they offer to the priest, shall be his. **So every man's holy gifts shall be his;** whatever any man gives to the priest, it becomes his."

Numbers 5:9–10

They burned the city with fire, and all that was in it. Only the silver and gold and articles of bronze and iron, **they put into the treasury of the house of the Lord.**

Joshua 6:24

"With all my ability I have provided for the house of my God the gold for the things of gold, and the silver for the things of silver, and the bronze for the things of bronze, the iron for the things of iron, and wood for the things of wood, onyx stones and inlaid stones, stones of antimony, and stones of various colors, and all kinds of precious stones, and alabaster in abundance. And moreover, in my delight in the house of my God, the treasure I have of gold and silver, I give to the house of my God, over and above all that I have already provided for the holy temple, namely, 3,000 talents of gold, of the gold of Ophir, and 7,000 talents of refined silver, to overlay the walls of the buildings; of gold for the things of gold, and of silver for the things of silver, that is, for all the work done by the craftsmen. Who then is willing to consecrate himself this day to the Lord?"

1 Chronicles 29:2–5

[Asa] **brought into the house of God** the dedicated things of his father and his own dedicated things: silver and gold and utensils.

2 Chronicles 15:18

They came to Hilkiah the high priest and delivered the money that was brought into the house of God, which the Levites, the doorkeepers, had collected from Manasseh and Ephraim, and from all the remnant of Israel, and from all Judah and Benjamin and the inhabitants of Jerusalem.

2 Chronicles 34:9

When they were bringing out the money which had been brought into the house of the Lord, **Hilkiah the priest found the book of the law of the Lord given by Moses.**

2 Chronicles 34:14

All those about them encouraged them with articles of silver, with gold, with goods, with cattle, and with valuables, aside from all that was given as a freewill offering.

Ezra 1:6

According to their ability they gave to the treasury for the work 61,000 gold drachmas, and 5,000 silver minas, and 100 priestly garments.

Ezra 2:69

"**Bring the silver and gold, which the king and his counselors have freely offered to the God of Israel,** whose dwelling is in Jerusalem, with all the silver and gold which you shall find in the whole province of Babylon, along with the freewill offering of the people and of the priests, who offered willingly for the house of their God which is in Jeru-

salem; with this money, therefore, you shall diligently buy
bulls, rams, and lambs, with their grain offerings and their
libations and offer them on the altar of the house of your
God which is in Jerusalem. And whatever seems good to
you and to your brothers to do with **the rest of the silver
and gold, you may do according to the will of your God."**

Ezra 7:15–18

Some from among the heads of fathers' households gave to
the work. The governor gave to the treasury 1,000 gold
drachmas, 50 basins, 530 priests' garments. And some of
the heads of fathers' households gave into the treasury of
the work 20,000 gold drachmas, and 2,200 silver minas.
And that which the rest of the people gave was 20,000 gold
drachmas and 2,000 silver minas, and 67 priests' garments.

Nehemiah 7:70–72

There is one who scatters, yet increases all the more, and
there is one who withholds what is justly due, but it results
only in want. **The generous man will be prosperous,** and he
who waters will himself be watered.

Proverbs 11:24–25

Many will entreat the favor of a generous man, and **every
man is a friend to him who gives gifts.**

Proverbs 19:6

He who is generous will be blessed, for he gives some of his
food to the poor.

Proverbs 22:9

He who gives to the poor will never want, but he who
shuts his eyes will have many curses.

Proverbs 28:27

They came into the house and saw the Child with Mary His
mother; and they fell down and worshiped Him; and open-
ing their treasures **they presented to Him gifts of gold and
frankincense and myrrh.**

Matthew 2:11

"**Give to him who asks of you,** and do not turn away from him who wants to borrow from you."

Matthew 5:42

He sat down opposite the treasury, and began observing **how the multitude were putting money into the treasury;** and many rich people were putting in large sums.

Mark 12:41

"Whoever hits you on the cheek, offer him the other also; and whoever takes away your coat, do not withhold your shirt from him either. **Give to everyone who asks of you,** and whoever takes away what is yours, do not demand it back."

Luke 6:29–30

"**Give, and it will be given to you;** good measure, pressed down, shaken together, running over, they will pour into your lap. For by your standard of measure it will be measured to you in return."

Luke 6:38

Mary therefore took a pound of very costly perfume of pure nard, and anointed the feet of Jesus, and wiped His feet with her hair; and the house was filled with the fragrance of the perfume. But Judas Iscariot, one of His disciples, who was intending to betray Him, said, "Why was this perfume not sold for three hundred denarii, and given to poor people?" Now he said this, not because he was concerned about the poor, but because he was a thief, and as he had the money box, he used to pilfer what was put into it. Jesus therefore said, "Let her alone, in order that she may keep it for the day of My burial."

John 12:3–7

Since we have gifts that differ according to the grace given to us, let each exercise them accordingly: . . . he who exhorts, in his exhortation; **he who gives, with liberality;** he who leads, with diligence; he who shows mercy, with cheerfulness.

Romans 12:6, 8

Let each one do just as he has purposed in his heart; not grudgingly or under compulsion; for God loves a cheerful giver.

2 Corinthians 9:7

He said to me, "It is done. I am the Alpha and the Omega, the beginning and the end. I will give to the one who thirsts from the spring of the water of life without cost. He who overcomes shall inherit these things, and I will be his God and he will be My son."

Revelation 21:6–7

The Spirit and the bride say, "Come." And let the one who hears say, "Come." And let the one who is thirsty come; let the one who wishes to take the water of life without cost.

Revelation 22:17

GIVING TO GET

S ome people require and even demand God's blessing because of what they consider their sacrificial giving. They are not in subjection to God but are trying to exercise control over Him. God promises that if we give out of a true and loving heart, He will return it multiplied, but He is under absolutely no requirement to return what is given to Him. However, God says there is nothing wrong with giving to get, as long as your attitude for getting more is to enable you to give more.

Perhaps the person I know who has best reflected this attitude is the developer of most of the road grading equipment in America—R. G. LeTourneau. He believed that his gift from God was the ability to give money. He always gave to get more, to give more, to get more, to give more, and so on. This is the attitude of giving to get that pleases God.

———————

"Who has given to Me that I should repay him? Whatever is under the whole heaven is Mine."

Job 41:11

Who has known the mind of the Lord, or who became His counselor? Or who has first given to him that it might be paid back to him again? For from Him and through Him and to Him are all things. To Him be the glory forever. Amen.

Romans 11:34–36

If I give all my possessions to feed the poor, and if I deliver my body to be burned, but do not have love, it profits me nothing.

1 Corinthians 13:3

179

GIVING TO OTHERS

Wouldn't it be great to see God's people open their hearts and give the way they should? We have enough money in North America to fund all the Christian work in the world if the people would just give. Unfortunately, money needed for ministering to others is often tied up in large monthly payments.

Obviously the government's goal for welfare is not to bring people to God. So it really should not be a government function to control, administer, or distribute people's daily needs. "Welfare" is the function of the Body of Christ. Not all giving consists of cash donations; you may donate your time, services, or noncash gifts, or something with an appreciating value, such as stocks, bond, jewelry, or real estate. If sacrificial giving is the result of good motives and attitudes, it will honor God.

It came about, when the camels had finished drinking, that **the man took a gold ring weighing a half-shekel and two bracelets for her wrists** weighing ten shekels in gold.
Genesis 24:22

The servant brought out articles of silver and articles of gold, and garments, and gave them to Rebekah; **he also gave precious things to her brother and to her mother.**
Genesis 24:53

"When my brother Esau meets you and asks you, saying, 'To whom do you belong, and where are you going, and to whom do these animals in front of you belong?' then you shall say, 'These belong to your servant Jacob; **it is a present sent to my lord Esau.** And behold, he also is behind us.' . . . After this manner you shall speak to Esau when you find him; and you shall say, 'Behold, your servant Jacob also is behind us.'" For he said, "**I will appease him with the present that goes before me.** Then afterward I will see his face; perhaps he will accept me."

Genesis 32:17–20

Jacob said, "No, please, if now I have found favor in your sight, **then take my present from my hand,** for I see your face as one sees the face of God, and you have received me favorably. Please take my gift which has been brought to you, because God has dealt graciously with me, and because I have plenty." Thus he urged him and he took it.

Genesis 33:10–11

Joseph gave orders to fill their bags with grain and **to restore every man's money** in his sack, and to give them provisions for the journey. . . . So they loaded their donkeys with their grain, and departed from there. And as one of them opened his sack to give his donkey fodder at the lodging place, he saw his money; and behold, it was in the mouth of his sack. Then he said to his brothers, "**My money has been returned,** and behold, it is even in my sack." And their hearts sank, and they turned trembling to one another, saying, "**What is this that God has done to us?**"

Genesis 42:25–28

It came about as they were emptying their sacks, that behold, **every man's bundle of money was in his sack;** and when they and their father saw their bundles of money, they were dismayed.

Genesis 42:35

So the men took this present, and they took double the money in their hand, and Benjamin; then they arose and went down to Egypt and stood before Joseph.

Genesis 43:15

The men were afraid, because they were brought to Joseph's house; and they said, "**It is because of the money that was returned in our sacks** the first time that we are being brought in, that he may seek occasion against us and fall upon us, and take us for slaves with our donkeys."

Genesis 43:18

When Joseph came home, they brought into the house to him the present which was in their hand and bowed to the ground before him.

Genesis 43:26

He commanded his house steward, saying, "**Fill the men's sacks** with food, as much as they can carry, and **put each man's money in the mouth of his sack.** And put my cup, the silver cup, in the mouth of the sack of the youngest, and his money for the grain." And he did as Joseph had told him.

Genesis 44:1–2

Pharaoh said to Joseph, "Say to your brothers, 'Do this: load your beasts and **go to the land of Canaan.**'"

Genesis 45:17

"'Do not concern yourselves with your goods, **for the best of all the land of Egypt is yours.**'"

Genesis 45:20

To each of them he gave changes of garments, but to Benjamin he gave three hundred pieces of silver and five changes of garments.

Genesis 45:22

Joseph settled his father and his brothers, and gave them a possession in the land of Egypt, in the best of the land, in the land of Rameses, as Pharaoh had ordered.

Genesis 47:11

"Take the Levites instead of all the first-born among the sons of Israel and the cattle of the Levites. And the Levites shall be Mine; I am the Lord. And for the ransom of the 273 of the first-born of the sons of Israel who are in excess beyond the Levites, you shall take five shekels apiece, per head; you shall take them in terms of the shekel of the sanctuary (the shekel is twenty gerahs), and give the money, the ransom of those who are in excess among them, to Aaron and to his sons." **So Moses took the ransom money from those who were in excess,** beyond those ransomed by the Levites.

Numbers 3:45–49

"Be careful that you do not forsake the Levite as long as you live in your land."

Deuteronomy 12:19

The servant answered Saul again and said, "Behold, I have in my hand a fourth of a shekel of silver; I will give it to the man of God and he will tell us our way."

1 Samuel 9:8

"Let this gift which your maidservant has brought to my lord be given to the young men who accompany my lord."

1 Samuel 25:27

Toi sent Joram his son to King David to greet him and bless him, because he had fought against Hadadezer and defeated him; for Hadadezer had been at war with Toi. And **Joram brought with him articles of silver, of gold and of bronze.** King David also dedicated these to the Lord, with the silver and gold that he had dedicated from all the nations which he had subdued.

2 Samuel 8:10–11

Hiram gave Solomon as much as he desired of the cedar and cypress timber. Solomon then gave Hiram 20,000 kors of wheat as food for his household, and twenty kors of beaten oil; thus **Solomon would give Hiram year by year.**

1 Kings 5:10–11

Hiram sent to the king 120 talents of gold.

1 Kings 9:14

They went to Ophir, and took four hundred and twenty talents of gold from there, and brought it to King Solomon.

1 Kings 9:28

So she came to Jerusalem with a very large retinue, with camels carrying spices and very much gold and precious stones. When she came to Solomon, she spoke with him about all that was in her heart.

1 Kings 10:2

She gave the king a hundred and twenty talents of gold, and a very great amount of spices and precious stones. Never again did such abundance of spices come in as that which the queen of Sheba gave King Solomon.

1 Kings 10:10

The weight of gold which came in to Solomon in one year was 666 talents of gold.

1 Kings 10:14

The king of Aram said, "Go now, and I will send a letter to the king of Israel." And he departed and took with him ten talents of silver and six thousand shekels of gold and ten changes of clothes.

2 Kings 5:5

When he returned to the man of God with all his company, and came and stood before him, he said, "Behold now, I **know that there is no God in all the earth, but in Israel;** so please take a present from your servant now." But he said, "As the Lord lives, before whom I stand, I will take nothing." And he urged him to take it, but he refused. And Naaman said, "If not, please let your servant at least be given two mules' load of earth; for your servant will no more offer burnt offering nor will he sacrifice to other gods, but to the Lord. In this matter may the Lord pardon your servant: when my master goes into the house of Rimmon to worship there, and he leans on my hand and I bow myself in the house of Rimmon, when I bow myself in the house of Rimmon, the Lord pardon your servant in this matter."

And he said to him, "Go in peace." So he departed from
him some distance. But Gehazi, the servant of Elisha the
man of God, thought, "Behold, my master has spared this
Naaman the Aramean, by not receiving from his hands
what he brought. As the Lord lives, I will run after him and
take something from him." So Gehazi pursed Naaman.
When Naaman saw one running after him, he came down
from the chariot to meet him and said, "Is all well?" And
he said, "All is well. My master has sent me, saying 'Behold, just now two young men of the sons of the prophets
have come to me from the hill country of Ephraim. **Please
give them a talent of silver and two changes of clothes.'"**
And Naaman said, "Be pleased to take two talents." And
he urged him, and bound two talents of silver in two bags
with two changes of clothes, and gave them to two of his
servants; and they carried them before him. When he came
to the hill, he took them from their hand and deposited
them in the house, and he sent the men away, and they
departed.

2 Kings 5:15–24

Ahaz took the silver and gold that was found in the house
of the Lord and in the treasuries of the king's house, and
sent a present to the king of Assyria.

2 Kings 16:8

**For his allowance, a regular allowance was given him by
the king,** a portion for each day, all the days of his life.

2 Kings 25:30

[They] took from there four hundred and fifty talents of
gold, and brought them to King Solomon.

2 Chronicles 8:18

[The queen of Sheba] **had a very large retinue,** with camels
carrying spices, and a large amount of gold and precious
stones; and when she came to Solomon, she spoke with
him about all that was on her heart. Then **she gave the
king one hundred and twenty talents of gold,** and a very
great amount of spices and precious stones; there had never

been spice like that which **the queen of Sheba** gave to King Solomon. And the servants of Huram and the servants of Solomon who brought gold from Ophir, also brought algum trees and precious stones.

2 Chronicles 9:1, 9–10

The weight of gold which came to Solomon in one year was 666 talents of gold.

2 Chronicles 9:13

They brought every man his gift, articles of silver and gold, garments, weapons, spices, horses, and mules, so much year by year.

2 Chronicles 9:24

Asa brought out silver and gold from the treasuries of the house of the Lord and the king's house, and **sent them to Ben-hadad king of Aram,** who lived in Damascus.

2 Chronicles 16:2

Some of the Philistines brought gifts and silver as tribute to Jehoshaphat; the Arabians also brought him flocks, 7,700 rams and 7,700 male goats.

2 Chronicles 17:11

A man's gift makes room for him, and **brings him before great men.**

Proverbs 18:16

"If you declare the dream and its interpretation, **you will receive from me gifts** and a reward and great honor; therefore declare to me the dream and its interpretation."

Daniel 2:6

Daniel answered and said before the king, "**Keep your gifts for yourself,** or give your rewards to someone else; however, I will read the inscription to the king and make the interpretation known to him."

Daniel 5:17

Belshazzar gave orders, and they clothed Daniel with purple and put a necklace of gold around his neck, and issued a proclamation concerning him that he **now** had authority as the third **ruler** in the kingdom.

Daniel 5:29

"Take silver and gold, make an ornate crown, and set it on the head of Joshua the son of Jehozadak, the high priest."

Zechariah 6:11

"When you give alms, do not let your left hand know what your right hand is doing that your alms may be in secret; and **your Father who sees in secret will repay you.**"

Matthew 6:3–4

"Let the man who has two tunics **share with him who has none;** and let him who has food do likewise."

Luke 3:11

"Just as you want people to treat you, treat them in the same way. . . . **Give, and it will be given to you;** good measure, pressed down, shaken together, running over, they will pour into your lap. For **by your standard of measure it will be measured to you** in return."

Luke 6:31, 38

"If you then, being evil, know how to give good gifts to your children, how much more shall your heavenly Father give the Holy Spirit to those who ask Him?"

Luke 11:13

Let each one do just as he has purposed in his heart; **not grudgingly or under compulsion;** for God loves a cheerful giver. . . . you will be enriched in everything for all liberality, which through us is producing thanksgiving to God.

2 Corinthians 9:7, 11

Let the one who is taught the word share all things with him who teaches.

Galatians 6:6

Be rich in good works . . . **be generous and ready to share.**

1 Timothy 6:18

Do not neglect doing good and sharing; for **with such sacrifices God is pleased.**

Hebrews 13:16

HELPING THE NEEDY

God's Word says there will always be needs in the world around us, and God expects us to help those in need. The needy are those who are doing the best they can with what they have, but what they have is insufficient to meet their needs.

The first generation church set an example for us when they sold their assets and surrendered the proceeds to meet the needs of other believers. So the question is whether we will be doers of the Word instead of hearers only. With literally millions of people starving in the world, the rewards of giving to them are saved lives as well as saved souls.

"You shall sow your land for six years and gather in its yield, but **on the seventh year you shall let it rest** and lie fallow, so that the needy of your people may eat; and whatever they leave the beast of the field may eat. You are to do the same with your vineyard and your olive grove."

Exodus 23:10–11

"**Nor shall you glean your vineyard,** nor shall you gather the fallen fruit of your vineyard; you shall leave them for the needy and for the stranger. I am the Lord your God."

Leviticus 19:10

"When you reap the harvest of your land, moreover, **you shall not reap to the very corners of your field,** nor gather the gleaning of your harvest; you are to leave them for the needy and the alien. I am the Lord your God."

Leviticus 23:22

"In case a countryman of yours becomes poor and his means with regard to you falter, then you are to sustain him, like a stranger or a sojourner, that he may live with you. Do not take usurious interest from him, but revere your God, that your countrymen may live with you. **You**

shall not give him your silver at interest, nor your food for gain."

Leviticus 25:35–37

"He executes justice for the orphan and the widow, and shows His love for the alien by giving him food and clothing. So show your love for the alien, for you were aliens in the land of Egypt."

Deuteronomy 10:18–19

"If there is a poor man with you, one of your brothers, in any of your towns in your land which the Lord your God is giving you, you shall not harden your heart, nor close your hand from your poor brother; but you shall **freely open your hand** to him, and shall generously lend him sufficient for his need in whatever he lacks. Beware, lest there is a base thought in your heart, saying, 'The seventh year, the year of remission is near,' and your eye is hostile toward your poor brother, and you give him nothing; then he may cry to the Lord against you, and it will be a sin in you. You shall **generously give** to him, and your heart shall not be grieved when you give to him, because for this thing the Lord your God will bless you in all your work and in all your undertakings. For **the poor will never cease to be in the land;** therefore I command you, saying, 'You shall freely open your hand to your brother, to your needy and poor in your land.'"

Deuteronomy 15:7–11

"You shall not oppress a hired servant who is poor and needy, whether he is one of your countrymen or one of your aliens who is in your land in your towns. **You shall give him his wages** on his day before the sun sets, for he is poor and sets his heart on it; so that he may not cry against you to the Lord and it become sin in you."

Deuteronomy 24:14–15

"When you reap your harvest in your field and have forgotten a sheaf in the field, **you shall not go back to get it;** it shall be for the alien, for the orphan, and for the widow, in

190

order that the Lord your God may bless you in all the work of your hands. When you beat your olive tree, you shall not go over the boughs again; it shall be for the alien, for the orphan, and for the widow. When you gather the grapes of your vineyard, you shall not go over it again; it shall be for the alien, for the orphan, and for the widow."

Deuteronomy 24:19–21

So Saul's servants spoke these words to David. But David said, "Is it trivial in your sight to become the king's son-in-law, since **I am a poor man and lightly esteemed?**"

1 Samuel 18:23

Everyone who was in distress, and **everyone who was in debt,** and everyone who was discontented, **gathered to him;** and he became captain over them. Now there were about four hundred men with him.

1 Samuel 22:2

Mordecai recorded these events, and he sent letters to all the Jews . . . obliging them to celebrate the fourteenth day of the month Adar, and the fifteenth day of the same month, annually, because . . . it was a month which was turned for them from sorrow into gladness and from mourning into a holiday; that they should make them days of feasting and rejoicing and **sending portions of food to one another and gifts to the poor.**

Esther 9:20–22

"**His sons favor the poor,** and his hands give back his wealth."

Job 20:10

"**I delivered the poor who cried for help, and the orphan who had no helper.**"

Job 29:12

"**I was a father to the needy,** and I investigated the case which I did not know."

Job 29:16

191

"Have I not wept for the one whose life is hard? **Was not my soul grieved for the needy?**"

Job 30:25

"**If I have kept the poor from their desire,** or have caused the eyes of the widow to fail, or have eaten my morsel alone, and the orphan has not shared it (but from my youth he grew up with me as with a father, and from infancy I guided her), if I have seen anyone perish for lack of clothing, or that the needy had no covering."

Job 31:16–19

The needy will not always be forgotten, nor the hope of the afflicted perish forever.

Psalm 9:18

"Because of the devastation of the afflicted, **because of the groaning of the needy, now I will arise,**" says the Lord; "I will set him in the safety for which he longs."

Psalm 12:5

This poor man cried and the Lord heard him, and saved him out of all his troubles.

Psalm 34:6

Since I am afflicted and needy, let the Lord be mindful of me; Thou art my help and my deliverer; do not delay, O my God.

Psalm 40:17

How blessed is he who considers the helpless; the Lord will deliver him in a day of trouble.

Psalm 41:1

God makes a home for the lonely; He leads out the prisoners into prosperity, only the rebellious dwell in a parched land.

Psalm 68:6

Thy creatures settled in it; **Thou didst provide in Thy goodness for the poor,** O God.

Psalm 68:10

The Lord hears the needy, and does not despise His who are prisoners.

Psalm 69:33

May he vindicate the afflicted of the people, **save the children of the needy, and crush the oppressor.**

Psalm 72:4

He will deliver the needy when he cries for help, the afflicted also, and him who has no helper. He will have compassion on the poor and needy, and the lives of the needy he will save. He will rescue their life from oppression and violence; and their blood will be precious in his sight.

Psalm 72:12–14

He pours contempt upon princes, and makes them wander in a pathless waste. But **He sets the needy securely on high** away from affliction, and makes his families like a flock.

Psalm 107:40–41

He stands at the right hand of the needy, to save him from those who judge his soul.

Psalm 109:31

He has given freely to the poor; His righteousness endures forever; His horn will be exalted in honor.

Psalm 112:9

He raises the poor from the dust, and lifts the needy from the ash heap, to make them sit with princes, with the princes of His people.

Psalm 113:7–8

Though the Lord is exalted, yet **He regards the lowly;** but the haughty He knows from afar.

Psalm 138:6

I know that **the Lord will maintain the cause of the afflicted,** and justice for the poor.

Psalm 140:12

He who despises his neighbor sins, but happy is he who is gracious to the poor.

Proverbs 14:21

He who oppresses the poor reproaches his Maker, but he who is gracious to the needy honors Him.

Proverbs 14:31

He who is gracious to a poor man lends to the Lord, and He will repay him for his good deed.

Proverbs 19:17

He who shuts his ear to the cry of the poor will also cry himself and not be answered.

Proverbs 21:13

He who gives to the poor will never want, but he who shuts his eyes will have many curses.

Proverbs 28:27

The righteous is concerned for the rights of the poor, the wicked does not understand such concern.

Proverbs 29:7

Open your mouth, **judge righteously,** and defend the rights of the afflicted and needy.

Proverbs 31:9

She extends her hand to the poor; and she stretches out her hands to the needy.

Proverbs 31:20

Thou hast been **a defense for the helpless,** a defense for the needy in his distress, a refuge from the storm, a shade from the heat; for the breath of the ruthless is like a rain storm against a wall.

Isaiah 25:4

"The afflicted and needy are seeking water, but there is none, and their tongue is parched with thirst; I, the Lord, will answer them Myself, as the God of Israel I will not forsake them."

Isaiah 41:17

"Is it not to divide your bread with the hungry, and bring the homeless poor into the house; when you see the naked, to cover him; and not to hide yourself from your own flesh?"

Isaiah 58:7

"He **pled the cause of the afflicted and needy;** then it was well. Is not that what it means to know Me?" declares the Lord.

Jeremiah 22:16

Some of the **poorest people** who had nothing, Nebuzaradan the captain of the bodyguard **left behind in the land of Judah,** and gave them vineyards and field at that time.

Jeremiah 39:10

"Behold, this was the guilt of your sister Sodom; she and her daughters had arrogance, abundant food, and careless ease, but **she did not help the poor and needy."**

Ezekiel 16:49

Break away now from your sins by doing righteousness, and from your iniquities **by showing mercy to the poor,** in case there may be a prolonging of your prosperity.

Daniel 4:27

"Whoever in the name of a disciple gives to one of these

little ones **even a cup of cold water to drink,** truly I say to you he shall not lose his reward."

Matthew 10:42

"The blind receive sight and the lame walk, the lepers are cleansed and the deaf hear, and the dead are raised up, and **the poor have the gospel preached to them.**"

Matthew 11:5

"But you say, 'Whoever shall say to his father or mother, "**Anything of mine you might have been helped by has been given to God,**" he is not to honor his father or his mother.' And thus you invalidated the word of God for the sake of your tradition."

Matthew 15:5–6

Jesus said to him, "**If you wish to be complete, go and sell your possessions** and give to the poor, and you shall have treasure in heaven; and come, follow Me."

Matthew 19:21

"'**For I was hungry, and you gave Me something to eat;** I was thirsty, and you gave Me drink; I was a stranger, and you invited Me in; naked, and you clothed Me; I was sick, and you visited Me; I was in prison, and you came to Me.' Then the righteous will answer Him, saying, 'Lord, when did we see You hungry, and feed you, or thirsty, and give You drink? And when did we see You a stranger, and invite You in, or naked, and clothe You? And when did we see You sick, or in prison, and come to You?' And the King will answer and say to them, 'Truly I say to you, **to the extent that you did it to one of these brothers of Mine,** even the least of them, **you did it to me.**' Then He will also say to those on His left, 'Depart from Me, accursed ones, into the eternal fire which has been prepared for the devil and his angels; **for I was hungry, and you gave Me nothing to eat;** I was thirsty, and you gave Me nothing to drink; I was a stranger, and you did not invite Me in; naked, and you did not clothe Me; sick, and in prison, and you did not visit Me.' Then they themselves also will answer, saying, 'Lord, when did we see You hungry, or thirsty, or a stranger, or naked, or sick, or in prison, and did not take care of You?' Then He will answer them, saying, 'Truly I say to you, **to the extent that you did not do it to one of the least of these, you did not do it to Me.'''**

Matthew 25:35–45

A woman came to him with an alabaster vial of very costly perfume, and she poured it upon His head as He reclined at the table. But the disciples were indignant when they saw this, and said, "Why this waste? For this perfume might have been sold for a high price and the money given to the poor." But Jesus, aware of this, said to them, "Why do you bother the woman? For she has done a good deed to Me. For **the poor you have with you always;** but you do not always have Me. For when she poured this perfume upon My body, she did it to prepare Me for burial."

Matthew 26:7–12

"'If a man says to his father or his mother, anything of mine you might have been helped by is Corban (that is to say, given to God),' you no longer permit him to do anything for his father or his mother."

Mark 7:11–12

Looking at him, Jesus felt a love for him, and said to him, **"One thing you lack: go and sell all you possess,** and give to the poor, and you shall have treasure in heaven; and come, follow Me." But at these words his face fell, and he went away grieved, for he was one who owned much property. And Jesus, looking around, said to His disciples, "How hard it will be for those who are wealthy to enter the kingdom of God!" And the disciples were amazed at His words. But Jesus answered again and said to them, "Children, how hard it is to enter the kingdom of God! It is easier for a camel to go through the eye of a needle than for a rich man to enter the kingdom of God." And they were even more astonished and said to Him, "Then who can be saved?"

Mark 10:21–26

While He was in Bethany at the home of Simon the leper, and reclining at the table, **there came a woman with an alabaster vial of very costly perfume** of pure nard; and she broke the vial and poured it over His head. But some were indignantly remarking to one another, "Why has this perfume been wasted? For this perfume might have been sold for over three hundred denarii, and the money given to the poor." And they were scolding her. But Jesus said, "Let her alone; why do you bother her? She has done a good deed to Me. For **the poor you always have with you, and whenever you wish, you can do them good;** but you do not always have Me."

Mark 14:3–7

He would answer and say to them, "**Let the man who has two tunics** share with him who has none; and let him who has food do likewise."

Luke 3:11

"The Spirit of the Lord is upon Me, because He anointed Me to **preach the gospel to the poor.** He has sent Me to proclaim release to the captives, and recovery of sight to the blind, to set free those who are downtrodden."

Luke 4:18

Turning His gaze on His disciples, He began to say, "**Blessed are you who are poor,** for yours is the kingdom of God."

Luke 6:20

He answered and said to them, "Go and report to John what you have seen and heard: the blind receive sight, the lame walk, the lepers are cleansed, and the deaf hear, the dead are raised up, **the poor have the gospel preached to them.**"

Luke 7:22

[He] said to them, "**Whoever receives this child in My name receives Me;** and whoever receives Me receives Him who sent Me; for he who is least among you, this is the one who is great."

Luke 9:48

"On the next day he took out two denarii and gave them to the innkeeper and said, '**Take care of him;** and whatever more you spend, when I return, **I will repay you.**'"

Luke 10:35

"**Sell your possessions** and give to charity; make yourselves purses which do not wear out, an unfailing treasure in heaven, where no thief comes near, nor moth destroys."

Luke 12:33

He also went on to say to the one who had invited Him, "When you give a luncheon or a dinner, do not invite your friends or your brother or your relatives or rich neighbors, lest they also invite you in return, and repayment come to you. But **when you give a reception, invite the poor,** the crippled, the lame, the blind, and you will be blessed, since they do not have the means to repay you; for you will be repaid at the resurrection of the righteous."

Luke 14:12–14

When Jesus heard this, He said to him, "One thing you still lack; **sell all that you possess, and distribute it to the poor,** and you shall have treasure in heaven; and come, follow Me." But when he heard these things, he became very sad; for he was extremely rich. And Jesus looked at him and said, "How hard it is for those who are wealthy to enter the kingdom of God! For it is easier for a camel to go through the eye of a needle, than for a rich man to enter the kingdom of God."

Luke 18:22–25

All **those who had believed were together, and had all things in common;** and they began selling their property and possessions, and were sharing them with all, as anyone might have need.

Acts 2:44–45

A certain man who had been lame from his mother's womb was being carried along, whom they used to set down every day at the gate of the temple which is called

Beautiful, in order to beg alms of those who were entering the temple. And when he saw Peter and John about to go into the temple, he began asking to receive alms. And Peter, along with John, fixed his gaze upon him and said, "Look at us!" And he began to give them his attention, expecting to receive something from them. But Peter said, "**I do not possess silver and gold, but what I do have I give to you:** In the name of Jesus Christ the Nazarene—walk!"

Acts 3:2–6

The congregation of those who believed were of one heart and soul; and **not one of them claimed that anything belonging to him was his own;** but all things were common property to them. And with great power the apostles were giving witness to the resurrection of the Lord Jesus, and abundant grace was upon them all. For there was not a needy person among them, for all who were owners of land or houses would sell them and bring the proceeds of the sales, and lay them at the apostles' feet; and they would be distributed to each, as any had need. And Joseph, a Levite of Cyprian birth, who was also called **Barnabas** by the apostles (which translated means, Son of Encouragement), and **who owned a tract of land,** sold it and brought the money and laid it at the apostles' feet.

Acts 4:32–37

At this time while the disciples were increasing in number, a complaint arose on the part of the Hellenistic Jews against the native Hebrews, because **their widows were being overlooked in the daily serving of food.** And the twelve summoned the congregation of the disciples and said, "It is not desirable for us to neglect the word of God in order to serve tables."

Acts 6:1–2

There was a certain man at Caesarea named Cornelius, . . . **a devout man,** and one who feared God with all his household, and **gave many alms to the Jewish people,** and prayed to God continually.

Acts 10:1–2

200

Fixing his gaze upon him and being much alarmed, he said, "What is it, Lord?" And he said to him, "**Your prayers and alms have ascended as a memorial before God.**"

Acts 10:4

"[Peter] said, 'Cornelius, your prayer has been heard and **your alms have been remembered before God.**'"

Acts 10:31

In the proportion that any of the disciples had means, **each of them determined to send a contribution** for the relief of the brethren living in Judea.

Acts 11:29

"After several years **I came to bring alms to my nation** and to present offerings."

Acts 24:17

Macedonia and Achaia have been pleased to make a contribution for the poor among the saints in Jerusalem. Yes, they were pleased to do so, and they are indebted to them. For if the Gentiles have shared in their spiritual things, they are indebted to minister to them also in material things.

Romans 15:26–27

Concerning the collection for the saints, as I directed the churches of Galatia, so do you also. On the first day of every week let each one of you put aside and save, as he may prosper, that no collections be made when I come.

1 Corinthians 16:1–2

In everything commending ourselves as servants of God, in much endurance, in afflictions, in hardships, in distresses, . . . as sorrowful yet always rejoicing, **as poor yet making many rich,** as having nothing yet possessing all things.

2 Corinthians 6:4, 10

In the churches of Macedonia . . . that in a great ordeal of affliction their abundance of joy and their deep poverty overflowed in the wealth of their liberality. For I testify that according to their ability, and beyond their ability **they gave of their own accord,** begging us with much entreaty for the favor of participation in the support of the saints, and this, not as we had expected, but they first gave themselves to the Lord and to us by the will of God.

2 Corinthians 8:1–5

You know the grace of our Lord Jesus Christ, that **though He was rich, yet for your sake He became poor,** that you through His poverty might become rich.

2 Corinthians 8:9

Finish doing it also; that just as there was the readiness to desire it, so there may be also the completion of it by your ability. For if the readiness is present, **it is acceptable according to what a man has,** not according to what he does not have. For **this is not for the ease of others and for your affliction, but by way of equality—at this present time your abundance being a supply for their want, that their abundance also may become a supply for your want, that there may be equality; as it is written, "He who** gathered **much did not have too much, and he who** gathered **little had no lack."**

2 Corinthians 8:11–15

God is able to make all grace abound to you, that always having all sufficiency in everything, **you may have an abundance for every good deed;** as it is written, "He **scattered abroad, He gave to the poor, His righteousness abides forever."** Now **He who supplies seed to the sower and bread for food, will supply and multiply your seed** for sowing and increase the harvest of your righteousness; you will be enriched in everything for all liberality, which through us is producing thanksgiving to God. For the ministry of this service is not only fully supplying the needs of the saints, but is also overflowing through many thanksgivings to God. Because of the proof given by this ministry they will glorify God for your obedience to your confession of the gospel of Christ, and for the liberality of your contribution to them and to all.

2 Corinthians 9:8–13

They only asked us **to remember the poor**—the very thing I also was eager to do.

Galatians 2:10

You yourselves also know, Philippians, that at the first preaching of the gospel, after I departed from Macedonia, no church shared with me in the matter of giving and receiving but you alone; for even in Thessalonica **you sent a gift more than once for my needs.** Not that I seek the gift itself, but I seek for the profit which increases to your account. But I have received everything in full, and have an abundance; I am amply supplied, having received from Epaphroditus what you have sent, a fragrant aroma, an acceptable sacrifice, well-pleasing to God.

Philippians 4:15–18

Honor widows who are widows indeed.

1 Timothy 5:3

She who is a widow indeed, and who has been left alone has fixed her hope on God, and continues in entreaties and prayers night and day.

1 Timothy 5:5

If any woman who is a believer has dependent widows, let her assist them, and let not the church be burdened, so that it may assist those who are widows indeed.

1 Timothy 5:16

Instruct them to do good, to be rich in good works, to **be generous and ready to share,** storing up for themselves the treasure of a good foundation for the future, so that they may take hold of that which is life indeed.

1 Timothy 6:18–19

You showed sympathy to the prisoners, and **accepted joy-
fully the seizure of your property,** knowing that you have
for yourselves a better possession and an abiding one.

Hebrews 10:34

This is pure and undefiled religion in the sight of our God
and Father, to **visit orphans and widows in their distress,**
and to keep oneself unstained by the world.

James 1:27

My brethren, **do not hold your faith in our glorious Lord
Jesus Christ with an attitude of personal favoritism.** For if
a man comes into your assembly with a gold ring and
dressed in fine clothes, and there also comes in a poor man
in dirty clothes, and you pay special attention to the one
who is wearing the fine clothes, and say, "You sit here in a
good place," and you say to the poor man, "You stand over
there, or sit down by my footstool," have you not made
distinctions among yourselves, and become judges with
evil motives? Listen, my beloved brethren; **did not God
choose the poor of this world** to be rich in faith and heirs of
the kingdom which He promised to those who love Him?
But you have dishonored the poor man. Is it not the rich
who oppress you and personally drag you into court? Do
they not blaspheme the fair name by which you have been
called? If, however, you are fulfilling the royal law, according to the Scripture, "**You shall love your neighbor as
yourself,**" you are doing well. But if you show partiality,
you are committing sin and are convicted by the law as
transgressors. For whoever keeps the whole law and yet
stumbles in one point, he has become guilty of all. For He
who said, "Do not commit adultery," also said, "Do not
commit murder." Now if you do not commit adultery, but
do commit murder, you have become a transgressor of the
law. So speak and so act, as those who are to be judged by
the law of liberty. For judgment will be merciless to one
who has shown no mercy; mercy triumphs over judgment.
What use is it, my brethren, if a man says he has **faith, but
he has no works?** Can that faith save him? **If a brother or
sister is without clothing and in need of daily food,** and

204

one of you says to them, "Go in peace, be warmed, and be filled," and yet you do not give them what is necessary for their body, what use it that?

James 2:1–16

Whoever has the world's goods, and beholds his brother in need and closes his heart against him, how does the love of God abide in him? Little children, let us not love with word or with tongue, but in deed and truth.

1 John 3:17–18

Beloved, you are acting faithfully in whatever you accomplish for the brethren, and especially when they are strangers; and they bear witness to your love before the church; and **you will do well to send them on their way in a manner worthy of God.**

3 John 5–6

"**They shall hunger no more,** neither thirst anymore; neither shall the sun beat down on them, nor any heat."

Revelation 7:16

INHERITANCE

This generation seems to be a people of extremes, and inheritance is no exception. One part of our society leaves enormous wealth to its generally untrained offspring, whereas another segment spends it all and leaves practically nothing to their families. Those who spend all they have without regard to their children are not good stewards. In fact, the legacy that many Christian parents leave today is one of debt. The primary inheritance we are to leave is spiritual; the secondary inheritance is financial.

Even a brief survey of the Bible reveals that God provided for each generation through inheritance. In biblical times, the sons inherited their father's properties and thus provided for the rest of their family. In most instances, the sons received their inheritance while their fathers were still living. Thus, a father was able to oversee their stewardship while they were learning.

Abram said, "O Lord God, what wilt Thou give me, since I am childless, and the **heir** of my house is Eliezer of Damascus?" And Abram said, "Since Thou hast given no offspring to me, one born in my house is my **heir**." Then behold, the word of the Lord came to him, saying, "This man will not be your heir; but **one who shall come forth from your own body, he shall be your heir.**"

Genesis 15:2–4

Abraham gave all that he had to Issac; but to the sons of his concubines, Abraham gave gifts while he was still living, and sent them away from his son Isaac eastward, to the land of the east. And these are all the years of Abraham's life that he lived, one hundred and seventy-five years. And Abraham breathed his last and died in a ripe

206

old age, an old man and satisfied with life; and he was gathered to his people.

Genesis 25:5–8

Jacob said, "**First sell me your birthright.**" And Esau said, "Behold, I am about to die; so of what use then is the birthright to me?" And Jacob said, "First swear to me"; so he swore to him, and sold his birthright to Jacob. . . . Thus Esau despised his birthright.

Genesis 25:31–34

It came about, as soon as Isaac **had finished blessing Jacob,** and Jacob had hardly gone out from the presence of Isaac his father, that Esau his brother came in from his hunting.

Genesis 27:30

Rachel and Leah answered and said to him, "**Do we still have any portion or inheritance in our father's house?** Are we not reckoned by him as foreigners? For he has sold us, and has also entirely consumed our purchase price. Surely all the wealth which God has taken away from our father belongs to us and our children; now then, do whatever God has said to you."

Genesis 31:14–16

The Lord said to Aaron, "**You shall have no inheritance in their land,** nor own any portion among them; I am your portion and your inheritance among the sons of Israel. And to the sons of Levi, behold, I have given all the tithe in Israel for an inheritance, in return for their service which they perform, the service of the tent of meeting."

Numbers 18:20–21

"**The tithe of the sons of Israel,** which they offer as an offering to the Lord, I have given to the Levites for an inheritance; therefore I have said concerning them, 'They shall have no inheritance among the sons of Israel.'"

Numbers 18:24

"**To the larger group you shall increase their inheritance**, and to the smaller group you shall diminish their inheritance; each shall be given their inheritance according to those who were numbered of them. But the land shall be divided by lot. **They shall receive their inheritance according to the names of the tribes** of their fathers. According to the selection by lot, their inheritance shall be divided between the larger and the smaller groups."

Numbers 26:54–56

"**The daughters of Zelophehad** are right in their statements. You shall surely give them a hereditary possession among their father's brothers, and **you shall transfer the inheritance of their father to them.** Further, you shall speak to the sons of Israel, saying, '**If a man dies and has no son, then you shall transfer his inheritance to his daughter.** And if he has no daughter, then you shall give his inheritance to his brothers. And if he has no brothers, then you shall give his inheritance to his father's brothers. And if his father has no brothers, then you shall give his inheritance to his nearest relative in his own family, and he shall possess it; and it shall be a statutory ordinance to the sons of Israel, just as the Lord commanded Moses.'"

Numbers 27:7–11

"**You shall inherit the land** by lot according to your families; to the larger you shall give more inheritance, and to the smaller you shall give less inheritance. Wherever the lot falls to anyone, that shall be his. You shall inherit according to the tribes of your fathers."

Numbers 33:54

"Command the sons of Israel that they **give to the Levites from the inheritance of their possession,** cities to live in; and you shall give to the Levites pasture lands around the cities."

Numbers 35:2

"As for the cities which you shall give from the possession of the sons of Israel, you shall take more from the larger and you shall take less from the smaller; each shall give some of his cities to the Levites in proportion to his possession which he inherits."

Numbers 35:8

"**If they marry one of the sons of the other tribes** of the sons of Israel, **their inheritance will be withdrawn** from the inheritance of our fathers and will be added to the inheritance of the tribe to which they belong; thus it will be withdrawn from our allotted inheritance. And when the jubilee of the sons of Israel comes, then their inheritance will be added to the inheritance of the tribe to which they belong; so their inheritance will be withdrawn from the inheritance of the tribe of our fathers."

Numbers 36:3–4

"'Let them marry whom they wish; only they must marry within the family of the tribe of their father.' Thus **no inheritance of the sons of Israel shall be transferred from tribe to tribe,** for the sons of Israel shall each hold to the inheritance of the tribe of his fathers."

Numbers 36:6–7

"**No inheritance shall be transferred from one tribe to another tribe,** for the tribes of the sons of Israel shall each hold to his own inheritance."

Numbers 36:9

"**The Levitical priests,** the whole tribe of Levi, **shall have no portion or inheritance with Israel;** they shall eat of the Lord's offerings by fire and His portion. And they shall have no inheritance among their countrymen; the Lord is their inheritance, as He promised them."

Deuteronomy 18:1–2

"**They shall eat equal portions,** except what they receive from the sale of their fathers' estates."

Deuteronomy 18:8

"**He shall acknowledge the first-born,** the son of the un-loved, **by giving him a double portion** of all that he has, for he is the beginning of his strength; to him belongs the right of the first-born."

Deuteronomy 21:17

Joshua took the whole land, according to all that the Lord had spoken to Moses, and **Joshua gave it for an inheritance to Israel** according to their divisions by their tribes. Thus the land had rest from war.

Joshua 11:23

Only to the tribe of Levi he did not give an inheritance; the offerings by fire to the Lord, the God of Israel, are their inheritance, as He spoke to him.

Joshua 13:14

To the tribe of Levi, Moses did not give an inheritance; **the Lord, the God of Israel, is their inheritance,** as He had promised to them.

Joshua 13:33

These are the territories which the sons of Israel inherited in the land of Canaan, which Eleazar the priest, and Joshua the son of Nun, and the heads of the households of the tribes of the sons of Israel **apportioned to them for an inheritance.**

Joshua 14:1

The sons of Joseph were two tribes, Manasseh and Ephraim, and they did not give a portion to the Levites in the land, except cities to live in, with their pasture lands for their livestock and for their property.

Joshua 14:4

Hebron became the inheritance of Caleb the son of Jephunneh the Kenizzite until this day, **because he followed the Lord God of Israel fully.**

Joshua 14:14

They came near before Eleazar the priest and before Joshua . . . saying, "The Lord commanded Moses to give us an inheritance among our brothers." So according to the command of the Lord he gave them an inheritance among their father's brothers. Thus there fell ten portions to Manasseh . . . because the **daughters of Manasseh received an inheritance** among his sons. And the land of Gilead belonged to the rest of the sons of Manasseh.

Joshua 17:4–6

They **buried the bones of Joseph,** which the sons of Israel brought up from Egypt, at Shechem, in the piece of ground which Jacob had brought from the sons of Hamor the father of Shechem for one hundred pieces of money; and they became the inheritance of Joseph's sons.

Joshua 24:32

Gilead's wife bore him sons; and when his wife's sons grew up, they drove **Jephthah** out and said to him, "You shall not have an inheritance in our father's house, for you are the son of another woman."

Judges 11:2

In those days there was no king of Israel; and in those days the tribe of the Danites was **seeking an inheritance for themselves to live in,** for until that day an inheritance had not been allotted to them as a possession among the tribes of Israel.

Judges 18:1

He said to the closest relative, "**Naomi,** who has come back from the land of Moab, has to sell the piece of land which belonged to our brother Elimelech. So I thought to inform you, saying, '**Buy it before those who are sitting here,** and before the elders of my people. If you will redeem it, redeem it; but if not, tell me that I may know; for there is no one but you to redeem it, and I am after you.'" And he said, "I will redeem it." Then Boaz said, "On the day you buy the field from the hand of Naomi, you must also acquire Ruth the Moabitess, the widow of the deceased, in order to raise up the name of the deceased on his inheritance." And the closest relative said, "**I cannot redeem it for myself, lest I jeopardize my own inheritance.** Redeem it for yourself; you may have my right of redemption, for I cannot redeem it." Now **this was the custom in former times in Israel concerning the redemption and the exchange of land to confirm any matter:** a man removed his sandal and gave it to another; and this was the manner of attestation in Israel.

Ruth 4:3–7

By the last words of David the sons of Levi were numbered, from twenty years old and upward. For their office is to assist the sons of Aaron with the service of the house of the Lord, in the courts and in the chambers and in the purifying of all holy things, even the work of the service of the house of God.

1 Chronicles 23:27–28

Their father gave them many gifts of silver, gold and precious things, with fortified cities in Judah, **but he gave the kingdom to Jehoram because he was the first-born.**

2 Chronicles 21:3

"**Never seek their peace or their prosperity, that you may be strong** and eat the good things of the land and leave it as an inheritance to your sons forever."

Ezra 9:12

Arise, O Lord, confront him, bring him low; deliver my soul from the wicked with Thy sword, **from men with Thy hand, O Lord, from men of the world, whose portion is in this life;** and whose belly Thou dost fill with Thy treasure; they are satisfied with children, and leave their abundance to their babes. As for me, I shall behold Thy face in righteousness; I will be satisfied with Thy likeness when I awake.

Psalm 17:13–15

A good man leaves an inheritance to his children's chil-

212

dren, and the wealth of the sinner is stored up for the righteous.

Proverbs 13:22

House and wealth are an inheritance from fathers, but **a prudent wife is from the Lord.**

Proverbs 19:14

An inheritance gained hurriedly at the beginning, will not be blessed in the end.

Proverbs 20:21

Thus I hated all the fruit of my labor for which I had labored under the sun, for I must leave it to the man who will come after me.

Ecclesiastes 2:18

When there is a man who has labored with wisdom, knowledge and skill, **then he gives his legacy to one who has not labored with them.** This too is vanity and a great evil.

Ecclesiastes 2:21

If a man fathers a hundred children and lives many years, however many they be, but his soul is not satisfied with good things, and **he does not even have a proper burial,** then I say, "Better the miscarriage than he," for it comes in futility and goes into obscurity; and its name is covered in obscurity.

Ecclesiastes 6:3–4

Our inheritance has been turned over to strangers, our houses to aliens.

Lamentations 5:2

Let the priests, the Lord's ministers, weep between the porch and the altar, and let them say, "Spare Thy people, O Lord, and **do not make thine inheritance a reproach,** a byword among the nations. Why should they among the peoples say, 'Where is their God?'"

Joel 2:17

"Listen to another parable. There was a landowner who planted a vineyard and put a wall around it and dug a wine press in it, and built a tower, and rented it out to vine-growers, and went on a journey. And when the harvest time approached, he sent his slaves to the vine-growers to receive his produce. And the vine-growers took his slaves and beat one, and killed another, and stoned a third. Again he sent another group of slaves larger than the first; and they did the same thing to them. But afterward he sent his son to them, saying, 'They will respect my son.' But when the vine-growers saw the son, they said among themselves, 'This is the heir; come, **let us kill him, and seize his inheritance.**' And they took him, and threw him out of the vineyard, and killed him. Therefore when the owner of the vineyard comes, what will he do to those vine-growers?" They said to Him, "He will bring those wretches to a wretched end, and will rent out the vineyard to other vine-growers, who will pay him the proceeds at the proper seasons."

Matthew 21:33–41

"The King will say to those on His right, 'Come, you who are blessed of My Father, inherit the kingdom prepared for you from the foundation of the world.'"

Matthew 25:34

He began to speak to them in parables: "A man planted a vineyard, and put a wall around it, and dug a vat under the wine press, and built a tower, and rented it out to vine-growers and went on a journey. And at the harvest time he sent a slave to the vine-growers, in order to receive some of the produce of the vineyard from the vine-growers. And they took him, and beat him, and sent him away empty-handed. And again he sent them another slave, and they wounded him in the head, and treated him shamefully. And he sent another, and that one they killed; and so with many others, beating some, and killing others. He had one more to send, a beloved son; he sent him last of all to them, saying, 'They will respect my son.' But those vine-growers said to one another, '**This is the heir; come, let us kill him,**

and the inheritance will be ours!' And they took him, and killed him, and threw him out of the vineyard. What will the owner of the vineyard do? He will come and destroy the vine-growers, and will give the vineyard to others."

Mark 12:1–9

He said, "**A certain man had two sons;** and the younger of them said to his father, 'Father, give me the share of the estate that falls to me.' And he divided his wealth between them. And not many days later, the younger son gathered everything together and went on a journey into a distant country, and there **he squandered his estate** with loose living. Now when he had spent everything, a severe famine occurred in that country, and he began to be in need. And he went and attached himself to one of the citizens of that country, and he sent him into his fields to feed swine. And he was longing to fill his stomach with the pods that the swine were eating, and no one was giving anything to him. But when he came to his senses, he said, 'How many of my father's hired men have more than enough bread, but I am dying here with hunger! I will get up and go to my father, and will say to him, "Father, I have sinned against heaven, and in your sight; I am no longer worthy to be called your son; make me as one of your hired men."' And he got up and came to his father. But while he was still a long way off, his father saw him, and felt compassion for him, and ran and embraced him, and kissed him. And the son said to him, 'Father, I have sinned against heaven and in your sight; I am no longer worthy to be called your son.' But the father said to his slaves, 'Quickly bring out the best robe and put it on him, and put a ring on his hand and sandals on his feet; and bring the fattened calf, kill it, and let us eat and be merry; for this son of mine was dead, and has come to life again; he was lost, and has been found.' And they began to be merry."

Luke 15:11–24

He began to tell the people this parable: "**A man planted a vineyard and rented it out to vine-growers,** and went on a journey for a long time. And at the harvest time he sent a

215

slave to the vine-growers, in order that they might give him some of the produce of the vineyard; but the vine-growers beat him and sent him away empty-handed. And he proceeded to send another slave; and they beat him also and treated him shamefully, and sent him away empty-handed. And he proceeded to send a third; and this one also they wounded and cast out. And the owner of the vineyard said, 'What shall I do? I will send my beloved son; perhaps they will respect him.' But when the vine-growers saw him, they reasoned with one another, saying, 'This is the heir; **let us kill him that the inheritance may be ours.'** And they threw him out of the vineyard and killed him. What, therefore, will the owner of the vineyard do to them? He will come and destroy these vine-growers and will give the vineyard to others." And when they heard it, they said, "May it never be!"

Luke 20:9–16

"When He had destroyed seven nations in the land of Canaan, **He distributed their land as an inheritance**—all of which took about four hundred and fifty years."

Acts 13:19

Here for this third time I am ready to come to you, and I will not be a burden to you; for I do not seek what is yours, but you; for children are not responsible to save up for their parents, but parents for their children.

2 Corinthians 12:14

Now I say, **as long as the heir is a child,** he does not differ at all from a slave although he is owner of everything.

Galatians 4:1

You are no longer a slave, but a son; and if a son, then an heir through God.

Galatians 4:7

See to it that no one comes short of the grace of God; that no root of bitterness springing up causes trouble, and by it

216

many be defiled; that there be no immoral or godless person **like Esau, who sold his own birthright** for a single meal. For you know that even afterwards, when he desired to inherit the blessing, he was rejected, for he found no place for repentance, though he sought for it with tears.

Hebrews 12:15–17

He said to me, "It is done. I am the Alpha and the Omega, the beginning and the end. I will give to the one who thirsts from the spring of the water of life without cost. **He who overcomes shall inherit these things,** and I will be his God and he will be My son."

Revelation 21:6–7

OFFERINGS

Sometimes it's difficult to separate all the levels of giving taught in God's Word. There are three basic levels of giving: (1) the tithe—this is the minimum of one-tenth; (2) the offering—this is above the tithe, given to meet specific needs; and (3) sacrificial giving—this often means giving up things we want because we see that others have greater needs.

An offering is the second level of giving. After you've given your tithe and God brings someone to your attention who has a legitimate need—perhaps a missionary who needs support or a family who doesn't have food or clothing for their children—at this point you give your offering. God never intended for everyone to give the same amount or to the same person or organization, but He wants us all to give bountifully and cheerfully.

So it came about in the course of time that **Cain brought an offering** to the Lord of the fruit of the ground. And Abel, on his part also brought of the firstlings of his flock and of their fat portions. And the Lord had regard for Abel and for his offering.

Genesis 4:3–4

"You shall not delay the offering from your harvest and your vintage. The first-born of your sons you shall give to Me."

Exodus 22:29

"**Tell the sons of Israel to raise a contribution for Me;** from every man whose heart moves him you shall raise My contribution. And this is the contribution which you are to raise from them: gold, silver and bronze."

Exodus 25:2–3

"When you take a census of the sons of Israel to number them, then **each one of them shall give a ransom for himself to the Lord,** when you number them, that there may be no plague among them when you number them. This is what everyone who is numbered shall give: half a shekel according to the shekel of the sanctuary (the shekel is twenty gerahs), half a shekel as a contribution to the Lord. Everyone who is numbered, from twenty years old and over, shall give the contribution to the Lord. **The rich shall not pay more, and the poor shall not pay less** than the half shekel, when you give the contribution to the Lord to make atonement for yourselves. And you shall take the atonement money from the sons of Israel, and shall give it for the service of the tent meeting, that it may be a memorial for the sons of Israel before the Lord, to make atonement for yourselves."

Exodus 30:12–16

"**Take from among you a contribution to the Lord;** whoever is of a willing heart, let him bring it as the Lord's contribution: gold, silver and bronze."

Exodus 35:5

Everyone whose heart stirred him and everyone whose spirit moved him came and **brought the Lord's contribution for the work of the tent of meeting** and for all its service and for the holy garments. Then all whose hearts moved them, both men and women, came and brought brooches and earrings and signet rings and bracelets, all articles of gold; so did every man who presented an offering of gold to the Lord.

Exodus 35:21–22

Everyone who could make a contribution of silver and bronze brought the Lord's contribution; and every man, who had in his possession acacia wood for any work of the service, brought it.

Exodus 35:24

219

They received from Moses all the contributions which the sons of Israel had brought to perform the work in the construction of the sanctuary. And **they still continued bringing to him freewill offerings every morning.**

Exodus 36:3

They said to Moses, "**The people are bringing much more than enough for the construction work** which the Lord commanded us to perform." So Moses issued a command, and a proclamation was circulated throughout the camp, saying, "Let neither man nor woman any longer perform work for the contributions of the sanctuary." Thus the people were restrained from bringing any more.

Exodus 36:5–6

"**If he is poor,** and his means are insufficient, **then he is to take one male lamb** for a guilt offering as a wave offering to make atonement for him, and one-tenth of an ephah of fine flour mixed with oil for a grain offering, and a log of oil, and two turtledoves or two young pigeons which are within his means, the one shall be a sin offering and the other a burnt offering."

Leviticus 14:21–22

"He shall then offer one of the turtledoves or young pigeons, which are within his means. **He shall offer what he can afford,** the one for a sin offering, and the other for a burnt offering, together with the grain offering. So the priest shall make atonement before the Lord on behalf of the one to be cleansed."

Leviticus 14:30–31

"**When a man offers a sacrifice of peace offerings** to the Lord to fulfill a special vow, or for a freewill offering, of the herd or of the flock, **it must be perfect** to be accepted; there shall be no defect in it."

Leviticus 22:21

"Speak to the sons of Israel, and say to them, 'When you enter the land which I am going to give to you and reap its harvest, then **you shall bring in the sheaf of the first fruits of your harvest** to the priest. And he shall wave the sheaf before the Lord for you to be accepted; on the day after the sabbath the priest shall wave it.'"

Leviticus 23:10–11

"**If he should ever wish to redeem it,** then he shall add one-fifth of it to your valuation."

Leviticus 27:13

"Yet **if the one who consecrates it should wish to redeem his house, then he shall add one-fifth of your valuation price to it,** so that it may be his. Again, if a man consecrates to the Lord part of the fields of his own property, then your valuation shall be proportionate to the seed needed for it: a homer of barley seed at fifty shekels of silver."

Leviticus 27:15–16

His offering was one silver dish whose weight was one hundred and thirty shekels, one silver bowl of seventy shekels, according to the shekel of the sanctuary, both of them full of fine flour mixed with oil for a grain offering; one gold pan of ten shekels, full of incense.

Numbers 7:13–14

"Or for a ram you shall prepare **as a grain offering** two-tenths of an ephah of fine flour mixed with one-third of a hin of oil; and for the libation you shall offer one-third of a hin of wine as a soothing aroma to the Lord."

Numbers 15:6–7

"Speak to the sons of Israel, and say to them, 'When you enter the land where I bring you, then it shall be, that when you eat of the food of the land, **you shall lift up an offering to the Lord.** Of the first of your dough you shall lift up a cake as an offering; as the offering of the threshing floor, so you shall lift if up. From the first of your dough

221

you shall give to the Lord an offering throughout your generations.'"

Numbers 15:18–21

The Lord spoke to Aaron, "Now behold, **I Myself have given you charge of My offerings,** even all the holy gifts of the sons of Israel, I have given them to you as a portion, and to your sons as a perpetual allotment. This shall be yours from the most holy gifts, reserved from the fire; every offering of theirs, even every grain offering and every sin offering and every guilt offering, which they shall render to Me, shall be most holy for you and for your sons."

Numbers 18:8–9

"So **we have bought as an offering to the Lord** what each man found, articles of gold, armlets and bracelets, signet rings, earrings and necklaces, to make atonement for ourselves before the Lord." And Moses and Eleazar the priest took the gold from them, all kinds of wrought articles. And all the gold of the offering which they offered up to the Lord, from the captains of thousands and the captains of hundreds, was 16,750 shekels. The men of war had taken booty, every man for himself. So Moses and Eleazar the priest took the gold from the captains of thousands and of hundreds, and brought it to the tent of meeting as a memorial for the sons of Israel before the Lord.

Numbers 31:50–54

"**There you shall bring your burnt offerings,** your sacrifices, your tithes, the contribution of your hand, your votive offerings, your freewill offerings, and the first-born of your herd and of your flock. There also you and your households shall eat before the Lord your God, and rejoice in all your undertakings in which the Lord your God has blessed you."

Deuteronomy 12:6–7

"It shall come about that the place in which the Lord your God shall choose for His name to dwell, **there you shall**

bring all that I command you; your burnt offerings and your sacrifices, your tithes and the contribution of your hand, and all your choice votive offerings which you will vow to the Lord."

Deuteronomy 12:11

"Every man shall give as he is able, according to the blessing of the Lord your God which He has given you."

Deuteronomy 16:17

"You shall not sacrifice to the Lord your God an ox or a sheep which has a blemish or any defect, for that is a detestable thing to the Lord your God."

Deuteronomy 17:1

The king said to Araunah, **"No, but I will surely buy it from you for a price, for I will not offer burnt offerings to the Lord my God which cost me nothing."** So David bought the threshing floor and the oxen for fifty shekels of silver.

2 Samuel 24:24

The king commanded, and they quarried great stones, costly stones, to lay the foundation of the house with cut stones.

1 Kings 5:17

The inner sanctuary was twenty cubits in length, twenty cubits in width, and twenty cubits in height, and he overlaid it with pure gold. He also overlaid the altar with cedar. So Solomon overlaid the inside of the house with pure gold. And he drew chains of gold across the front of the inner sanctuary; and he overlaid it with gold. And he overlaid the whole house with gold, until all the house was finished. Also the whole altar which was by the inner sanctuary he overlaid with gold.

1 Kings 6:20–22

He also overlaid the cherubim with gold.

1 Kings 6:28

All the work that King Solomon performed in the house of the Lord was finished. And Solomon brought in the things dedicated by his father David, the silver and the gold and the utensils, and he put them in the treasuries of the house of the Lord.

1 Kings 7:51

King Solomon made 200 large shields of beaten gold, using 600 shekels of gold on each large shield. And he made 300 shields of beaten gold, using three minas of gold on each shield, and the king put them in the house of the forest of Lebanon. Moreover, the king made a great throne of ivory and overlaid it with refined gold.

1 Kings 10:16–18

He brought into the house of the Lord the dedicated things of his father and his own dedicated things: silver and gold and utensils.

1 Kings 15:15

Jehoash said to the priests, "All the money of the sacred things which is brought into the house of the Lord, in current money, both the money of each man's assessment and all the money which any man's heart prompts him to bring into the house of the Lord, let the priests take it for themselves, each from his acquaintance; and they shall repair the damages of the house wherever any damage may be found." But it came about that in the twenty-third year of King Jehoash the priests had not repaired the damages of the house. Then King Jehoash called for Jehoiada the priest, and for the other priests and said to them, "Why do you not repair the damages of the house? Now therefore take no more money from your acquaintances, but pay it for the damages of the house."

2 Kings 12:4–7

Jehoiada the priest took a chest and bored a hole in its lid, and put it beside the altar, on the right side as one comes into the house of the Lord; and the priests who guarded the threshold put in it all the money which was brought into the house of the Lord. And when they saw that there was much money in the chest, the king's scribe and the high priest came up and tied it in bags and counted the money which was found in the house of the Lord. And they gave the money which was weighed out into the hands of those who did the work, who had the oversight of the house of the Lord; and they paid it out to the carpenters and the builders, who worked on the house of the Lord; and to the masons and the stonecutters, and for buying timber and hewn stone to repair the damages to the house of the Lord, and for all that was laid out for the house to repair it. But there were not made for the house of the Lord silver cups, snuffers, bowls, trumpets, any vessels of gold, or vessels of silver from the money which was brought into the house of the Lord; **for they gave that to those who did the work, and with it they repaired the house of the Lord.** Moreover, they did not require an accounting from the men into whose hand they gave the money to pay to those who did the work, for they dealt faithfully. The money from the guilt offerings and the money from the sin offerings, was not brought in to the house of the Lord; it was for the priests.

2 Kings 12:9–16

"Go up to Hilkiah the high priest that he may count the money brought in to the house of the Lord which the door-keepers have gathered from the people. And let them deliver it into the hand of the workmen who have the oversight of the house of the Lord, and **let them give it to the workmen who are in the house of the Lord to repair the damages of the house.**"

2 Kings 22:4–5

Hilkiah the high priest said to Shaphan the scribe, "I have found the book of the law in the house of the Lord." And Hilkiah gave the book to Shaphan who read it. And Shaphan the scribe came to the king and brought back word to the king and said, "Your servants have emptied out the money that was found in the house, and have delivered it into the hand of the workmen who have the oversight of the house of the Lord."

2 Kings 22:8–9

Ornan said to David, "**Take it for yourself**; and let my lord the king do what is good in his sight. See, I will give the oxen for burnt offerings and the threshing sledges for wood and the wheat for the grain offering; I will give it all."

1 Chronicles 21:23

This Shelomoth and his relatives had charge of all the treasures of the dedicated gifts, which King David and the heads of the fathers' households, the commanders of thousands and hundreds, and commanders of the army, had dedicated. **They dedicated part of the spoil won in battles to repair the house of the Lord.**

1 Chronicles 26:26–27

For the service for the house of God they gave 5,000 talents and 10,000 darics of gold, and 10,000 talents of silver, and 18,000 talents of brass, and 100,000 talents of iron.

1 Chronicles 29:7

It came about whenever the chest was brought in to the king's officer by the Levites, and when they saw that there was much money, then the king's scribe and the chief priest's officer would come, empty the chest, take it, and return it to its place. Thus they did daily and collected much money. And the king and Jehoiada gave it to those who did the work of the service of the house of the Lord; and they hired masons and carpenters to restore the house of the Lord, and also workers in iron and bronze to repair the house of the Lord.

2 Chronicles 24:11–12

When they had finished, they brought the rest of the money before the king and Jehoiada; and it was made into utensils for the house of the Lord, utensils for the service and the burnt offering, and pans and utensils of gold and silver. And they offered burnt offerings in the house of the Lord continually all the days of Jehoiada.

2 Chronicles 24:14

Kore the son of Imnah the Levite, the keeper of the eastern gate, was over the freewill offerings of God, to apportion the contributions for the Lord and the most holy things. And under his authority were Eden, Miniamin, Jeshua, Shemaiah, Amariah, and Shecaniah in the cities of the priests, to distribute faithfully their portions to their brothers by divisions, whether great or small.

2 Chronicles 31:14–15

"**Every survivor,** at whatever place he may live, **let the men of that place support him with silver and gold,** with goods and cattle, together with a freewill offering for the house of God which is in Jerusalem."

Ezra 1:4

I weighed out to them the silver, the gold, and the utensils, the offering for the house of our God which the king and his counselors and his princes, and all Israel present there, had offered. Thus I weighed into their hands **650 talents of silver,** and silver utensils worth 100 talents, and gold talents, and 20 gold bowls, worth 1,000 darics; and two utensils of fine shiny bronze, precious as gold.

Ezra 8:25–27

The priests and the Levites accepted and weighed out silver and gold and the utensils, to bring them to Jerusalem to the house of our God.

Ezra 8:30

We cast lots for the supply of wood among the priests, the Levites, and the people in order that they might bring it to the house of our God, according to our fathers' households, at fixed time annually, to burn on the altar of the Lord our God as it is written in the law; and in order that they might bring the first fruits of our ground and the first fruits of all the fruit of every tree to the house of the Lord annually.

Nehemiah 10:34–35

"When I had brought them into the land which I swore to give to them, then they saw every high hill and every leafy tree, and they **offered there their sacrifices,** and **there they presented the provocation of their offering.** There also they made their soothing aroma, and there they poured out their libations."

Ezekiel 20:28

"As for you, O house of Israel," thus says the Lord God, "Go, serve every one his idols; but later, you will surely listen to Me, and My holy name you will profane no longer with your gifts and with your idols. For on My holy mountain, on the high mountain of Israel," declares the Lord God, "there the whole house of Israel, all of them, will serve Me in the land; there I shall accept them, and there **I shall seek your contributions** and the choicest of your gifts, with all your holy things."

Ezekiel 20:39–40

He said to me, "The north chambers and the south chambers, which are opposite the separate area, they are the holy chambers where the priests who are near to the Lord shall eat the most holy things. There they shall lay the most holy things, the grain offering, the sin offering, and the guilt offering; for the place is holy."

Ezekiel 42:13

"Offer **a thank offering** also from that which is leavened, and proclaim freewill offerings, make them known. For so you love to do, you sons of Israel," declares the Lord God.

Amos 4:5

"He will sit as a smelter and purifier of silver, and He will purify the sons of Levi and refine them like gold and silver,

so that they may present to the Lord offerings in righteousness."

Malachi 3:3

A poor widow came and put in two small copper coins, which amount to a cent. And calling His disciples to Him, He said to them, "Truly I say to you, this poor widow put in more than all the contributors to the treasury; for they all put in out of their surplus, but she, out of her poverty, **put in all she owned,** all she had to live on."

Mark 12:42–44

While He was in Bethany at the home of Simon the leper, and reclining at the table, **there came a woman with an alabaster vial of very costly perfume** of pure nard; and she broke the vial and poured it over His head. But some were indignantly remarking to one another, "Why has this perfume been wasted? For this perfume might have been sold for over three hundred denarii, and the money given to the poor." And they were scolding her. But Jesus said, "Let her alone; why do you bother her? She has done a good deed to Me. For the poor you always have with you, and whenever you wish, you can do them good; but you do not always have Me."

Mark 14:3–7

He looked up and saw the rich putting their gifts into the treasury. And He saw **a certain poor widow putting in two small copper coins.** And He said, "Truly I say to you, this poor widow put in more than all of them; for they all out of their surplus put into the offering; but she out of her poverty put in all that she had to live on."

Luke 21:1–4

Joseph, a Levite of Cyprian birth, who was also called **Barnabas** by the apostles (which translated means, Son of Encouragement), and **who owned a tract of land,** sold it and brought the money and laid it at the apostles' feet.

Acts 4:36–37

"Take them and purify yourself along with them, and **pay their expenses** in order that they may shave their heads; and all will know that there is nothing to the things which they have been told about you, but that you yourself also walk orderly, keeping the Law."

Acts 21:24

"After several years **I came to bring alms** to my nation and to present offerings."

Acts 24:17

This I say, **he who sows sparingly shall also reap sparingly;** and he who sows bountifully shall also reap bountifully.

2 Corinthians 9:6

Honor widows who are widows indeed.

1 Timothy 5:3

We ought to support such men, that we may be fellow workers with the truth.

3 John 8

PLANNING

Planning is a part of a Christian's walk with God and essential in any financial program. It is literally committing spiritual goals to written form. In Proverbs God says that someone who plans well will foresee dangers and avoid them, but the foolish person (the one who doesn't plan) will rush ahead, do whatever is convenient, and end up paying the penalties.

Just as we can't build houses without blueprints, we can't have the financial structure of stewardship without blueprints (or plans). God wants us to be able to live on a budget—a short-term plan. And then we are to look forward—to see eventual needs and try to meet them—a long-term plan.

"Let Pharaoh take action to appoint overseers in charge of the land, and **let him exact a fifth of the produce of the land of Egypt** in the seven years of abundance. Then let them gather all the food of these good years that are coming, and store up the grain for food in the cities under Pharaoh's authority, and let them guard it. And let the food become as a reserve for the land for the seven years of famine which will occur in the land of Egypt, so that the land may not perish during the famine."

Genesis 41:34–36

"**At the harvest you shall give a fifth to Pharaoh,** and four-fifths shall be your own for seed of the field and for your food and for those of your households and as food for your little ones."

Genesis 47:24

David said, "My son Solomon is young and inexperienced, and the house that is to be built for the Lord shall be exceedingly magnificent, famous and glorious throughout all lands. Therefore I will make preparation for it." **So David made ample preparations before his death.**

1 Chronicles 22:5

"Now behold, with great pains **I have prepared for the house of the Lord 100,000 talents of gold and 1,000,000 talents of silver,** and bronze and iron beyond weight, for they are in great quantity; also timber and stone I have prepared, and you may add to them."

1 Chronicles 22:14

The plans of the heart belong to man, but the answer of the tongue is from the Lord.

Proverbs 16:1

Commit your works to the Lord, and your plans will be established.

Proverbs 16:3

The mind of man plans his way, but the Lord directs his steps.

Proverbs 16:9

Many are the plans in a man's heart, but the counsel of the Lord, it will stand.

Proverbs 19:21

A plan in the heart of a man is like deep water, but a man of understanding draws it out.

Proverbs 20:5

The plans of the diligent lead surely to advantage, but everyone who is hasty comes surely to poverty.

Proverbs 21:5

The prudent sees the evil and hides himself, but the naive go on, and are punished for it.

Proverbs 22:3

By wisdom a house is built, and **by understanding it is established;** and by knowledge the rooms are filled with all precious and pleasant riches.

Proverbs 24:3–4

Prepare your work outside, and make it ready for yourself in the field; afterwards, then, build your house.

Proverbs 24:27

A prudent man sees evil and hides himself, the naive proceed and pay the penalty.

Proverbs 27:12

Know well the condition of your flocks, and pay attention to your herds; for riches are not forever, nor does a crown endure to all generations.

Proverbs 27:23–24

The ants are not a strong folk, but they prepare their food in the summer.

Proverbs 30:25

"Which one of you, **when he wants to build a tower,** does not first sit down and calculate the cost, to see if he has enough to complete it? Otherwise, when he has laid a foundation, and is not able to finish, all who observe it begin to ridicule him, saying, 'This man began to build and was not able to finish.'"

Luke 14:28–30

PROVISION

There's a great difference between provision as our grandparents knew it—enough to get by—and as we know it in our generation. Provision does mean that you have enough to get by, but we've gone far beyond that. God does not promise to supply enough money to satisfy our every whim and desire. His promise is to meet our needs and provide an abundance (and here's the key) so that we can help others. It's when we accept this principle that God will multiply our abundance as well.

Additionally, as God provides for us, He admonishes us to provide for those in our families. For the head of a household, this is not limited to life alone but extends to providing even after death.

"The officers also shall speak to the people, saying, '**Who is the man that has built a new house** and has not dedicated it? Let him depart and return to his house, lest he die in the battle and another man dedicate it.'"

Deuteronomy 20:5

He said to them, "Therefore every scribe who has become a disciple of the kingdom of heaven is like a head of a household, **who brings forth out of his treasure things new and old.**"

Matthew 13:52

If any one does not provide for his own, and especially for those of his household, he has denied the faith, and is worse than an unbeliever.

1 Timothy 5:8

If anyone advocates a different doctrine, and does not agree with sound words, those of our Lord Jesus Christ, and with the doctrine conforming to godliness, he is conceited and **understands nothing;** but he has a morbid interest in controversial questions and disputes about words, out of which arise envy, strife, abusive language, evil suspicions, and constant friction between **men of depraved mind** and deprived of the truth, **who suppose that godliness is a means of gain.** But godliness actually is a means of great gain, when accompanied by contentment. For we have brought nothing into the world, so we cannot taken anything out of it either. And if we have food and covering, with these we shall be content.

1 Timothy 6:3–8

Storing up for themselves the treasure of a good foundation for the future, so that they may **take hold of that which is life indeed.**

1 Timothy 6:19

STOREHOUSE

The Jews, who gave produce rather than money, needed a place to bring their tithes of produce, grain, and animals. This place was the storehouse, which had a multi-function. The tribe of Levi would get their provision from there because they owned the land. The temple priests would get their provision there. The traveling evangelists (those we would have called prophets in the Old Testament) would get their provision there. The Hebrew and Gentile widows, orphans, and poor would get their provision from the storehouse.

The storehouse was a physical place that God's people used to store their goods until there was a need. Today, ideally, the equivalent of the storehouse is the local church. God's Word instructs us to bring our tithes into the storehouse.

The Levites, their relatives, had charge of the treasures of the house of God, and of the treasures of the dedicated gifts.

1 Chronicles 26:20

The sons of Jehieli, Zetham and Joel his brother, **had charge of the treasures** of the house of the Lord.

1 Chronicles 26:22

Shebuel the son of Gershom, the son of Moses, was officer over the treasures.

1 Chronicles 26:24

On that day men were also appointed over the chambers for the stores, **the contributions, the first fruits, and the tithes,** to gather into them from the fields of the cities the

portions required by the law for the priests and Levites; for Judah rejoiced over the priests and Levites who served.
Nehemiah 12:44

[Eliashib the priest] had prepared a large room for him, where formerly they put the grain offerings, the frankincense, the utensils, and the tithes of grain, wine and oil prescribed for the Levites, the singers and the gatekeepers, and the contributions for the priests.
Nehemiah 13:5

In charge of the storehouses I appointed Shelemiah the priest, Zadok the scribe, and Pedaiah of the Levites, and in addition to them was Hanan the son of Zaccur, the son of Mattaniah; for they were considered reliable, and it was their task to distribute to their kinsmen.
Nehemiah 13:13

"Bring the whole tithe into the storehouse, so that there may be food in My house, and test Me now in this," says the Lord of hosts, "if I will not open for you the windows of heaven, and pour out for you a blessing until it overflows."
Malachi 3:10

TITHE

The word *tithe* means one-tenth. It's the *minimum* portion that a Christian should tithe. The tithe's purpose is to be a testimony of God's ownership, and thus it is meant to be individualized.

The Jews gave a tithe that was far in excess of one-tenth. In fact, they gave three tithes: one tithe each year to the storehouse; a second tithe for the widows and orphans of the Hebrews; and a third tithe, every third year, to the widows and orphans of the Gentiles. So, the Jews tithed an average of 23⅓ percent. Certainly God's people, living under grace, should be able to out-tithe the Jews, who were living under the law.

"Blessed be God Most High, Who has delivered your enemies into your hand." And **he gave him a tenth of all.**

Genesis 14:20

"This stone, which I have set up as a pillar, will be God's house; and of all that Thou dost give me **I will surely give a tenth to Thee.**"

Genesis 28:22

"Thus **all the tithe of the land,** of the seed of the land or of the fruit of the tree, is the Lord's; it is holy to the Lord. **If, therefore, a man wishes to redeem part of his tithe, he shall add to it one-fifth of it.** And for every tenth part of herd or flock, whatever passes under the rod, the tenth one shall be holy to the Lord. He is not to be concerned whether it is good or bad, nor shall he exchange it; or if he does exchange it, then both it and its substitute shall become holy. It shall not be redeemed."

Leviticus 27:30–33

"Moreover, you shall speak to the Levites and say to them, 'When you take from the sons of Israel the tithe which I have given you from them for your inheritance; then you shall present an offering from it to the Lord, a tithe of the tithe.'"

Numbers 18:26

"You shall also present an offering to the Lord from your tithes, which you receive from the sons of Israel; and **from it you shall give the Lord's offering to Aaron the priest.** Out of all your gifts you shall present every offering due to the Lord, from all the best of them, the sacred part from them."

Numbers 18:28–29

"**There you shall bring your burnt offerings,** your sacrifices, your tithes, the contribution of your hand, your votive offerings, your freewill offerings, and the first-born of your herd and of your flock. There also you and your households shall eat before the Lord your God, and rejoice in all your undertakings in which the Lord your God has blessed you."

Deuteronomy 12:6–7

"It shall come about that the place in which the Lord your God shall choose for His name to dwell, **there you shall bring all that I command you:** your burnt offerings and your sacrifices, your tithes and the contribution of your hand, and all your choice votive offerings which you will vow to the Lord."

Deuteronomy 12:11

"**You are not allowed to eat within your gates the tithe of your grain,** or new wine, or oil, or the first-born of your herd or flock, or any of your votive offerings which you vow, or your freewill offerings, or the contribution of your hand."

Deuteronomy 12:17

"**You shall surely tithe all the produce from what you sow,** which comes out of the field every year. And you shall eat in the presence of the Lord your God, at the place where

He chooses to establish His name, **the tithe of your grain,** your new wine, your oil, and the first-born of your herd and your flock, in order that you may learn to fear the Lord your God always. And if the distance is so great for you that you are not able to bring the tithe, since the place where the Lord your God chooses to set His name is too far away from you when the Lord your God blesses you, then you shall exchange it for money, and bind the money in your hand and go to the place which the Lord your God chooses. And you may spend the money for whatever your heart desires, for oxen, or sheep, or wine, or strong drink, or whatever your heart desires; and there you shall eat in the presence of the Lord your God and rejoice, you and your household. Also you shall not neglect the Levite who is in your town, for he has no portion or inheritance among you. At the end of every third year you shall bring out all **the tithe of your produce** in that year, and shall deposit it in your town. And the Levite, because he has no portion or inheritance among you, and the alien, the orphan and the widow who are in your town, shall come and eat and be satisfied, in order that the Lord your God may bless you in all the work of your hand which you do."

Deuteronomy 14:22–29

"'Now behold, I have brought the first of the produce of the ground which Thou, O Lord has given me.' And you shall set it down before the Lord your God, and worship before the Lord your God; and you and the Levite and the alien who is among you shall rejoice in all the good which the Lord your God has given you and your household. When you have finished paying all **the tithe of your increase in the third year, the year of tithing, then you shall give it to the Levite,** to the stranger, to the orphan and to the widow, that they may eat in your towns, and be satisfied. And you shall say before the Lord your God, 'I have removed the sacred portion from my house, and also have given it to the Levite and the alien, the orphan and the widow, according to all Thy commandments which Thou hast commanded me; I have not transgressed or forgotten any of Thy commandments.'"

Deuteronomy 26:10–13

We will also bring the first of our dough, our contributions, the fruit of every tree, the new wine and the oil to the priests at the chambers of the house of our God, and the tithe of our ground to the Levites, for the Levites are they who receive the tithes in all the rural towns. And the priest, the son of Aaron, shall be with the Levites when the Levites receive tithes, and the Levites shall bring up the tenth of the tithes to the house of our God, to the chambers of the storehouse. For the sons of Israel and **the sons of Levi shall bring the contribution of the grain,** the new wine and the oil, to the chambers; there are the utensils of the sanctuary, the priests who are ministering, the gatekeepers, and the singers. Thus we will not neglect the house of our God.

Nehemiah 10:37–39

On that day men were also appointed over the chambers for the stores, **the contributions, the first fruits, and the tithes,** to gather into them from the fields of the cities the portions required by the law for the priests and Levites; for Judah rejoiced over the priests and Levites who served.

Nehemiah 12:44

[Eliashib the priest] had prepared a large room for him, where formerly they put the grain offerings, the frankincense, the utensils, and the tithes of grain, wine and oil prescribed for the Levites, the singers and the gatekeepers, and **the contributions for the priests.**

Nehemiah 13:5

All Judah then brought **the tithe of the grain,** wine, and oil into the storehouses. And **in charge of the storehouses I appointed Shelemiah** the priest, Zadok the scribe, and Pedaiah of the Levites, and in addition to them was Hanan the son of Zaccur, the son of Mattaniah; for they were considered reliable, and it was their task to distribute to their kinsmen.

Nehemiah 13:12–13

"Enter Bethel and transgress; in Gilgal multiply transgression! **Bring your sacrifices every morning**, your tithes every three days."

Amos 4:4

"From the days of your fathers you have turned aside from My statutes, and have not kept them. Return to Me, and I will return to you," says the Lord of hosts. "But you say, 'How shall we return?' **Will a man rob God?** Yet you are robbing Me! But you say, 'How have we robbed Thee?' **In tithes and offerings.** You are cursed with a curse, for you are robbing Me, the whole nation of You! Bring the whole tithe into the storehouse, so that there may be food in My house, and test Me now in this," says the Lord of hosts, "if I will not open for you the windows of heaven, and pour out for you a blessing until it overflows. Then I will rebuke the devourer for you, so that it may not destroy the fruits of the ground; nor will your vine in the field cast its grapes," says the Lord of hosts.

Malachi 3:7–11

"Woe to you, scribes and Pharisees, hypocrites! **For you tithe mint and dill and cummin,** and have neglected the weightier provisions of the law; justice and mercy and faithfulness; but these are the things you should have done without neglecting the others."

Matthew 23:23

"Woe to you Pharisees! **For you pay tithe of mint** and rue and every kind of garden herb, and yet disregard justice and the love of God; but these are the things you should have done without neglecting the others."

Luke 11:42

This Melchizedek, king of Salem, priest of the Most High God, who met Abraham as he was returning from the slaughter of the kings and blessed him, to whom also Abraham apportioned a tenth part of all the spoils, was first of all, by the translation of his name, king of righteousness, and then also king of Salem, which is king of peace. Without father, without mother, without genealogy, having neither beginning of days nor end of life, but made like the Son of God, he abides a priest perpetually. Now observe how great this man was to whom Abraham, the patriarch, **gave a tenth of the choicest spoils.** And those indeed of the sons of Levi who receive the priest's office have commandment in the Law to collect a tenth from the people, that is, from their brethren, although these are descended from Abraham. But the one whose genealogy is not traced from them collected a tenth from Abraham, and blessed the one who had the promises. But without any dispute the lesser is blessed by the greater. And in this case mortal men receive tithes, but in that case one receives them, of whom it is witnessed that he lives on. And, so to speak, through **Abraham even Levi, who received tithes, paid tithes.**

Hebrews 7:1–9

WORTHLESS GIFTS

I t's a sad commentary today that many Christians give into God's kingdom things they simply don't want. When we give gifts and offerings, we aren't just giving to a church, an individual, or a charity; we are giving it to God and, therefore, God wants the best of what we have—not the leftovers.

God does not want us to give our worn-out clothes, broken lawn mowers, and beat-up cars to the people who have needs. God wants us to give our best. Things that are old, broken, or worn out should be given to a charitable organization that can restore them and profit from their sale. Fill the needs of others with your best.

"You shall never seek their peace or their prosperity all your days."

Deuteronomy 23:6

"**You shall not bring the hire of a harlot** or the wages of a dog into the house of the Lord your God for any votive offering, for both of these are an abomination to the Lord your God."

Deuteronomy 23:18

"**Why do you kick at My sacrifice and at My offering** which I have commanded in My dwelling, and honor your sons above Me, by making yourselves fat with the choicest of every offering of My people Israel?"

1 Samuel 2:29

"You also say, 'My, how tiresome it is!' And you disdainfully sniff at it," says the Lord of hosts, "and you bring what was taken by robbery, and **what is lame or sick; so you bring the offering!** Should I receive that from your hand?" says the Lord.

Malachi 1:13

"As for the man who does this, may the Lord cut off from the tents of Jacob everyone who awakes and answers, or who presents an offering to the Lord of hosts."

Malachi 2:12

A certain man named Ananias, with his wife Sapphira, sold a piece of property, and kept back some of the price for himself, with his wife's full knowledge, and bringing a portion of it, he laid it at the apostles' feet. But Peter said, "Ananias, why has Satan filled your heart to lie to the Holy Spirit, and to keep back some of the price of the land? While it remained unsold, did it not remain your own? And after it was sold, was it not under your control? Why is it that you have conceived this deed in your heart? You have not lied to men, but to God." And as he heard these words, Ananias fell down and breathed his last; and great fear came upon all who heard of it. And the young men arose and covered him up, and after carrying him out, they buried him. Now there elapsed an interval of about three hours, and his wife came in, not knowing what had happened. And Peter responded to her, "Tell me whether you sold the land for such and such a price?" And she said, "Yes, that was the price." Then Peter said to her, "Why is it that you have agreed together to put the Spirit of the Lord to the test? Behold, the feet of those who have buried your husband are at the door, and they shall carry you out as well." And she fell immediately at his feet, and breathed her last; and the young men came in and found her dead, and they carried her out and buried her beside her husband.

Acts 5:1–10

SECTION FIVE

GOD'S BLESSINGS AND CURSES

This section deals with God's supernatural intervention in the lives of His people to provide their needs and, many times, to punish their enemies. A good example of this can be seen in the word of the prophet Malachi to the people of Israel. When he confronted them with the fact that they didn't love God, they denied it and said, "We do love God." Malachi confronted them again by saying "If a man loves God, would he cheat or rob God?" Malachi told them that if they would trust God and give Him the first fruits of everything they had He would bless them. But if they withheld those first fruits, God would allow the devourer to come among them and take everything they had.

So, we will look at the difference between God's blessings in providing for the people who have obeyed Him and God's curses upon those who have disobeyed Him.

BLESSINGS

We must believe that God wants to bless us. There are many examples of God blessing people throughout Scripture. More often than not we associate His blessings with only material things, as in the case of Abraham and David and Solomon. They were all wealthy men but, indeed, the blessings of the Lord are more than just money.

God's blessings, other than material, might be a happy marriage, children, good relationships with family and friends, career satisfaction, specific answers to prayer, protection, healing, and the list goes on and on. Our blessings come as a result of trust and faith in Jesus Christ. Many Christians fail to experience God's blessings because they conform to the image of the world.

"I will also judge the nation whom they will serve; and afterward **they will come out with many possessions.**"
Genesis 15:14

"**The Lord has greatly blessed my master,** so that he has become rich; and He has given him flocks and herds, and silver and gold, and servants and maids, and camels and donkeys. . . . and he has given him all that he has."
Genesis 24:35–36

"Sojourn in this land and I will be with you and bless you, for to you and **to your descendants I will give all these lands,** and I will establish the oath which I swore to your father Abraham."
Genesis 26:3

Isaac sowed in that land, and reaped in the same year a hundredfold. And **the Lord blessed him, and the man became rich,** and continued to grow richer until he became

very wealthy; for he had possessions of flocks and herds and a great household, so that the Philistines envied him.
Genesis 26:12–14

"**God has taken away your father's livestock** and given them to me."
Genesis 31:9

The Lord was with Joseph, so he became a successful man. And he was in the house of his master, the Egyptian. Now his master saw that the Lord was with him and how the Lord caused all that he did to prosper in his hand. . . . all that he owned he put in his charge. . . . the Lord blessed the Egyptian's house on account of Joseph; **thus the Lord's blessing was upon all that he owned,** in the house and in the field. So he left everything he owned in Joseph's charge.
Genesis 39:2–6

He refused and said to his master's wife, "Behold, with me here, my master does not concern himself with anything in the house, and he has put all that he owns in my charge."
Genesis 39:8

The chief jailer did not supervise anything under Joseph's charge because the Lord was with him; and **whatever he did, the Lord made to prosper.**
Genesis 39:23

"He has filled him with the Spirit of God, in wisdom, in understanding and in knowledge and in all craftsmanship; to make designs for working in gold and in silver and in bronze."
Exodus 35:31–32

"**The Lord will command the blessing upon you** in your barns and in all that you put your hand to, and He will bless you in the land which the Lord your God gives you."
Deuteronomy 28:8

"**The Lord will make you abound in prosperity,** in the off-spring of your body and in the offspring of your beast and in the produce of your ground, in the land which the Lord swore to your fathers to give you."

Deuteronomy 28:11

"Keep the words of this covenant to do them, **that you may prosper** in all that you do."

Deuteronomy 29:9

"You shall again obey the Lord, and observe all His com-mandments which I command you today. Then **the Lord your God will prosper you abundantly in all the work of your hand,** in the offspring of your body and in the off-spring of your cattle and in the produce of your ground, for the Lord will again rejoice over you for good, just as He rejoiced over your fathers; if you obey the Lord your God to keep His commandments and His statutes which are written in this book of the law, if you turn to the Lord your God with all your heart and soul. For this commandment which I command you today is not too difficult for you, nor is it out of reach."

Deuteronomy 30:8–11

"**This book of the law shall not depart from your mouth,** but you shall meditate on it day and night, so that you may be careful to do according to all that is written in it; for then you will make your way prosperous, and then you will have success."

Joshua 1:8

He said, "May you be blessed of the Lord, my daughter. You have shown your last kindness to be better than the first by not going after young men, whether poor or rich."

Ruth 3:10

All the people who were in the court, and the elders, said, "We are witnesses. May the Lord make the woman who is coming into your home like Rachel and Leah, both of

whom built the house of Israel; and may you achieve
wealth in Ephrathah and become famous in Bethlehem."

Ruth 4:11

"**Those who honor Me I will honor,** and those who despise
Me will be lightly esteemed."

1 Samuel 2:30

He died in a ripe old age, **full of days, riches and honor;**
and his son Solomon reigned in his place.

1 Chronicles 29:28

All King Solomon's drinking vessels were of gold, and all
the vessels of the house of the forest of Lebanon were of
pure gold; silver was not considered valuable in the days
of Solomon . . . the ships of Tarshish came bringing gold
and silver, ivory and apes and peacocks. So King Solomon
became greater than all the kings of the earth in riches and
wisdom.

2 Chronicles 9:20–22

Jehoshaphat had great riches and honor; and he allied
himself by marriage with Ahab.

2 Chronicles 18:1

"If they hear and serve Him, **they shall end their days in
prosperity,** and their years in pleasures."

Job 36:11

The Lord loves justice, and does not forsake His godly
ones; They are preserved forever; but the descendants of
the wicked will be cut off. **The righteous will inherit the
land,** and dwell in it forever.

Psalm 37:28–29

Behold, **children are a gift of the Lord;** the fruit of the
womb is a reward.

Psalm 127:3

A faithful man will abound with blessings, but he who makes haste to be rich will not go unpunished.

Proverbs 28:20

An excellent wife, who can find? For her worth is far above jewels.

Proverbs 31:10

COUNSEL OF GOD

When we are truly seeking the total counsel of God, we must be willing to accept God's provision—whether it be heavy or slight. We don't serve God because of what He can do for us; we serve Him because He is God. The apostle Paul said "Learn to get along in all conditions—whether in plenty or in want." So, in the counsel of God, we can't limit it to provision. We also must be willing to accept that counsel when something is withheld. Fortunately, God's value system is based on spiritual worth and is measured by our willingness to accept His direction.

Laban said to Jacob, "Because you are my relative, **should you therefore serve me for nothing? Tell me, what shall your wages be?**"

Genesis 29:15

The men of Israel took some of their provisions, and did not ask for the counsel of the Lord. And **Joshua made peace with them and made a covenant with them,** to let them live; and the leaders of the congregation swore an oath to them.

Joshua 9:14–15

I will instruct you and teach you in the way which you should go; **I will counsel you with My eye upon you.** Do not be as the horse or as the mule which have no understanding.

Psalm 32:8–9

"They hated knowledge, and did not choose the fear of the Lord. They would not accept my counsel, they spurned all my reproof. So they shall eat of the fruit of their own way, and be satiated with their own devices. **For the waywardness of the naive shall kill them,** and the complacency of

254

fools shall destroy them. But he who listens to me shall live securely, and shall be at ease from the dread of evil."

Proverbs 1:29–33

Lest strangers be filled with your strength, and **your hard-earned goods go to the house of an alien.**

Proverbs 5:10

"**Take my instruction, and not silver,** and knowledge rather than choicest gold. For wisdom is better than jewels; and all desirable things can not compare with her. I, wisdom, dwell with prudence, and I find knowledge and discretion."

Proverbs 8:10–11

Many are the plans in a man's heart, but the counsel of the Lord, it will stand.

Proverbs 19:21

"If you were of the world, the world would love its own; but because you are not of the world, but I chose you out of the world, therefore the world hates you."

John 15:19

DISCIPLINE

Many times God disciplines His people by withholding material things and by removing material things from their possession. A classic example of that is found in the nation of Israel: quite often God not only withheld His blessings but actually took away from them—even their freedom and sent them into slavery—because they would not obey God's Word. God is still a righteous God and, although He loves us, He will discipline as necessary in order to get us to obey His direction.

The difference between discipline and a curse from God is that discipline is applied in love to redirect, while a curse is to make a clear example of those so afflicted.

They captured and looted all their wealth and all their little ones and their wives, even all that was in the houses.

Genesis 34:29

Asa took all the silver and the gold which were left in the treasuries of the house of the Lord and the treasuries of the king's house, and **delivered them into the hand of his servants.** And King Asa sent them to Ben-hadad the son of Tabrimmon, the son of Hezion, king of Aram, who lived in Damascus.

1 Kings 15:18

He took all the gold and silver and all the utensils which were found in the house of the Lord, and in the treasuries of the king's house, the hostages also, and returned to Samaria.

2 Kings 14:14

He carried out from there all the treasures of the house of the Lord, and the treasures of the king's house, and cut in pieces all the vessels of gold which Solomon king of Israel had made in the temple of the Lord, just as the Lord had said. Then he led away into exile all Jerusalem and all the captains and all the mighty men of valor, ten thousand captives, and all the craftsmen and the smiths. **None remained except the poorest people of the land.**

2 Kings 24:13–14

The captain of the guard also took away the firepans and the basins, what was fine gold and what was fine silver.

2 Kings 25:15

So **Shishak** king of Egypt came up against Jerusalem, and **took the treasures of the house of the Lord** and the treasures of the king's palace. He took everything; he even took the golden shields which Solomon had made.

2 Chronicles 12:9

Ahaz took a portion out of the house of the Lord and out of the palace of the king and of the princes, and **gave it to the king of Assyria; but it did not help him.**

2 Chronicles 28:21

"**Whoever will not observe the law of your God** and the law of the king, **let judgment be executed upon him strictly,** whether for death or for banishment or for confiscation of goods or for imprisonment."

Ezra 7:26

My son, do not reject the discipline of the Lord, or loathe His reproof, for whom the Lord loves He reproves, even as a father, the son in whom he delights.

Proverbs 3:11–12

Teaching is light; and reproofs for discipline are the way of life.

Proverbs 6:23

He who **walks in integrity** walks securely, but he who perverts his ways will be found out.

Proverbs 10:9

Whoever loves discipline loves knowledge, but he who hates reproof is stupid.

Proverbs 12:1

A wise son accepts his father's discipline, but a scoffer does not listen to rebuke.

Proverbs 13:1

Poverty and shame will come to him who neglects discipline, but he who regards reproof will be honored.

Proverbs 13:18

A fool rejects his father's discipline, but he who regards reproof is prudent.

Proverbs 15:5

He who neglects discipline despises himself, but he who listens to reproof acquires understanding.

Proverbs 15:32

All the ways of a man are clean in his own sight, but **the Lord weighs the motives.**

Proverbs 16:2

Discipline your son while there is hope, and do not desire his death.

Proverbs 19:18

Train up a child in the way he should go, even when he is old he will not depart from it.

Proverbs 22:6

Foolishness is bound up in the heart of a child; the rod of discipline will remove it far from him.

Proverbs 22:15

Do not hold back discipline from the child, although you beat him with the rod, he will not die.

Proverbs 23:13

The rod and reproof give wisdom, but a child who gets his own way brings shame to his mother.

Proverbs 29:15

Correct your son, and he will give you comfort; he will also delight your soul.

Proverbs 29:17

God will bring every act to judgment, everything which is hidden, whether it is good or evil.

Ecclesiastes 12:14

"Behold, the days are coming when all that is in your house, and **all that your fathers have laid up in store** to this day shall be carried to Babylon; **nothing shall be left,**" says the Lord.

Isaiah 39:6

"**The shepherds** have become stupid and **have not sought the Lord; therefore they have not prospered,** and all their flock is scattered."

Jeremiah 10:21

"**Your wealth and your treasures I will give for booty** without cost, even for all your sins and within all your borders."

Jeremiah 15:13

"O mountain of Mine in the countryside, **I will give over your wealth and all your treasures for booty,** your high places for sin throughout your borders."

Jeremiah 17:3

"O you who dwell by many waters, **abundant in treasures, your end has come,** the measure of your end."

Jeremiah 51:13

[If he] **oppresses the poor and needy,** commits robbery, does not restore a pledge, but lifts up his eyes to the idols, and commits abomination, he lends money on interest and takes increase; will he live? He will not live! He has committed all these abominations, he will surely be put to death; his blood will be on his own head.

Ezekiel 18:12–13

"I will judge you, O house of Israel, each according to his conduct," declares the Lord God. "Repent and turn away from all your transgressions, **so that iniquity may not become a stumbling block to you.** . . . I have no pleasure in the death of anyone who dies," declares the Lord God. "Therefore, repent and live."

Ezekiel 18:30, 32

"Also **they will make a spoil of your riches** and a prey of your merchandise, break down your walls and destroy your pleasant houses, and throw your stones and your timbers and your debris into the water."

Ezekiel 26:12

"By the abundance of your trade you were internally filled with violence, and you sinned; therefore I have cast you as profane from the mountain of God. And I have destroyed you, O covering cherub, from the midst of the stones of fire."

Ezekiel 28:16

"By the multitude of your iniquities, in **the unrighteousness of your trade,** you profaned your sanctuaries. Therefore I have brought fire from the midst of you; it has consumed you, and I have turned you to ashes on the earth in the eyes of all who see you."

Ezekiel 28:18

"**I shall turn the fortunes of Egypt** and shall make them return to the land of Pathros, to the land of their origin; and there they will be a lowly kingdom."

Ezekiel 29:14

"It will come about at that time that I will search Jerusalem with lamps, and **I will punish** the men who are stagnant in spirit, who say in their hearts, 'The Lord will not do good or evil!' Moreover, their wealth will become plunder, and their houses desolate; yes, they will build houses but not inhabit them, and plant vineyards but not drink their wine."

Zephaniah 1:12–13

"You look for much, but behold, it comes to little; when you bring it home, I blow it away. Why?" declares the Lord of hosts, "Because of My house which lies desolate, **while each of you runs to his own house.**"

Haggai 1:9

"I will draw near to you for judgment; and I will be a swift witness against the sorcerers and against the adulterers and against those who swear falsely, and **against those who oppress the wage earner in his wages,** the widow and the orphan, and those who turn aside the alien, and do not fear Me," says the Lord of hosts.

Malachi 3:5

"**Whoever has, to him shall more be given,** and he shall have an abundance; but whoever does not have, even what he has shall be taken away from him."

Matthew 13:12

"My son, do not regard lightly the discipline of the Lord, nor faint when you are reproved by Him, for **those whom the Lord loves He disciplines,** and He scourges every son whom He receives." It is for discipline that you endure; God deals with you as with sons; for what son is there whom his father does not discipline? But if you are without discipline, of which all have become partakers, then you are illegitimate children and not sons. Furthermore, we had earthly fathers to discipline us, and we respected them; shall we not much rather be subject to the Father of spirits, and live? For they disciplined us for a short time as seemed best to them, but **He disciplines us for our good,**

that we may share His holiness. All discipline for the moment seems not to be joyful, but sorrowful; yet to those who have been trained by it, afterwards **it yields the peaceful fruit of righteousness.**

Hebrews 12:5–11

"'Those whom I love, I reprove and discipline; be zealous therefore, and repent.'"

Revelation 3:19

"The fruit you long for has gone from you, and all things that were luxurious and splendid have passed away from you and men will no longer find them. **The merchants of these things, who became rich from her,** will stand at a distance because of the fear of her torment, weeping and mourning, saying, 'Woe, woe, the great city, she who was clothed in fine linen and purple and scarlet, and adorned with gold and precious stones and pearls; for in one hour such great wealth has been laid waste!' And every shipmaster and every passenger and sailor, and as many as make their living by the sea, stood at a distance, and were crying out as they saw the smoke of her burning, saying, 'What city is like the great city?' And they threw dust on their heads and were crying out, weeping and mourning, saying, 'Woe, woe, the great city, in which all who had ships at sea became rich by her wealth, for in one hour she has been laid waste!'"

Revelation 18:14–19

FALSE GODS

In our society today, false gods are commonplace. They don't look like the golden calf made by Aaron, but they are still false gods. The false god of government provision teaches us to trust more in the government than we do in God. The false god of financial security for the future, through retirement plans and savings plans (though these are essential to being good stewards and planning for the future), also can be a means to draw us away from God and cause us to trust more in the provision than the Provider. Intangible false gods are usually pride, position, fame, success—anything that detours our commitment to God.

"You shall not worship [other gods] or serve them; for I, the Lord your God, am a jealous God, **visiting the iniquity of the fathers on the children,** on the third and the fourth generations of those who hate Me, but showing lovingkindness to thousands, to those who love Me and keep My commandments."

Exodus 20:5–6

"**You shall not make other gods besides Me;** gods of silver or gods of gold, you shall not make for yourselves."

Exodus 20:23

Aaron said to them, "Tear off the gold rings which are in the ears of your wives, your sons, and your daughters, and bring them to me." Then **all the people tore off the gold rings which were in their ears, and brought them to Aaron.**

Exodus 32:2–3

"I said to them, '**Whoever has any gold, let them tear it off.**' So they gave it to me, and I threw it into the fire, and out came this calf."

Exodus 32:24

"**They have made a god of gold** for themselves."

Exodus 32:31

The earth opened its mouth and swallowed them up, and their households, and all the men who belonged to Korah, with their possessions.

Numbers 16:32

The Lord gave Jehoiakim king of Judah into his hand, along with some of the vessels of the house of God; and he brought them to the land of Shinar, to the house of his god, and he **brought the vessels into the treasury of his god.**

Daniel 1:2

Then they brought the gold vessels that had been taken out of the temple, the house of God which was in Jerusalem; and the king and his nobles, his wives, and his concubines drank from them. They drank the wine and **praised the gods of gold and silver,** of bronze, iron, wood, and stone.

Daniel 5:3–4

"You have exalted yourself against the Lord of heaven; and they have brought the vessels of His house before you, and you and your nobles, your wives and your concubines have been drinking wine from them; and **you have praised the gods of silver and gold,** of bronze, iron, wood and stone, which do not see, hear or understand. But the God in whose hand are your life-breath and your ways, you have not glorified."

Daniel 5:23

"I will tell you the truth. Behold, **three more kings are going to arise in Persia.** Then a fourth will gain far more riches than all of them; as soon as he becomes strong through his riches, he will arouse the whole empire against the realm of Greece."

Daniel 11:2

"Their gods with their metal images and their precious vessels of silver and gold he will take into captivity to

Egypt, and he on his part will refrain from attacking the king of the North for some years."

Daniel 11:8

"In his place one will arise who will send an oppressor through the Jewel of his kingdom; yet within a few days he will be shattered, though neither in anger nor in battle."

Daniel 11:20

"He will honor a god of fortresses, a god whom his fathers did not know; **he will honor him with gold,** silver, costly stones, and treasures."

Daniel 11:38

They have set up kings, but not by Me; they have appointed princes, but I did not know it. With their silver and gold **they have made idols** for themselves, that they might be cut off.

Hosea 8:4

They sin more and more, and make for themselves molten images, **idols skillfully made** from their silver, all of them the work of craftsmen. They say of them, "Let the men who sacrifice kiss the calves!"

Hosea 13:2

"Though he flourishes among the reeds, an east wind will come, the wind of the Lord coming up from the wilderness; and his fountain will become dry, and his spring will be dried up; **it will plunder his treasury** of every precious article."

Hosea 13:15

"**Woe to you, blind guides,** who say, 'Whoever swears by the temple, that is nothing; but whoever swears by the gold of the temple, he is obligated.' You fools and blind men; which is more important, the gold, or the temple that sanctified the gold?"

Matthew 23:16–17

False Gods

"Being then the offspring of God, we ought not to think that the Divine Nature is like gold or silver or stone, an image formed by the art and thought of man."

Acts 17:29

Consider the members of your earthly body as dead to immorality, impurity, passion, evil desire, and greed, which amounts to idolatry.

Colossians 3:5

The rest of mankind, who were not killed by these plagues, **did not repent of the works of their hands, so as not to worship demons, and the idols of gold and of silver and of brass and of stone and of wood, which can neither see nor hear nor walk.**

Revelation 9:20

He causes all, **the small and the great, and the rich and the poor,** and the free men and the slaves, **to be given a mark** on their right hand, or on their forehead.

Revelation 13:16

"All nations have drunk of the wine of the passion of her immorality, and the kings of the earth have committed acts of immorality with her, and **the merchants of the earth have become rich by the wealth** of her sensuality."

Revelation 18:3

JUSTICE

To question why the unrighteous aren't punished by God is to question His wisdom. Proverbs says those who walk in integrity walk securely, but those who pervert their ways will be found out. Too often we expect God to practice justice by bringing vengeance upon those who mistreat us. God has promised that justice is His, and wrath is His, but He doesn't promise that we'll see that in this lifetime. In fact, many times God's justice is delayed . . . until the day of judgment.

You shall not distort justice; you shall not be partial, and you shall not take a bribe, for a bribe blinds the eyes of the wise and perverts the words of the righteous. **Justice, and only justice, you shall pursue,** that you may live and possess the land which the Lord your God is giving you.

Deuteronomy 16:19–20

"This we will do to them, even let them live, lest wrath be upon us for the oath which we swore to them."

Joshua 9:20

When these lepers came to the outskirts of the camp, they entered one tent and ate and drank, and carried from there silver and gold and clothes, and went and hid them; and they returned and entered another tent and carried from there also, and went and hid them. Then they said to one another, "We are not doing right. This day is a day of good news, but we are keeping silent; if we wait until morning light, punishment will overtake us. Now therefore come, let us go and tell the king's household."

2 Kings 7:8–9

Then Mordecai went out from the presence of the king in royal robes of blue and white, with a large crown of gold and a garment of fine linen and purple; and the city of Susa shouted and rejoiced.

Esther 8:15

The rest of the Jews . . . assembled, to defend their lives and rid themselves of their enemies, and kill 75,000 of those who hated them; but they did not lay their hands on the plunder.

Esther 9:16

"He saves from the sword of their mouth, and the poor from the hand of the mighty."

Job 5:15

"He will not become rich, nor will his wealth endure; and his grain will not bend down to the ground."

Job 15:29

"He swallows riches, but will vomit them up; God will expel them from his belly."

Job 20:15

"Complete darkness is held in reserve for his treasures, and unfanned fire will devour him; it will consume the survivor in his tent."

Job 20:26

"The increase of his house will depart; his possessions will flow away in the day of His anger. This is the wicked man's portion from God, even the heritage decreed to him by God."

Job 20:28–29

"They spend their days in prosperity, and suddenly they go down to Sheol."

Job 21:13

"It would be fire that consumes to Abaddon, and would uproot all my increase."

Job 31:12

Each one gave him one piece of money, and each a ring of gold.

Job 42:11

Until I came into the sanctuary of God; then I perceived their end. **Surely Thou dost set them in slippery places;** Thou dost cast them down to destruction.

Psalm 73:17–18

I know that the Lord will maintain the cause of the afflicted, and justice for the poor.

Psalm 140:12

[The Lord] is a shield to those who walk in integrity, **guarding the paths of justice,** and He preserves the way of His godly ones. Then you will discern righteousness and justice and equity and every good course.

Proverbs 2:7–9

"Riches and honor are with me, enduring wealth and righteousness. . . . I walk in the way of righteousness, **in the midst of the paths of justice.**"

Proverbs 8:18, 20

He who **walks in integrity** walks securely, but he who perverts his ways will be found out.

Proverbs 10:9

A wicked man receives a bribe from the bosom to pervert the ways of justice.

Proverbs 17:23

To do righteousness and **justice is desired by the Lord rather than sacrifice.**

Proverbs 21:3

God will bring every act to judgment, everything which is hidden, whether it is good or evil.

Ecclesiastes 12:14

Behold, I am going to stir up the Medes against them, who will not value silver or take pleasure in gold.

Isaiah 13:17

"Let the outcasts of Moab stay with you; be a hiding place to them from the destroyer." For the extortioner has come to an end, destruction has ceased, **oppressors** have completely disappeared from the land.

Isaiah 16:4

"I shall also give over all the wealth of this city, all its produce, and all its costly things; even all the treasures of the kings of Judah I shall give over to the hand of their enemies, and they will plunder them, take them away, and bring them to Babylon."

Jeremiah 20:5

"O you who dwell by many waters, **abundant in treasures, your end has come,** the measure of your end."

Jeremiah 51:13

"Violence has grown into a rod of wickedness. None of them shall remain, none of their multitude, none of their wealth, nor anything eminent among them."

Ezekiel 7:11

"They shall fling their silver into the streets, and their gold shall become an abhorrent thing; their silver and their gold shall not be able to deliver them in the day of the wrath of the Lord. They cannot satisfy their appetite, nor can they fill their stomachs, for their iniquity has become an occasion of stumbling."

Ezekiel 7:19

"As for his father, because he practiced extortion, robbed his brother, and did what was not good among his people, behold, he will die for his iniquity."

Ezekiel 18:18

"They will make a spoil of your riches and a prey of your merchandise, break down your walls and destroy your pleasant houses, and throw your stones and your timbers and your debris into the water."

Ezekiel 26:12

I lifted my eyes and looked, and behold, there was a certain man dressed in linen, whose waist was girded with a belt of pure gold of Uphaz. His body also was like beryl, his face had the appearance of lightning, his eyes were like flaming torches, his arms and feet like the gleam of polished bronze, and the sound of his words like the sound of a tumult.

Daniel 10:5–6

"They will go because of destruction; Egypt will gather them up, Memphis will bury them. **Weeds will take over their treasures of silver;** thorns will be in their tents."

Hosea 9:6

"Though he flourishes among the reeds, an east wind will come, the wind of the Lord coming up from the wilderness; and his fountain will become dry, and his spring will be dried up; **it will plunder his treasury** of every precious article."

Hosea 13:15

"The seeds shrivel under their clods; **the storehouses are desolate,** the barns are torn down, for the grain is dried up."

Joel 1:17

"Since you have taken My silver and My gold, brought My precious treasures to your temples, and sold the sons of Judah and Jerusalem to the Greeks in order to remove them far from their territory, behold, I am going to arouse them from the place where you have sold them, and return your recompense on your head. Also **I will sell your sons and your daughters into the hand of the sons of Judah,** and they will sell them to the Sabeans, to a distant nation," for the Lord has spoken.

Joel 3:5–8

Thus says the Lord God, "An enemy, even one surrounding the land, will pull down your strength from you and **your citadels will be looted.**"

Amos 3:11

"All of her idols will be smashed, **all of her earnings will be burned with fire,** and all of her images I will make desolate, for she collected them from a harlot's earnings, and to the earnings of a harlot they will return."

Micah 1:7

"Arise and thresh, daughter of Zion, for your horn I will make iron and your hoofs I will make bronze, that you may pulverize many peoples, that **you may devote to the Lord their unjust gain** and their wealth to the Lord of all the earth."

Micah 4:13

What does the Lord require of you but to do justice, to love kindness, and to walk humbly with your God?

Micah 6:8

"**Plunder the silver!** Plunder the gold! For there is no limit to the treasure—wealth from every kind of desirable object."

Nahum 2:9

Neither their silver nor their gold will be able to deliver them on the day of the Lord's wrath; and all the earth will be devoured in the fire of His jealousy, for He will make a complete end, indeed a terrifying one, of all the inhabitants of the earth.

Zephaniah 1:18

Then he said to me, "This is the curse that is going forth over the face of the whole land; **surely everyone who steals will be purged** away according to the writing on one side, and everyone who swears will be purged away according to the writing on the other side. I will make it go forth," declares the Lord of hosts, "and it will enter the house of the thief and the house of the one who swears falsely by My

272

name; and it will spend the night within that house and consume it with its timber and stones."

Zechariah 5:3–4

Thus has the Lord of hosts said, "**Dispense true justice,** and practice kindness and compassion each to his brother."

Zechariah 7:9

Tyre built herself a fortress and piled up silver like dust, and gold like the mire of the streets. Behold, **the Lord will dispossess her and cast her wealth into the sea;** and she will be consumed with fire.

Zechariah 9:3–4

"**In the way you judge, you will be judged;** and by your standard of measure, it will be measured to you."

Matthew 7:2

Since he did not have the means to repay, his lord commanded him to be sold, along with his wife and children and all that he had, and **repayment to be made.**

Matthew 18:25

"**He has filled the hungry with good things;** and sent away the rich empty-handed."

Luke 1:53

"**There was a certain rich man, and he habitually dressed in purple** and fine linen, gaily living in splendor every day. And a certain poor man named Lazarus was laid at his gate, covered with sores, and longing to be fed with the crumbs which were falling from the rich man's table; besides, even the dogs were coming and licking his sores. Now it came about that the poor man died and he was carried away by the angels to Abraham's bosom; and the rich man also died and was buried. And in Hades he lifted up his eyes, being in torment, and saw Abraham far away, and Lazarus in his bosom. And he cried out and said, 'Father Abraham, have mercy on me, and send Lazarus, that he may dip the tip of his finger in water and cool off my tongue; for I am in agony in this flame.' But Abraham said, 'Child, remember that during your life you received your good things, and likewise Lazarus bad things; but now he is being comforted here, and you are in agony.'"

Luke 16:19–25

The kings of the earth and the great men and the commanders and **the rich and the strong and every slave and free man,** hid themselves in the caves and among the rocks of the mountains.

Revelation 6:15

"The fruit you long for has gone from you, and all things that were luxurious and splendid have passed away from you and men will no longer find them. **The merchants of these things, who became rich from her,** will stand at a distance because of the fear of her torment, weeping and mourning, saying, 'Woe, woe, the great city, she who was clothed in fine linen and purple and scarlet, and adorned with gold and precious stones and pearls; for in one hour such great wealth has been laid waste!' And every shipmaster and every passenger and sailor, and as many as make their living by the sea, stood at a distance, and were crying out as they saw the smoke of her burning, saying, 'What city is like the great city?' And they threw dust on their heads and were crying out, weeping and mourning, saying, '**Woe, woe, the great city,** in which all who had ships at sea became rich by her wealth, for in one hour she has been laid waste!'"

Revelation 18:14–19

PROMISES OF GOD

God promises that He will bless those who obey and serve Him. He will provide for those who trust Him. Many times we equate provision with great wealth—according to the standards of the rest of the world. But the promises of God do not include wealth. Many people in our society believe they are being deprived as a result of not owning a home. God does not promise ownership of a home to everybody.

God's promises deal with what He says He will give us in order to accomplish His plan for our lives. The more we act as good stewards and manage God's resources according to His direction, the more God will entrust to us. If we really trust God with everything we have, He will satisfy all our needs as He promised.

"As for Asher, his food shall be rich, and he shall yield royal dainties."

Genesis 49:20

"I have heard the grumblings of the sons of Israel; speak to them, saying, 'At twilight you shall eat meat, and in the morning you shall be filled with bread; and **you shall know that I am the Lord your God.**'"

Exodus 16:12

"The Lord your God is the God of gods and the Lord of lords, the great, the mighty, and the awesome **God who does not show partiality,** nor take a bribe."

Deuteronomy 10:17

"Boast no more so very proudly, do not let arrogance come out of your mouth; for the Lord is a God of knowledge, and with Him actions are weighed."

1 Samuel 2:3

"The Lord makes poor and rich; He brings low, He also exalts."

1 Samuel 2:7

God said to him, "Because you have asked this thing and have not asked for yourself long life, nor have asked riches for yourself, nor have you asked for the life of your enemies, but have asked for yourself discernment to understand justice, behold, I have done according to your words. Behold, I have given you a wise and discerning heart, so that there has been no one like you before you, nor shall one like you arise after you. And **I have also given you what you have not asked, both riches and honor, so that there will not be any among the kings like you all your days.**"

1 Kings 3:11–13

So King **Solomon became greater than all the kings of the earth in riches and in wisdom.**

1 Kings 10:23

God said to Solomon, "Because you had this in mind, and did not ask for riches, wealth, or honor, or the life of those who hate you, nor have you even asked for long life, but you have asked for yourself wisdom and knowledge, that you may rule My people, over whom I have made you king, wisdom and knowledge have been granted to you. And **I will give you riches and wealth and honor,** such as none of the kings who were before you has possessed, nor those who will come after you."

2 Chronicles 1:11–12

The king made silver and gold as plentiful in Jerusalem as stones, and he made cedars as plentiful as sycamores in the lowland.

2 Chronicles 1:15

All King Solomon's drinking vessels were of gold, and all the vessels of the house of the forest of Lebanon were of pure gold; silver was not considered valuable in the days

of Solomon. . . . the ships of Tarshish came bringing gold
and silver, ivory and apes and peacocks. So King Solomon
became greater than all the kings of the earth in riches and
wisdom.

2 Chronicles 9:20–22

The Spirit of God came on Azariah the son of Oded, and he
went out to meet Asa and said to him, "Listen to me, Asa,
and all Judah and Benjamin; the Lord is with you when
you are with Him. And if you seek Him, He will let you find
Him; but if you forsake Him, He will forsake you."

2 Chronicles 15:1–2

The Lord established the kingdom in his control, and all
Judah brought tribute to Jehoshaphat, and he had great
riches and honor.

2 Chronicles 17:5

He continued to seek God in the days of Zechariah, who
had understanding through the vision of God; and as long
as he sought the Lord, **God prospered him.**

2 Chronicles 26:5

Hezekiah had immense riches and honor; and he made for
himself treasuries for silver, gold, precious stones, spices,
shields and all kinds of valuable articles, storehouses also
for the produce of grain, wine and oil, pens for all kinds of
cattle and sheepfolds for the flocks. And he made cities for
himself, and acquired flocks and herds in abundance; for
God had given him very great wealth.

2 Chronicles 32:27–29

"[Grant me] timber to make beams for the gates of the fortress which is by the temple, for the wall of the city, and
for the house to which I will go." . . . The king granted
them to me **because the good hand of my God was on me.**

Nehemiah 2:8

I answered them and said to them, "**The God of heaven
will give us success;** therefore we His servants will arise

277

and build, but you have no portion, right, or memorial in Jerusalem."

Nehemiah 2:20

"Behold, how happy is the man whom God reproves, so do not despise the discipline of the Almighty. For He inflicts pain, and gives relief; He wounds, and His hands also heal. From six troubles He will deliver you, even in seven evil will not touch you. **In famine He will redeem you from death,** and in war from the power of the sword."

Job 5:17–20

"Place your gold in the dust, and the gold of Ophir among the stones of the brooks, then **the Almighty will be your gold and choice silver to you.**"

Job 22:24–25

"When He has tried me, **I shall come forth as gold.**"

Job 23:10

"**Who shows no partiality to princes,** nor regards the rich above the poor, for they all are the work of His hands?"

Job 34:19

"If they hear and serve Him, **they shall end their days in prosperity,** and their years in pleasures."

Job 36:11

The Lord restored the fortunes of Job when he prayed for his friends, and the Lord increased all that Job had two-fold.

Job 42:10

O Lord, who may abide in Thy tent? Who may dwell on Thy holy hill? **He who walks with integrity,** and works righteousness, and speaks truth in his heart.

Psalm 15:1–2

Many are the afflictions of the righteous; but the Lord delivers him out of them all.

Psalm 34:19

The Lord loves justice, and does not forsake His godly ones; they are preserved forever; but the descendants of the wicked will be cut off. **The righteous will inherit the land, and dwell in it forever.**

Psalm 37:28–29

"**Offer to God a sacrifice of thanksgiving,** and **pay your vows to the Most High;** and call upon Me in the day of trouble; I shall rescue you, and you will honor Me."

Psalm 50:14–15

He brought them out with silver and gold; and among His tribes there was not one who stumbled.

Psalm 105:37

He raises the poor from the dust, and lifts the needy from the ash heap, to make them sit with princes, with the princes of His people.

Psalm 113:7–8

May the Lord give you increase, you and your children.

Psalm 115:14

"May peace be within your walls, and **prosperity within your palaces.**"

Psalm 122:7

The Lord bless you from Zion, and **may you see the prosperity of Jerusalem** all the days of your life.

Psalm 128:5

The Lord gives wisdom; from His mouth come knowledge and understanding.

Proverbs 2:6

Length of days and years of life, and peace they will add to you. **Do not let kindness and truth leave you;** bind them around your neck, write them on the tablet of your heart. So you will find favor and good repute in the sight of God and man.

Proverbs 3:2–4

"**Take my instruction, and not silver,** and knowledge rather than choicest gold. For wisdom is better than jewels; and all desirable things can not compare with her. I, wisdom, dwell with prudence, and I find knowledge and discretion."

Proverbs 8:10–12

"He who finds me finds life, and obtains favor from the Lord."

Proverbs 8:35

The wages of the righteous is life, the income of the wicked, punishment.

Proverbs 10:16

It is the blessing of the Lord that makes rich, and He adds no sorrow to it.

Proverbs 10:22

A gracious woman attains honor, and violent men attain riches.

Proverbs 11:16

Do not say, "I will repay evil"; wait for the Lord, and He will save you.

Proverbs 20:22

The rich and the poor have a common bond, but the Lord is the maker of them all.

Proverbs 22:2

"Many waters cannot quench love, nor will rivers overflow it; **if a man were to give all the riches of his house for love, it would be utterly despised.**"

Song of Solomon 8:7

With righteousness He will judge the poor, and decide with fairness for the afflicted of the earth; and He will strike the earth with the rod of His mouth, and with the breath of His lips He will slay the wicked.

Isaiah 11:4

"You will see and be radiant, and your heart will thrill and rejoice; **because the abundance of the sea will be turned to you,** the wealth of the nations will come to you."

Isaiah 60:5

"**Instead of bronze I will bring gold,** and instead of iron I will bring silver, and instead of wood, bronze, and instead of stones, iron. And I will make peace your administrators, and righteousness your overseers."

Isaiah 60:17

Thus says the Lord God, "Now **I shall restore the fortunes of Jacob,** and have mercy on the whole house of Israel; and I shall be jealous for My holy name."

Ezekiel 39:25

"**She does not know that it was I who gave her the grain,** the new wine, and the oil, and lavished on her silver and gold, which they used for Baal."

Hosea 2:8

"The coast will be for the remnant of the house of Judah, they will pasture on it. In the houses of Ashkelon they will lie down at evening; for the Lord their God will care for them and restore their fortune."

Zephaniah 2:7

"I will shake all the nations; and they will come with the wealth of all nations; and I will fill this house with glory," says the Lord of hosts. **"The silver is Mine, and the gold is Mine,"** declares the Lord of hosts.

Haggai 2:7–8

Again, proclaim, saying, "Thus says the Lord of hosts, '**My cities will again overflow with prosperity, and the Lord will again comfort Zion and again** choose Jerusalem.'"

Zechariah 1:17

The Lord will possess Judah as His portion in the holy land, and will again choose Jerusalem.

Zechariah 2:12

"I will bring the third part through the fire, refine them as silver is refined, and test them as gold is tested. They will call on My name, and I will answer them; I will say, 'They are My people,' and they will say, 'The Lord is my God.'"

Zechariah 13:9

Judah also will fight at Jerusalem; and **the wealth of all the surrounding nations will be gathered,** gold and silver and garments in great abundance.

Zechariah 14:14

"Rejoice, and be glad, for your reward in heaven is great, for so they persecuted the prophets who were before you."

Matthew 5:12

"Whoever wishes to save his life shall lose it; but whoever loses his life for My sake shall find it."

Matthew 16:25

"Whoever has, to him shall more be given; and whoever does not have, even what he has shall be taken away from him."

Mark 4:25

Jesus said, "Truly I say to you, **there is no one who has left house or brothers or sisters** or mother or father or children or farms, for My sake and for the gospel's sake, but that he shall receive a hundred times as much now in the present age, houses and brothers and sisters and mothers and children and farms, along with persecutions; and in the age to come, eternal life."

Mark 10:29–30

"For all these things the nations of the world eagerly seek; but your Father knows that you need these things. But seek for His kingdom, and **these things shall be added to you.**"

Luke 12:30–31

The Lord said, "Who then is the faithful and sensible steward, whom his master will put in charge of his servants, to give them their rations at the proper time?"

Luke 12:42

"Truly I say to you, that **he will put him in charge of all his possessions.**"

Luke 12:44

"If you ask Me anything in My name, **I will do it.**"

John 14:14

"**In that day you will ask in My name,** and I do not say to you that I will request the Father on your behalf; for the Father Himself loves you, because you have loved Me, and have believed that I came forth from the Father."

John 16:26–27

The Scripture says, "**Whoever believes in Him will not be disappointed.**" For there is no distinction between Jew and Greek; **for the same Lord is Lord of all, abounding in riches** for all who call upon Him.

Romans 10:11–12

My God **shall supply all your needs** according to His riches in glory in Christ Jesus.

Philippians 4:19

PROVISION OF GOD

T he *minimum* provision that God promised is that He will not allow His people to go hungry or to beg bread. And the very fact that there are many people, including Christians, who are hungry and begging bread says that many of God's people have failed the fundamental concept that God put in His Word—the concept of sharing.

We're reminded of what Paul said: "Share with those in need in your time of plenty; in your time of need they will share from their plenty." Paul also wrote that God would supply all our needs according to His riches in glory by Christ Jesus. That is His *maximum* provision.

The gold of that land is good; the bdellium and the onyx stone are there.

Genesis 2:12

Abram took Sarai his wife and Lot his nephew, and all their possessions which they had accumulated, and the persons which they had acquired in Haran, and they set out for the land of Canaan; thus they came to the land of Canaan.

Genesis 12:5

Abram was very rich in livestock, in silver and in gold.

Genesis 13:2

The land could not sustain them while dwelling together; for their possessions were so great that they were not able to remain together.

Genesis 13:6

They took all the goods of Sodom and Gomorrah and all their food supply, and departed. And they also took Lot,

Abram's nephew, and his possessions and departed, for he was living in Sodom.

Genesis 14:11–12

He brought back all the goods, and also brought back his relative Lot with his possessions, and also the women, and the people.

Genesis 14:16

"I will not take a thread or a sandal thong or anything that is yours, **lest you should say, 'I have made Abram rich.'**"

Genesis 14:23

"May He also give you the blessing of Abraham, to you and to your descendants with you; that **you may possess the land of your sojournings,** which God gave to Abraham."

Genesis 28:4

Leah said, "**God has endowed me with a good gift;** now my husband will dwell with me, because I have borne him six sons." So she named him Zebulun.

Genesis 30:20

The man became exceedingly prosperous, and had large flocks and female and male servants and camels and donkeys.

Genesis 30:43

He named the second Ephraim, "For," he said, "**God has made me fruitful in the land of my affliction.**"

Genesis 41:52

Joseph said to his brothers, "Please come closer to me." And they came closer. And he said, "I am your brother Joseph, whom you sold into Egypt. And now do not be grieved or angry with yourselves, because you sold me here; **for God sent me before you to preserve life.**"

Genesis 45:4–5

They took their livestock and their property, which they had acquired in the land of Canaan, and came to Egypt, Jacob and all his descendants with him.

Genesis 46:6

"I will grant this people favor in the sight of the Egyptians; and it shall be that when you go, you will not go empty-handed. But every woman shall ask of her neighbor and the woman who lives in her house, articles of silver and articles of gold, and clothing; and you will put them on your sons and daughters. **Thus you will plunder the Egyptians.**"

Exodus 3:21–22

"**I will bring you to the land which I swore to give to Abraham,** Isaac, and Jacob, and I will give it to you for a possession; I am the Lord."

Exodus 6:8

"The Lord will make a distinction between the livestock of Israel and the livestock of Egypt, so that **nothing will die of all that belongs to the sons of Israel.**"

Exodus 9:4

"Speak now in the hearing of the people **that each man ask from his neighbor and each woman from her neighbor for articles of silver and articles of gold.**" And the Lord gave the people favor in the sight of the Egyptians.

Exodus 11:2–3

The sons of Israel had done according to the word of Moses, for they had requested from the Egyptians articles of silver and articles of gold, and clothing; **and the Lord had given the people favor in the sight of the Egyptians, so that they let them have their request. Thus they plundered the Egyptians.**

Exodus 12:35–36

The Lord said to Moses, "Behold, **I will rain bread from heaven for you;** and the people shall go out and gather a

286

day's portion every day, that I may test them, whether or not they will walk in My instruction."

Exodus 16:4

"This is what the Lord has commanded, '**Gather of it every man as much as he should eat;** you shall take an omer apiece according to the number of persons each of you has in his tent.'"

Exodus 16:16

When they measured it with an omer, he who gathered much had no excess, and he who had gathered little had no lack; **every man gathered as much as he should eat.** And Moses said to them, "**Let no man leave any of it until morning.**" But they did not listen to Moses, and some left part of it until morning, and it bred worms and became foul; and Moses was angry with them. And they gathered it morning by morning, every man as much as he should eat; but when the sun grew hot, it would melt.

Exodus 16:18–21

Moses said, "This is what the Lord has commanded, '**Let an omerful of it be kept throughout your generations,** that they may see the bread that I fed you in the wilderness, when I brought you out of the land of Egypt.'"

Exodus 16:32

"Behold, I will stand before you there on the rock at Horeb; and you shall strike the rock, and **water will come out of it, that the people may drink.**" And Moses did so in the sight of the elders of Israel.

Exodus 17:6

"The land will yield its produce, so that you can eat your fill and live securely on it."

Leviticus 25:19

"**We have bought as an offering to the Lord** what each man found, articles of gold, armlets and bracelets, signet rings, earrings and necklaces, to make atonement for ourselves

287

before the Lord." And Moses and Eleazar the priest took
the gold from them, all kinds of wrought articles. And all
the gold of the offering which they offered up to the Lord,
from the captains of thousands and the captains of hundreds, was 16,750 shekels. The men of war had taken booty, every man for himself. So Moses and Eleazar the priest
took the gold from the captains of thousands and of hundreds, and brought it to the tent of meeting as a memorial
for the sons of Israel before the Lord.

Numbers 31:50–54

"The Lord your God has blessed you in all that you have
done; He has known your wanderings through this great
wilderness. These forty years the Lord your God has been
with you; you have not lacked a thing."

Deuteronomy 2:7

"You shall remember the Lord your God, for it is He who
is giving you power to make wealth, that He may confirm
His covenant which He swore to your fathers, as it is this
day."

Deuteronomy 8:18

"He executes justice for the orphan and the widow, and
shows His love for the alien by giving him food and clothing. So show your love for the alien, for you were aliens in
the land of Egypt."

Deuteronomy 10:18–19

[He] said to them, **"Return to your tents with great riches**
and with very much livestock, with silver, gold, bronze,
iron, and with very many clothes; divide the spoil of your
enemies with your brothers."

Joshua 22:8

"I gave you a land on which you had not labored, and cities which you had not built, and you have lived in them;
you are eating of vineyards and olive groves which you did
not plant."

Joshua 24:13

Elijah said to her, "Do not fear; go, do as you have said, but make me a little bread cake from it first, and bring it out to me, and afterward you may make one for yourself and for your son. For thus says the Lord God of Israel, '**The bowl of flour shall not be exhausted, nor shall the jar of oil be empty, until the day that the Lord sends rain on the face of the earth.**'"

1 Kings 17:13–14

The bowl of flour was not exhausted nor did the jar of oil become empty, according to the word of the Lord which He spoke through Elijah.

1 Kings 17:16

The people went out and plundered the camp of the Arameans. Then a measure of fine flour was sold for a shekel and two measures of barley for a shekel, according to the word of the Lord.

2 Kings 7:16

"**Both riches and honor come from Thee, and Thou dost rule over all,** and in Thy hand is power and might; and it lies in Thy hand to make great, and to strengthen everyone. Now therefore, our God, we thank Thee, and praise Thy glorious name. But who am I and who are my people that we should be able to offer as generously as this? For all things come from Thee, and from Thy hand we have given Thee."

1 Chronicles 29:12–14

The porch which was in front of the house was as long as the width of the house, twenty cubits, and the height 120; and inside he overlaid it with pure gold. And he overlaid the main room with cypress wood and overlaid it with fine gold, and ornamented it with palm trees and chains. Further, he adorned the house with precious stones; and the gold was gold from Parvaim. He also overlaid the house with gold—the beams, the thresholds, and its walls, and its doors; and he carved cherubim on the walls.

2 Chronicles 3:4–7

Solomon also made all the things that were in the house of God: even the golden altar, the tables with the bread of the Presence on them, the lampstands with their lamps of pure gold, to burn in front of the inner sanctuary in the way prescribed; the flowers, the lamps, and the tongs of gold, of purest gold; and the snuffers, the bowls, the spoons, and the firepans of pure gold; and the entrance of the house, its inner doors for the holy of holies, and the doors of the house, that is, of the nave, of gold.

2 Chronicles 4:19–22

Even the silver and the gold and all of the utensils, and put them in the treasuries of the house of God.

2 Chronicles 5:1

This was their number: 30 gold dishes, 1,000 silver dishes, 29 duplicates; 30 gold bowls, 410 silver bowls of a second kind, and 1,000 other articles. **All the articles of gold and silver numbered 5,400.** Sheshbazzar brought them all up with the exiles who went up from Babylon to Jerusalem.

Ezra 1:9–11

"The gold and silver utensils of the house of God which Nebuchadnezzar had taken from the temple in Jerusalem, and brought them to the temple of Babylon, these King Cyrus took from the temple of Babylon, and they were given to one whose name was Sheshbazzar, whom he had appointed governor."

Ezra 5:14

"If it pleases the king let a search be conducted in the king's treasure house, which is there in Babylon, if it be that **a decree was issued by king Cyrus to rebuild this house** of God at Jerusalem; and let the king send to us his decision concerning this matter."

Ezra 5:17

King Darius issued a decree, and search was made in the archives, where the treasures were stored in Babylon.

Ezra 6:1

"[Let the temple be rebuilt] with three layers of huge stones, and one layer of timbers. And let the cost be paid from the royal treasury. And also let the gold and silver utensils of the temple of God, which Nebuchadnezzar took from the temple in Jerusalem and brought to Babylon, be returned and brought to their places in the temple in Jerusalem; and you shall put them in the house of God."

Ezra 6:4–5

"[Grant me] timber to make beams for the gates of the fortress which is by the temple, for the wall of the city, and for the house to which I will go." . . . The king granted them to me **because the good hand of my God was on me.**

Nehemiah 2:8

"Indeed, forty years **Thou didst provide for them in the wilderness** and they were not in want; their clothes did not wear out, nor did their feet swell."

Nehemiah 9:21

He said, "**Naked I came from my mother's womb, and naked I shall return there.** The Lord gave and the Lord has taken away. Blessed be the name of the Lord."

Job 1:21

He said to her, "You speak as one of the foolish women speaks. **Shall we indeed accept good from God and not accept adversity?**" In all this Job did not sin with his lips.

Job 2:10

Each one gave him one piece of money, and each a ring of gold.

Job 42:11

Thou dost make him to rule over the works of Thy hands; Thou has put all things under his feet.

Psalm 8:6

The earth is the Lord's, and all it contains, the world, and those who dwell in it.

Psalm 24:1

Who is the man who fears the Lord? He will instruct him in the way he should choose. **His soul will abide in prosperity,** and his descendants will inherit the land.

Psalm 25:12–13

Behold, **the eye of the Lord is on those who fear Him,** on those who hope for His lovingkindness, to deliver their soul from death, and **to keep them alive in famine.**

Psalm 33:18–19

O fear the Lord, you His saints; **for to those who fear Him, there is no want.**

Psalm 34:9

Contend, O Lord, with those who contend with me; fight against those who fight against me.

Psalm 35:1

Delight yourself in the Lord, and He will give you the desires of your heart.

Psalm 37:4

Rest in the Lord and wait patiently for Him; **do not fret because of him who prospers in his way,** because of the man who carries out wicked schemes. Cease from anger, and forsake wrath; do not fret, it leads only to evildoing. For evildoers will be cut off, but those who wait for the Lord, they will inherit the land.

Psalm 37:7–9

The Lord knows the days of the blameless; and their inheritance will be forever. They will not be ashamed in the time of evil; and in the days of famine they will have abundance.

Psalm 37:18–19

I have been young, and now I am old; yet **I have not seen the righteous forsaken,** or his descendants begging bread.
Psalm 37:25

Wait for the Lord, and keep His way, and He will exalt you to inherit the land; when the wicked are cut off, you will see it.
Psalm 37:34

"**If I were hungry, I would not tell you; for the world is Mine,** and all it contains."
Psalm 50:12

Once God has spoken; twice I have heard this; that power belongs to God; and lovingkindness is Thine, O Lord, for **Thou dost recompense a man according to his work.**
Psalm 62:11–12

That I may see the prosperity of Thy chosen ones, that I may rejoice in the gladness of Thy nation, that I may glory with Thine inheritance.
Psalm 106:5

Wealth and riches are in his house, and his righteousness endures forever.
Psalm 112:3

O Lord, do save, we beseech Thee; O Lord, we beseech Thee, do **send prosperity!**
Psalm 118:25

"Had it not been the Lord who was on our side," let Israel now say, "Had it not been the Lord who was on our side, when men rose up against us; then they would have swallowed us alive, when their anger was kindled against us."
Psalm 124:1–3

"I will abundantly bless her provision; **I will satisfy her needy with bread.**"
Psalm 132:15

"**Riches and honor are with me, enduring wealth and righteousness.** My fruit is better than gold, even pure gold, and my yield than choicest silver. I walk in the way of righteousness, in the midst of the paths of justice, to endow those who love me with wealth, that I may fill their treasuries."

Proverbs 8:18–21

It is the blessing of the Lord that makes rich, and He adds no sorrow to it.

Proverbs 10:22

The poor man and the oppressor have this in common: **the Lord gives light to the eyes of both.**

Proverbs 29:13

"**My hand reached to the riches of the peoples** like a nest, and as one gathers abandoned eggs, I gathered all the earth; and there was not one that flapped its wing or opened its beak or chirped."

Isaiah 10:14

He will give you rain for the seed which you will sow in the ground, and bread from the yield of the ground, and **it will be rich and plenteous;** on that day your livestock will graze in a roomy pasture.

Isaiah 30:23

"I will give you the treasures of darkness, and **hidden wealth of secret places,** in order that you may know that it is I, the Lord, the God of Israel, who calls you by your name."

Isaiah 45:3

"I have aroused him in righteousness, and I will make all his ways smooth; he will build My city, and will **let my exiles go free, without any payment or reward,**" says the Lord of hosts.

Isaiah 45:13

"In their riches you will boast."

Isaiah 61:6

"Men shall buy fields for money, sign and seal deeds, and call in witnesses in the land of Benjamin, in the environs of Jerusalem, in the cities of Judah, in the cities of the hill country, in the cities of the lowland, and in the cities of the Negev; for I will restore their fortunes," declares the Lord.

Jeremiah 32:44

"I also clothed you with embroidered cloth, and put sandals of porpoise skin on your feet; **and I wrapped you with fine linen and covered you with silk. And I adorned you with ornaments,** put bracelets on your hands, and a necklace around your neck. I also put a ring in your nostril, earrings in your ears, and a beautiful crown on your head. Thus you were adorned with gold and silver, and your dress was of fine linen, silk, and embroidered cloth. You ate fine flour, honey, and oil; so you were exceedingly beautiful and advanced to royalty."

Ezekiel 16:10–13

"You were in Eden, the garden of God; every precious stone was your covering: the ruby, the topaz, and the diamond; the beryl, the onyx, and the jasper; the lapis lazuli, the turquoise, and the emerald; and the gold, the workmanship of your settings and sockets, was in you. On the day that you were created they were prepared."

Ezekiel 28:13

"I will shake all the nations; and they will come with the wealth of all nations; and I will fill this house with glory," says the Lord of hosts. **"The silver is Mine, and the gold is Mine,"** declares the Lord of hosts.

Haggai 2:7–8

He took the five loaves and the two fish, and looking up toward heaven, He blessed the food and broke the loaves and He kept giving them to the disciples to set before them; and He divided up the two fish among them all.

Mark 6:41

So then let no one boast in men. For all things belong to you, whether Paul or Apollos or Cephas or the world or life or death or things present or things to come; **all things belong to you, and you belong to Christ;** and Christ belongs to God.

1 Corinthians 3:21–23

My God shall supply all your needs according to His riches in glory in Christ Jesus.

Philippians 4:19

Godliness actually is a means of great gain, when accompanied by contentment. For we have brought nothing into the world, so we cannot take anything out of it either. And if we have food and covering, with these we shall be content.

1 Timothy 6:6–8

SURPLUS

It is a fact that God has provided a great surplus to many Christians. God is not against prosperity. It is one of His blessings to those who love and obey Him. For one person, a surplus of money represents a trust from God that can be used for current and future needs. For another, it represents a trap of Satan to lead him out of God's path. Scripture warns that there is a greater danger in having a surplus than in having a need. For people with a surplus of money provided by God to meet future needs, good stewardship is required.

The important thing is to have a plan for the use of potential surpluses—planning before the money becomes available. Prosperity can require a great deal of time and attention. The urgency of our materialistic lifestyles becomes a tyranny that demands most of our energies. The possession of things has become a scorecard to determine success.

I was envious of the arrogant, as I saw the prosperity of the wicked.

Psalm 73:3

Go to the ant, O sluggard, observe her ways and be wise, which, having no chief, officer or ruler, prepares her food in the summer, and gathers her provision in the harvest.

Proverbs 6:6–8

"The one who had received the five talents came up and brought five more talents, saying, 'Master, you entrusted five talents to me; see, I have gained five more talents.'"

Matthew 25:20

Surplus

"To everyone who has shall more be given, and he shall have an abundance; but from the one who does not have, even what he does have shall be taken away."

Matthew 25:29

"He who is **faithful in a very little thing is faithful also in much;** and he who is unrighteous in a very little thing is unrighteous also in much. If therefore you have not been faithful in the use of unrighteous mammon, who will entrust the true riches to you?"

Luke 16:10–11

Jesus looked at him and said, "How hard it is for those who are wealthy to enter the kingdom of God! For it is easier for a camel to go through the eye of a needle, than for a rich man to enter the kingdom of God."

Luke 18:24–25

If anyone does not provide for his own, and especially for those of his household, he has denied the faith, and is worse than an unbeliever.

1 Timothy 5:8

Godliness actually is a means of great gain, when accompanied by contentment. For we have brought nothing into the world, so we cannot take anything out of it either.

1 Timothy 6:6–7

Those who want to get rich fall into temptation and a snare and many **foolish and harmful desires which plunge men into ruin and destruction.** For the love of money is a root of all sorts of evil, and some by longing for it have wandered away from the faith, and pierced themselves with many a pang.

1 Timothy 6:9–10

Instruct those who are rich in this present world not to be conceited or to fix their hope on the uncertainty of riches, but on God, **who richly supplies us with all things to enjoy.**

1 Timothy 6:17

Whatever we ask we receive from Him, because we keep His commandments and do the things that are pleasing in His sight.

1 John 3:22

WEALTH

What is wealth according to God's Word? Well, it certainly isn't having material things or living lavishly. God says that wealth includes salvation, peace, creative abilities, and even health; and it is His plan that we honor Him with our wealth. There's no amount of money that can buy the wealth of God. It comes only as a result of being obedient to God's Word.

Wealth can be corruptive—used to purchase influence, bribes, illegal transactions, or guns and bombs. But, on the other hand, wealth can be creative—used to spread God's Word, build hospitals and churches, feed the poor, or take care of orphans.

"The earth is the Lord's."

Exodus 9:29

You shall overlay it with pure gold, inside and out you shall overlay it, and you shall make a gold molding around it.

Exodus 25:11

You shall make **a mercy seat of pure gold,** two and a half cubits long and one and a half cubits wide. And you shall make two cherubim of gold, make them of hammered work at the two ends of the mercy seat.

Exodus 25:17–18

You shall overlay it **with pure gold and make a gold border around it.** And you shall make it for a rim of a handbreadth around it; and you shall make a gold border for the rim around it. And you shall make four gold rings for it.

Exodus 25:24–26

You shall make the poles of acacia wood and overlay them with gold, so that with them the table may be carried. And you shall make its dishes and its pans and its jars and its bowls, with which to pour libations; **you shall make them of pure gold.** Then you shall **make a lampstand of pure gold.**

Exodus 25:28–29, 31

Their bulbs and their branches shall be of one piece with it; **all of it shall be one piece of hammered work of pure gold.**

Exodus 25:36

Its snuffers and their trays shall be of pure gold. It shall be made from a **talent of pure gold,** with all these utensils.

Exodus 25:38–39

You shall make fifty clasps of **gold.** . . . You shall make fifty clasps of bronze . . . and their forty sockets of **silver.**

Exodus 26:6, 11, 21

There shall be eight boards with their **sockets of silver,** sixteen sockets; two sockets under one board and two sockets under another board.

Exodus 26:25

You shall overlay the boards **with gold and make their rings of gold** as holders for the bars; and you shall overlay the bars with gold.

Exodus 26:29

You shall hang it on four pillars of **acacia overlaid with gold,** their hooks also being of gold, on **four sockets of silver.**

Exodus 26:32

You shall make five pillars of acacia for the screen, and overlay them with **gold, their hooks also being of gold,** and you shall cast five sockets of bronze for them.

Exodus 26:37

Its pillars shall be twenty, with their twenty sockets of bronze; the hooks of the pillars and their **bands shall be of silver.** And likewise for the north side . . . the hooks of the pillars and their **bands shall be of silver.**

Exodus 27:10–11

All the pillars around the court shall be furnished with **silver bands with their hooks of silver** and their sockets of bronze.

Exodus 27:17

They shall take the gold and the blue and the purple and the scarlet material and the fine linen. They shall also make the **ephod of gold,** of blue and purple and scarlet material and **fine twisted linen,** the work of the skillful workman.

Exodus 28:5–6

Of the same material: of gold. . . . You shall set them in **filigree settings of gold.**

Exodus 28:8, 11

You shall make **filigree settings of gold, and two chains of pure gold.** . . . You shall make a breastpiece of judgment, the work of a skillful workman; like the work of the ephod you shall make it; of gold, of blue and purple and scarlet material and **fine twisted linen** you shall make it.

Exodus 28:13–15

You shall make on the breastpiece chains of twisted cordage work in pure gold . . . two **rings of gold.** . . . You shall put the **cords of gold** on the two rings at the ends of the breastpiece. . . . You shall make **two rings of gold.**

Exodus 28:22–24, 26

You shall make **two rings of gold.**

Exodus 28:27

Bells of gold between them all around: a golden bell and a pomegranate, a **golden bell** and a pomegranate, all around on the hem of the robe.

Exodus 28:33–34

You shall also make a **plate of pure gold** and shall engrave on it, like the engravings of a seal, "Holy to the Lord."

Exodus 28:36

You shall **overlay it with pure gold,** its top and its side all around, and its horns; and you shall make a gold molding all around for it . . . make **two gold rings.** . . . overlay them with gold.

Exodus 30:3–5

When you take a census of the sons of Israel to number them, then each one of them shall give a ransom for himself to the Lord, when you number them, that there may be no plague among them when you number them. This is what everyone who is numbered shall give: half a shekel according to the shekel of the sanctuary (the shekel is twenty gerahs), half a shekel as a contribution to the Lord. Everyone who is numbered, from twenty years old and over, shall give the contribution to the Lord. The rich shall not pay more, and the poor shall not pay less than the half shekel, when you give the contribution to the Lord to make atonement for yourselves. And you shall take the atonement money from the sons of Israel, and shall give it for the service of the tent of meeting, that it may be a memorial for the sons of Israel before the Lord, to make atonement for yourselves.

Exodus 30:12–16

Make artistic designs for **work in gold, in silver, and in bronze.** . . . The table also and its utensils, and the pure **gold lampstand** with all its utensils, and the altar of incense.

Exodus 31:4, 8

He made fifty **clasps of gold,** and joined the curtains to one another with the clasps, so that the tabernacle was a unit.

Exodus 36:13

He made **forty sockets of silver** under the twenty boards . . . and their forty sockets of silver.

Exodus 36:24, 26

He made a mercy seat of pure gold. He made **two cherubim of gold.**

Exodus 37:6–7

He made the **utensils which were on the table,** its dishes and its pans and its bowls and its jars, with which to pour out libations, **of pure gold.** Then he made the **lampstand of pure gold.**

Exodus 37:16–17

Their bulbs and their branches were of one piece with it; the whole of it was **a single hammered work of pure gold.** And he made its seven lamps with its snuffers and its **trays of pure gold.** He made it and all its utensils from a talent of pure gold.

Exodus 37:22–24

Bands were of silver. . . . **Bands were of silver.** . . . **Bands were of silver.** . . . Bands, of silver; and the overlaying of their tops, of silver. . . . **Hooks were of silver, . . . bands were of silver.**

Exodus 38:10–12, 17, 19

All the **gold that was used for the work,** in all the work of the sanctuary, even the gold of the wave offering, was 29 talents and 730 shekels, according to the shekel of the sanctuary. And the silver of those of the congregation who were numbered was 100 talents and 1,775 shekels, according to the shekel of the sanctuary.

Exodus 38:24–25

He made the ephod of gold. . . . Then they **hammered out gold sheets.**

Exodus 39:2–3

He placed the **gold altar in the tent of meeting** in front of the veil.

Exodus 40:26

"This is the statute of the law which the Lord has commanded Moses: only the gold and the silver, the bronze, the iron, the tin and the lead."

Numbers 31:21–22

"You shall remember the Lord your God, for **it is He who is giving you power to make wealth,** that He may confirm His covenant which He swore to your fathers."

Deuteronomy 8:18

All King Solomon's drinking vessels were of gold, and all the vessels of the house of the forest of Lebanon were of pure gold. None was of silver; it was not considered valuable in the days of Solomon.

1 Kings 10:21

King **Solomon became greater than all the kings of the earth in riches and in wisdom.**

1 Kings 10:23

The king made silver as common as stones in Jerusalem, and he made cedars as plentiful as sycamore trees that are in the lowland.

1 Kings 10:27

David took the shields of gold which were carried by the servants of Hadadezer, and brought them to Jerusalem.

1 Chronicles 18:7

Hadoram brought all kinds of articles of gold and silver and bronze. **King David also dedicated these to the Lord** with the silver and the gold which he had carried away from all the nations: from Edom, Moab, the sons of Ammon, the Philistines, and from Amalek.

1 Chronicles 18:10–11

David took the crown of their king from his head, and he found it to weigh a talent of gold, and there was a precious stone in it; and it was placed on David's head. And he brought out the spoil of the city, a very great amount.

1 Chronicles 20:2

David gave to his son Solomon the plan of the porch of the temple, its buildings, its storehouses, its upper rooms, its inner rooms, . . . and the plan of all that he had in mind, for the courts of the house of the Lord, and for all the surrounding rooms, for the storehouses of the house of God, and for the storehouses of the dedicated things; . . . **for the golden utensils,** the weight of gold for all utensils for every kind of service; for the silver utensils, the weight of silver for all utensils for every kind of service; and the weight of gold for the golden lampstands and their golden lamps, with the weight of each lampstand and its lamps; and the weight of silver for the silver lampstands, with the weight of each lampstand and its lamps according to the use of each lampstand; and the gold by weight for the tables of showbread, for each table; and silver for the silver tables; and the forks, the basins, and the pitchers of pure gold; and for the golden bowls with the weight for each bowl; and for the silver bowls with the weight for each bowl; and for the altar of incense refined gold by weight; and gold for the model of the chariot, even the cherubim, that spread out their wings, and covered the ark of the covenant of the Lord.

1 Chronicles 28:11–18

He made **the ten golden lampstands** in the way prescribed for them, and he set them in the temple, five on the right side and five on the left. He also made ten tables and placed them in the temple, five on the right side and five on the left. And he made one hundred golden bowls.

2 Chronicles 4:7–8

King Solomon made 200 large shields of beaten gold, using 600 shekels of beaten gold on each large shield. And he made 300 shields of beaten gold, using three hundred shekels of gold on each shield, and the king put them in the house of the forest of Lebanon. Moreover, **the king made a great throne of ivory and overlaid it with pure gold.** And there were six steps to the throne and a footstool in gold attached to the throne, and arms on each side of the seat, and two lions standing beside the arms.

2 Chronicles 9:15–18

The king made silver as common as stones in Jerusalem, and he made cedars as plentiful as sycamore trees that are in the lowland.

2 Chronicles 9:27

There were hangings of fine white and violet linen held by cords of fine purple linen on silver rings and marble columns, and couches of gold and silver on a mosaic pavement of porphyry, marble, mother-of-pearl, and precious stones. **Drinks were served in golden vessels** of various kinds, and the royal wine was plentiful according to the king's bounty.

Esther 1:6–7

His possessions also were 7,000 sheep, 3,000 camels, 500 yoke of oxen, 500 female donkeys, and very many servants; and that man was the greatest of all the men of the east.

Job 1:3

"**Surely there is a mine for silver,** and a place where they refine gold."

Job 28:1

"**Its rocks are the source of sapphires,** and its dust contains gold."

Job 28:6

By the word of the Lord the heavens were made, and by the breath of His mouth all their host.

Psalm 33:6

Honor the Lord from your wealth.

Proverbs 3:9

Their land has also been filled with silver and gold, and there **is no end to their treasures.**

Isaiah 2:7

"I will give you the treasures of darkness, and **hidden wealth of secret places, in order that you may know that it is I, the Lord,** the God of Israel, who calls you by your name."

Isaiah 45:3

In the beginning was the Word, and the Word was with God, and the Word was God. He was in the beginning with God. **All things came into being by Him,** and apart from Him nothing came into being that has come into being.

John 1:1–3

The earth is the Lord's, and all it contains.

1 Corinthians 10:26

Now Christ has been raised from the dead, the first fruits of those who are asleep. For since by a man came death, by a man also came the resurrection of the dead. For as in Adam all die, so also in Christ all shall be made alive. But each in his own order: **Christ the first fruits,** after that those who are Christ's at His coming.

1 Corinthians 15:20–23

WICKEDNESS

There always will be liars and thieves taking advantage of those who obey godly principles; and, it is quite possible that the ways of the wicked will cause them to prosper. God recognized in His Word that there were, and will be, many wicked people on earth, but He said that the prosperity of the wicked will not stand, because their prosperity ends when they die, as everyone must.

The prosperity of the righteous does not die; it begins at death, because for all of eternity God said that the wicked will be punished and the righteous will be blessed. Keep that in mind when looking at the prosperity of the wicked.

"[The Lord] repays those who hate Him to their faces, to destroy them; **He will not delay with him who hates Him,** He will repay him to his face."

Deuteronomy 7:10

"The anger of the Lord will be kindled against you, and **He will shut up the heavens** so that there will be no rain and the ground will not yield its fruit; and you will perish quickly from the good land which the Lord is giving you."

Deuteronomy 11:17

"It shall come about, if you will not obey the Lord your God, to observe to do all His commandments and His statutes with which I charge you today, that all these curses shall come upon you and overtake you. Cursed shall you be in the city, and cursed shall you be in the country. Cursed shall be your basket and your kneading bowl. Cursed shall be the offspring of your body and the produce of your ground, the increase of your herd and the young of your flock. Cursed shall you be when you come in, and cursed shall you be when you go out. The Lord will send upon you curses, confusion, and rebuke, in all you undertake to do, until you are destroyed and until you perish quickly, on account of the evil of your deeds, because you have forsaken Me."

Deuteronomy 28:15–20

"The Lord will bring you back to Egypt in ships, by the way about which I spoke to you, 'You will never see it again!' And there **you shall offer yourselves for sale to your enemies** as male and female slaves, but there will be no buyer."

Deuteronomy 28:68

Joshua called for them and spoke to them, saying, "Why have you deceived us, saying, 'We are very far from you,' when you are living within our land? Now therefore, you are cursed, and you shall never cease being slaves, both hewers of wood and drawers of water for the house of my God."

Joshua 9:22–23

The anger of the Lord was kindled against Israel, so that **He sold them into the hands of Cushan-rishathaim** king of Mesopotamia; and the sons of Israel served Cushan-rishathaim eight years. And when the sons of Israel cried to the Lord, the Lord raised up a deliverer for the sons of Israel to deliver them, Othniel the son of Kenaz, Caleb's younger brother.

Judges 3:8–9

The sons of Israel again did evil in the sight of the Lord, after Ehud died. And **the Lord sold them into the hand of Jabin** king of Canaan, who reigned in Hazor; and the commander of his army was Sisera, who lived in Harosheth-hagoyim.

Judges 4:1–2

The anger of the Lord burned against Israel, and **He sold them into the hands of the Philistines,** and into the hands of the sons of Ammon.

Judges 10:7

"I have told him that **I am about to judge his house forever** for the iniquity which he knew, because his sons brought a curse on themselves and **he did not rebuke them.**"

1 Samuel 3:13

"They forgot the Lord their God, so **He sold them into the hand of Sisera,** captain of the army of Hazor, and into the hand of the Philistines and into the hand of the king of Moab, and they fought against them."

1 Samuel 12:9

It came about in the fifth year of King Rehoboam, that Shishak the king of Egypt came up against Jerusalem. And he **took away the treasures of the house of the Lord** and the treasures of the king's house, and he took everything, even taking all the shields of gold which Solomon had made.

1 Kings 14:25–26

Ahab said to Elijah, "Have you found me, O my enemy?" And he answered, "I have found you, because **you have sold yourself to do evil** in the sight of the Lord."

1 Kings 21:20

Surely **there was no one like Ahab who sold himself to do evil** in the sight of the Lord, because Jezebel his wife incited him.

1 Kings 21:25

The royal officer answered the man of God and said, "Now behold, if the Lord should make windows in heaven, could such a thing be?" And he said, "Behold, you shall see it with your own eyes, but you shall not eat of it." And **so it happened to him, for the people trampled on him at the gate, and he died.**

2 Kings 7:19–20

When **Jehoshaphat and his people came to take their spoil,** they found much among them, including goods, garments, and valuable things which they took for themselves, more than they could carry. And they were three days taking the spoil because there was so much.

2 Chronicles 20:25

He took all the gold and silver, and all the utensils which were found in the house of God with Obed-edom, and the treasures of the king's house, the hostages also, and returned to Samaria.

2 Chronicles 25:24

All the articles of the house of God, great and small, and the treasures of the house of the Lord, and the treasures of the king and of his officers, **he brought them all to Babylon.**

2 Chronicles 36:18

"He frustrates the plotting of the shrewd, so that their hands cannot attain success. **He captures the wise by their own shrewdness** and the advice of the cunning is quickly thwarted."

Job 5:12–13

"The arrows of the Almighty are within me; their poison my spirit drinks; the terrors of God are arrayed against me."

Job 6:4

"**This is the portion of a wicked man** from God, and the inheritance which tyrants receive from the Almighty. Though his sons are many, they are destined for the sword; and his descendants will not be satisfied with bread. His survivors will be buried because of the plague, and their widows will not be able to weep. "**Though he piles up silver like dust, and prepares garments as plentiful as the clay; he may prepare it, but the just will wear it,** and the innocent will divide the silver."

Job 27:13–17

"**He lies down rich, but never again;** he opens his eyes, and it is no more. Terrors overtake him like a flood; a tempest steals him away in the night."

Job 27:19–20

How blessed is the man who does not walk in the counsel of the wicked, nor stand in the path of sinners, nor sit in the seat of scoffers! The wicked are not so, but they are like chaff which the wind drives away. Therefore the wicked will not stand in the judgment, nor sinners in the assembly of the righteous. For the Lord knows the way of the righteous, but **the way of the wicked will perish.**

Psalm 1:1, 4–6

Many are the sorrows of the wicked; but he who trusts in the Lord, lovingkindness shall surround him.

Psalm 32:10

Mark the blameless man, and behold the upright; for the man of peace will have a posterity. But transgressors will be altogether destroyed; **the posterity of the wicked will be cut off.**

Psalm 37:37–38

The Lord protects the strangers; **He supports the fatherless and the widow;** but He thwarts the way of the wicked.

Psalm 146:9

Do not enter the path of the wicked, and do not proceed in the way of evil men.

Proverbs 4:14

The way of the wicked is like darkness; they do not know over what they stumble.

Proverbs 4:19

The Lord will not allow the righteous to hunger, but He will thrust aside the craving of the wicked.

Proverbs 10:3

The fear of the Lord prolongs life, but the years of the wicked will be shortened.

Proverbs 10:27

The wicked earns deceptive wages, but he who sows righteousness gets a true reward.

Proverbs 11:18

The light of the righteous rejoices, but the lamp of the wicked goes out.

Proverbs 13:9

Adversity pursues sinners, but the righteous will be rewarded with prosperity.

Proverbs 13:21

The righteous has enough to satisfy his appetite, **but the stomach of the wicked is in want.**

Proverbs 13:25

Much wealth is in the house of the righteous, but trouble is in the income of the wicked.

Proverbs 15:6

The sacrifice of the wicked is an abomination, how much more when he brings it with evil intent!

Proverbs 21:27

When the righteous increase, the people rejoice, but when a wicked man rules, people groan.

Proverbs 29:2

To a person who is good in His sight He has given wisdom and knowledge and joy, while to the sinner He has given the task of gathering and collecting so that he may give to one who is good in God's sight. This too is vanity and striving after wind.

Ecclesiastes 2:26

Let the wicked forsake his way, and the unrighteous man his thoughts; and let him return to the Lord . . . for He will abundantly pardon.

Isaiah 55:7

The wicked are like the tossing sea, for it cannot be quiet, and its waters toss up refuse and mud. "**There is no peace,**" says my God, "**for the wicked.**"

Isaiah 57:20–21

Her adversaries have become her masters, **her enemies prosper;** for the Lord has caused her grief **because of the multitude of her transgressions;** her little ones have gone away as captives before the adversary.

Lamentations 1:5

"They will burn your houses with fire and execute judgments on you in the sight of many women. Then I shall stop you from playing the harlot, and you will also no longer pay your lovers."

Ezekiel 16:41

"Son of man, the house of Israel has become dross to Me; all of them are bronze and tin and iron and lead in the furnace; they are the dross of silver. Therefore, thus says the Lord God, 'Because all of you have become dross, therefore, behold, I am going to gather you into the midst of Jerusalem. As they gather silver and bronze and iron and lead and tin into the furnace to blow fire on it in order to melt it, so **I shall gather you in My anger and in My wrath,** and I shall lay you there and melt you.'"

Ezekiel 22:18–20

"**Tarshish was your customer because of the abundance of all kinds of wealth; with silver, iron, tin, and lead, they paid for your wares.**"

Ezekiel 27:12

"All the inhabitants of the coastlands are appalled at you, and their kings are horribly afraid; they are troubled in

315

countenance. The merchants among the peoples hiss at you; . . . and you will be no more."

Ezekiel 27:35–36

"A sword will come upon Egypt, and anguish will be in Ethiopia, when the slain fall in Egypt, **they take away her wealth,** and her foundations are torn down."

Ezekiel 30:4

"'As for the wickedness of the wicked, he will not stumble because of it in the day when he turns from his wickedness. . . .' But when I say to the wicked, 'You will surely die,' and he turns from his sin and practices justice and righteousness, **if a wicked man restores a pledge, pays back what he has taken by robbery, walks by the statues which ensure life without committing iniquity, he will surely live;** he shall not die. None of his sins that he has committed will be remembered against him. He has practiced justice and righteousness; he will surely live."

Ezekiel 33:12, 14–15

"They shall not come near to Me to serve as a priest to Me, nor come near to any of My holy things, to the things that are most holy; but they shall bear their shame and their abominations which they have committed."

Ezekiel 44:13

The Lord gave Jehoiakim king of Judah into his hand, along with some of the vessels of the house of God; and he brought them to the land of Shinar, to the house of his god and he brought the vessels into the treasury of his god.

Daniel 1:2

"I will also smite the winter house together with the summer house; the houses of ivory will also perish and the great houses will come to an end," declares the Lord.

Amos 3:15

Woe to those who are at ease in Zion, and to **those who feel secure in the mountain** of Samaria, the distinguished men of the foremost of nations, to whom the house of Israel comes. Go over to Calneh and look, and go from there to Hamath the great, then go down to Gath of the Philistines. Are they better than these kingdoms, or is their territory greater than yours? Do you put off the day of calamity, and would you bring near the seat of violence? Those who recline on beds of ivory and sprawl on their couches, and eat lambs from the flock and calves from the midst of the stall, who improvise to the sound of the harp, and like David have composed songs for themselves, who drink wine from sacrificial bowls while they anoint themselves with the finest of oils, yet they have not grieved over the ruin of Joseph. Therefore, they will now go into exile at the head of the exiles, and the sprawlers' banqueting will pass away.

Amos 6:1–7

"You have sown much, but harvest little; you eat, but there is not enough to be satisfied; you drink, but there is not enough to become drunk; you put on clothing, but no one is warm enough; and **he who earns, earns wages to put into a purse with holes.**"

Haggai 1:6

Tyre built herself a fortress and piled up silver like dust, and gold like the mire of the streets. Behold, **the Lord will dispossess her and cast her wealth into the sea;** and she will be consumed with fire.

Zechariah 9:3–4

"**The kingdom of heaven is like a landowner who went out early in the morning to hire laborers for his vineyard.** And when he had agreed with the laborers for a denarius for the day, he sent them into his vineyard. And he went out about the third hour and saw others standing idle in the market place; and to those he said, 'You too go into the vineyard, and whatever is right I will give you.' And so they went. Again he went out about the sixth and the ninth hour, and did the same thing. And about the eleventh hour he went out, and found others standing; and he said to them, 'Why have you been standing here idle all day long?'

317

They said to him, 'Because no one hired us.' He said to them, 'You too go into the vineyard.' And when evening had come, the owner of the vineyard said to his foreman, 'Call the laborers and pay them their wages, beginning with the last group to the first.' And when those hired about the eleventh hour came, each one received a denarius. And when those hired first came, they thought that they would receive more; and they also received each one a denarius. And when they received it, they grumbled at the landowner, saying, 'These last men have worked only one hour, and you have made them equal to us who have borne the burden and the scorching heat of the day.' But he answered and said to one of them, 'Friend, I am doing you no wrong; did you not agree with me for a denarius? Take what is yours and go your way, but I wish to give to this last man the same as to you. Is it not lawful for me to do what I wish with what is my own? Or is your eye envious because I am generous?' Thus the last shall be first, and the first last.''

Matthew 20:1–6

"There shall certainly be a resurrection of both the righteous and the wicked."

Acts 24:15

The **wages of sin is death,** but the free gift of God is eternal life in Christ Jesus our Lord.

Romans 6:23

Submit yourselves for the Lord's sake to every human institution, whether to a king as the one in authority, or to governors as sent by him for the **punishment of evildoers and the praise of those who do right.** For such is the will of God that by doing right you may silence the ignorance of foolish men.

1 Peter 2:13–15

SECTION SIX

GOVERNMENT

There is a legitimate role in God's Word for government. Most of the references in the Bible for government are found in the Old Testament, and at that time government was a theocracy. There was very little separation between the government of Israel and the church. We see more separation in the New Testament as a result of the Roman Empire ruling over the people of God and, yet, we are also admonished in God's Word to honor the authorities above us. Bear in mind that the admonition came at a time when one of the most wicked governments designed by men was in charge of the people of Israel. It doesn't mean that we have to blindly follow the government and its disobedience to God, but it does mean that we should honor the authority that God has put above us.

Today there's a great confusion on the part of Christians about their relationship to our government, because much of what's discussed concerns constitutional rights, not biblical rights. According to

God's Word, He did not guarantee us freedom . . . nor prosperity . . . nor an honorable government. Those guarantees come out of the Constitution and we, as individuals, and certainly as Christians as well, have a right to expect the Constitution to guarantee our rights. But we do not have a right to expect God to guarantee them.

ADMINISTRATIVE TAX

There were actually two taxes levied upon the people of God in Christ's day: administrative and church. The administrative tax was levied on the people by the government of Rome. We are admonished to render unto Caesar the things that are Caesar's, so the taxes that we owe the government should be paid to the government. We might question having to pay taxes to the government, which then go to support individuals through welfare, Social Security, Medicare, and the other administrative devices we have. Does that supersede or reduce our commitment to support the church and its role in welfare? It does not. That is an administrative tax—no different than what was levied upon the people of Israel by the government of Rome.

Joseph made it a statute concerning the land of Egypt valid to this day, that Pharaoh should have the fifth; only the land of the priests did not become Pharaoh's.

Genesis 47:26

"**He will take the best of your fields** and your vineyards and your olive groves, **and give them to his servants.** And he will take a tenth of your seed and of your vineyards, and give to his officers and to his servants. He will also take your male servants and your female servants and your best young men and your donkeys, and use them for his work. **He will take a tenth of your flocks,** and you yourselves will become his servants. Then you will cry out in that day because of your king whom you have chosen for yourselves, but the Lord will not answer you in that day." Nevertheless, the people refused to listen to the voice of Samuel, and they said, "No, but there shall be a king over us."

1 Samuel 8:14–19

David put garrisons among the Arameans of Damascus, and **the Arameans became servants to David, bringing tribute.** And the Lord helped David wherever he went. And David took the shields of gold which were carried by the servants of Hadadezer, and brought them to Jerusalem.

2 Samuel 8:6–7

Mesha king of Moab was a sheep breeder, and **used to pay the king of Israel** 100,000 lambs and the wool of 100,000 rams.

2 Kings 3:4

Pul, king of Assyria, came against the land, and Menahem gave Pul a thousand talents of silver so that his hand might be with him to strengthen the kingdom under his rule. **Then Menahem exacted the money from Israel,** even from all the mighty men of wealth, from each man fifty shekels of silver to pay the king of Assyria. So the king of Assyria returned and did not remain there in the land.

2 Kings 15:19–20

Shalmaneser king of Assyria came up against him, and **Hoshea because his servant and paid him tribute.** But the king of Assyria found conspiracy in Hoshea, who had sent messengers to [the] king of Egypt and had offered no tribute to the king of Assyria, as he had done year by year; so the king of Assyria shut him up and bound him in prison.

2 Kings 17:3–4

Hezekiah king of Judah sent to the king of Assyria at Lachish, saying, "I have done wrong. **Withdraw from me; whatever you impose on me I will bear.**" So the king of Assyria required of Hezekiah king of Judah three hundred talents of silver and thirty talents of gold. And Hezekiah gave him all the silver which was found in the house of the Lord, and in the treasuries of the king's house. At that time Hezekiah cut off the gold from the doors of the temple of the Lord, and from the doorposts which Hezekiah king of Judah had overlaid, and gave it to the king of Assyria.

2 Kings 18:14–16

Pharaoh Neco imprisoned him at Riblah in the land of Hamath, that he might not reign in Jerusalem; and **he imposed on the land a fine of one hundred talents of silver** and a talent of gold.

2 Kings 23:33

Jehoiakim gave the silver and gold to Pharaoh, but he taxed the land in order to give the money at the command of Pharaoh. He exacted the silver and gold from the people of the land, each according to his valuation, to give it to Pharaoh Neco.

2 Kings 23:35

So the Lord established the kingdom in his control, and all **Judah brought tribute to Jehoshaphat,** and he had great riches and honor.

2 Chronicles 17:5

The Ammonites also gave tribute to Uzziah, and his fame extended to the border of Egypt, for he became very strong.

2 Chronicles 26:8

He fought also with the king of the Ammonites and prevailed over them so that the **Ammonites gave him during that year one hundred talents of silver,** ten thousand kors of wheat and ten thousand of barley. The Ammonites also paid him this amount in the second and in the third year.

2 Chronicles 27:5

"They have also emptied out the money which was found in the house of the Lord, and have delivered it into the hands of the supervisors and the workmen."

2 Chronicles 34:17

Then the king of Egypt deposed him at Jerusalem, and **imposed on the land a fine of one hundred talents of silver** and one talent of gold.

2 Chronicles 36:3

"Now let it be known to the king, that if that city is rebuilt and the walls are finished, **they will not pay tribute,** custom, or toll, and it will damage the revenue of the kings."

Ezra 4:13

"[It has been discovered] that mighty kings have ruled over Jerusalem, governing all the provinces beyond the River, and that **tribute, custom, and toll were paid to them.** So, now issue a decree to make these men stop work, that the city may not be rebuilt until a decree is issued by me."

Ezra 4:20–21

"Moreover, I issue a decree concerning what you are to do for these elders of Judah in the rebuilding of this house of God; **the full cost is to be paid to these people from the royal treasury out of the taxes** of the provinces beyond the River, and that without delay."

Ezra 6:8

"I, even **I King Artaxerxes, issue a decree** to all the treasurers who are in the provinces beyond the River, that whatever Ezra the priest, the scribe of the law of the God of heaven, may require of you, it shall be done diligently, even up to 100 talents of silver, 100 kors of wheat, 100 baths of wine, 100 baths of oil, and salt as needed."

Ezra 7:21–22

"We also inform you that **it is not allowed to impose tax, tribute or toll on any of the priests,** Levites, singers, door-keepers, Nethinim, or servants of this house of God."

Ezra 7:24

There were those who said, "We, our sons and our daughters, are many; therefore let us get grain that we may eat and live." And there were others who said, "**We are mortgaging our fields,** our vineyards, and our houses that we might get grain because of the famine." Also there were those who said, "We have borrowed money for the king's tax on our fields and our vineyards. And now our flesh is like the flesh of our brothers, our children like their children. Yet behold, we are forcing our sons and our daughters to be slaves, and some of our daughters are forced into bondage already, and we are helpless because our fields and vineyards belong to others."

Nehemiah 5:2–5

King Ahasuerus laid a tribute on the land and on the coastlands of the sea.

Esther 10:1

When they had come to Capernaum, those who collected the two-drachma tax came to Peter, and said, "**Does your teacher not pay the two-drachma tax?" He said, "Yes." And when he came into the house, Jesus spoke to him first, saying, "What do you think, Simon? From whom do the kings of the earth collect customs or poll-tax, from their sons or from strangers?" And upon his saying, "From strangers," Jesus said to him, "Consequently the sons are exempt. But, lest we give them offense, go to the sea, and throw in a hook, and take the first fish that comes up; and when you open its mouth, you will find a stater. Take that and give it to them for you and Me."**

Matthew 17:24–27

"Tell us therefore, what do You think? **Is it lawful to give a poll-tax to Caesar,** or not?" But Jesus perceived their malice, and said, "Why are you testing Me, you hypocrites? Show Me the coin used for the poll-tax." And they brought Him a denarius. And He said to them, "Whose likeness and inscription is this?" They said to Him, "Caesar's." Then He said to them, "Then render to Caesar the things that are Caesar's; and to God the things that are God's."

Matthew 22:17–21

They came and said to Him, "Teacher, we know that You are truthful, and defer to no one; for You are not partial to any, but teach the way of God in truth. **Is it lawful to pay a poll-tax to Caesar, or not?** Shall we pay, or shall we not pay?" But He, knowing their hypocrisy, said to them, "Why are you testing me? Bring Me a denarius to look at." And they brought one. And He said to them, "Whose likeness and inscription is this?" And they said to Him, "Caesar's." And Jesus said to them, "Render to Caesar the things that are Caesar's, and to God the things that are God's." And they were amazed at Him.

Mark 12:14–17

Some tax-gatherers also came to be baptized, and they said to him, "Teacher, what shall we do?" And he said to them, **"Collect no more than what you have been ordered to."**

Luke 3:12–13

"Is it lawful for us to pay taxes to Caesar, or not?"

Luke 20:22

He said to them, "Then render to Caesar the things that are Caesar's, and to God the things that are God's."

Luke 20:25

They began to accuse Him, saying, **"We found this man** misleading our nation and **forbidding to pay taxes to Caesar,** and saying that He Himself is Christ, a King."

Luke 23:2

Let every person be in subjection to the governing authorities. For there is no authority except from God, and those which exist are established by God.

Romans 13:1

Because of this you also pay taxes, for rulers are servants of God, devoting themselves to this very thing. Render to all what is due them; tax to whom tax is due; custom to whom custom; fear to whom fear; honor to whom honor.

Romans 13:6–7

CHURCH TAX

In the Lord's day the church tax was levied upon the people of Israel. Today there is no church tax because we don't live in a theocracy, in which the church literally can tax its people. Today, church tax is more commonly known as the tithe—a voluntary contribution given by God's people.

The principle of the tithe is as applicable to a twentieth-century Christian as it was to Abraham, who gave the first tithe 430 years before the law was given to man. We are told to surrender the tithe into the storehouse of God, as an acknowledgment of God's sovereignty over everything we have.

"You and Eleazar the priest and the heads of the fathers' households of the congregation, take a count of the booty that was captured, both of man and of animal; and divide the booty between the warriors who went out to battle and all the congregation. And levy **a tax for the Lord from the men of war who went out to battle,** one in five hundred of the persons and of the cattle and of the donkeys and of the sheep; take it from their half and give it to Eleazar the priest, as an offering to the Lord."

Numbers 31:26–29

He gathered the priests and Levites, and said to them, "Go out to the cities of Judah, and **collect money from all Israel to repair the house of your God annually,** and you shall do the matter quickly." But the Levites did not act quickly.

2 Chronicles 24:5

They made a proclamation in Judah and Jerusalem to **bring to the Lord the levy fixed by Moses the servant of God** on Israel in the wilderness.

2 Chronicles 24:9

It came about whenever the chest was brought in to the king's officer by the Levites, and when they saw that there was much money, then the king's scribe and the chief priest's officer would come, empty the chest, take it, and return it to its place. Thus they did daily and collected much money. And the king and Jehoiada gave it to those who did the work of the service of the house of the Lord; and they hired masons and carpenters to restore the house of the Lord, and also workers in iron and bronze to repair the house of the Lord.

2 Chronicles 24:11–12

After that He went out, and noticed **a tax-gatherer named Levi,** sitting in the tax office, and He said to him, "Follow Me."

Luke 5:27

SECTION SEVEN
INVESTING

Investing applies to the management of funds to generate a potential profit. Sometimes Christians are confused about the concept of investing. Some dedicate their entire lives to investing, thinking that somehow they can buffer themselves from all the world's ills simply by having enough finances. And others, to take the contrary view, believe that investing is a secular enterprise and Christians should have nothing to do with it. Both are unbalanced and both are wrong.

God talks a great deal in His Word about investing, but it's always to satisfy future needs: educating children, supplementing income in old age, and many other activities that are perfectly legitimate under God's Word, including the need to store up some wealth for future needs within the body of Christ. So it is not investing in and of itself that is unscriptural. It is the attitude that often surrounds the concept of investing.

BUYING

We, as Christians, were bought with a price and the Bible tells us that we are to glorify God in our bodies. Jesus paid that price for that purchase. Whether we glorify God might depend on what kind of consumers we are. The critical perspective is that we buy what we need rather than what we want or desire. That doesn't mean that God will not allow us to have material possessions beyond our basic necessities; He just wants us to be good stewards. Our buying usually reflects our value systems.

"Every male among you who is eight days old shall be circumcised throughout your generations, **a servant who is born in the house or who is bought with money** from any foreigner, who is not of your descendants. A servant who is born in your house **or who is bought with your money** shall surely be circumcised; thus shall My covenant be in your flesh for an everlasting covenant."

Genesis 17:12–13

Abraham took Ishmael his son, and all the servants who were born in his house and **all who were bought with his money,** every male among the men of Abraham's household, and circumcised the flesh of their foreskin in the very same day, as God had said to him.

Genesis 17:23

All the men of his household, **who were born in the house or bought with money from a foreigner,** were circumcised with him.

Genesis 17:27

To Sarah he said, "Behold, **I have given your brother a thousand pieces of silver;** behold, it is your vindication be-

fore all who are with you, and before all men you are
cleared."

Genesis 20:16

"[Approach Ephron] that he may give me the cave of Machpelah which he owns, which is at the end of his field; for
**the full price let him give it to me in your presence for a
burial site."**

Genesis 23:9

"My lord, listen to me; a piece of land worth four hundred
shekels of silver, what is that between me and you? So
bury your dead." And Abraham listened to Ephron; and
Abraham weighed out for Ephron the silver which he had
named in the hearing of the sons of Heth, four hundred
shekels of silver, commercial standard. So Ephron's field,
which was in Machpelah, which faced Mamre, the field
and cave which was in it, and all the trees which were in
the field, that were within all the confines of its border,
were deeded over to Abraham for a possession.

Genesis 23:15–18

[In] **the field which Abraham purchased from the sons of
Heth;** there Abraham was buried with Sarah his wife.

Genesis 25:10

Jacob loved Rachel, so he said, "**I will serve you seven
years for your younger daughter Rachel."**

Genesis 29:18

He bought the piece of land where he had pitched his tent
from the hand of the sons of Hamor, Shechem's father, for
one hundred pieces of money.

Genesis 33:19

"You shall live with us, and the land shall be open before
you; live and **trade in it, and acquire property in it."** Shechem also said to her father and to her brothers, "If I find
favor in your sight, then I will give whatever you say to
me. **Ask me ever so much bridal payment and gift,** and I

will give according as you say to me; but give me the girl in marriage."

Genesis 34:10–12

The people of all the earth came to Egypt to buy grain from Joseph, because the famine was severe in all the earth.

Genesis 41:57

He said, "Behold, I have heard that there is grain in Egypt; **go down there and buy some for us** from that place, so that we may live and not die." Then ten brothers of Joseph went down to buy grain from Egypt.

Genesis 42:2–3

Joseph's brothers came and bowed down to him with their faces to the ground. . . . "Where have you come from?" And they said, "**From the land of Canaan, to buy food.**" But Joseph had recognized his brothers, although they did not recognize him. And Joseph remembered the dreams which he had about them, and said to them, "You are spies; you have come to look at the undefended parts of our land." Then they said to him, "No, my lord, but your servants have come to buy food."

Genesis 42:6–10

"If you send our brother with us, we will go down and buy you food."

Genesis 43:4

"**Take double the money** in your hand, and take back in your hand the money that was returned in the mouth of your sacks; perhaps it was a mistake."

Genesis 43:12

They came near to Joseph's house steward . . . and said, "Oh, my lord, we indeed came down the first time to buy food, and it came about when we came to the lodging place, that we opened our sacks, and behold, each man's money was in the mouth of his sack, our money in full. So we have brought it back in our hand. We have also brought down other money in our hand to buy food; we do not know who put our money in our sacks." And he said, "**Be at ease and do not be afraid. Your God and the God of your father has given you treasure** in your sacks; I had your money." Then he brought Simeon out to them.

Genesis 43:19–23

"Behold, the money which we found in the mouth of our sacks we have brought back to you from the land of Canaan. How then could we steal silver or gold from your lord's house?"

Genesis 44:8

Joseph gathered all the money that was found in the land of Egypt and in the land of Canaan for the grain which they bought, and Joseph brought the money into Pharaoh's house. And when the money was all spent in the land of Egypt and in the land of Canaan, all the Egyptians came to Joseph and said, "Give us food, for why should we die in your presence? For our money is gone." Then Joseph said, "Give up your livestock, and I will give you food for your livestock, since your money is gone." **So they brought their livestock to Joseph,** and Joseph gave them food in exchange for the horses and the flocks and the herds and the donkeys; and he fed them with food in exchange for all their livestock that year. And when that year was ended, they came to him the next year and said to him, "We will not hide from my lord that **our money is all spent,** and the cattle are my lord's. There is nothing left for my lord except our bodies and our lands. . . . Buy us and our land for food, and **we and our land will be slaves to Pharaoh."** . . . So **Joseph bought all the land of Egypt for Pharaoh,** for every Egyptian sold his field, because the famine was severe upon them. Thus the land became Pharaoh's. And as for the people, he removed them to the cities from one end of Egypt's border to the other. **Only the land of the priests he did not buy,** for the priests had an allotment from Pharaoh, and they lived off the allotment which Pharaoh gave them. Therefore, they did not sell their land. Then Joseph said to the people, "Behold, I have today bought you and your land for Pharaoh; now, here is seed for you, and you may sow the land."

Genesis 47:14–23

The Lord said to Moses and Aaron, "This is the ordinance of the Passover; no foreigner is to eat of it; **but every man's slave purchased with money,** after you have circumcised him, then he may eat of it."

Exodus 12:43–44

"If you buy a Hebrew slave, he shall serve for six years; but on the seventh he shall go out as a free man without payment."

Exodus 21:2

"If a priest buys a slave as his property with his money, that one may eat of it, and those who are born in his house may eat of his food."

Leviticus 22:11

"On this year of jubilee each of you shall return to his own property. If you make a sale, moreover, to your friend, or buy from your friend's hand, you shall not wrong one another. Corresponding to the number of years after the jubilee, you shall buy from your friend; he is to sell to you according to the number of years of crops. In proportion to the extent of the years you shall increase its price, and in proportion to the fewness of the years, you shall diminish its price; for it is a number of crops he is selling to you. So you shall not wrong one another, but you shall fear your God; for I am the Lord your God."

Leviticus 25:13–17

"If a fellow countryman of yours becomes so poor he has to sell part of his property, then his nearest kinsman is to come and buy back what his relative has sold. Or in case a man has no kinsman, but so recovers his means as to find sufficient for its redemption, then he shall calculate the years since its sale and refund the balance to the man to whom he sold it, and so return to his property. But if he

335

has not found sufficient means to get it back for himself, then what he has sold shall remain in the hands of its purchaser until the year of jubilee; but at the jubilee it shall revert, that he may return to his property."

Leviticus 25:25–28

Again, the sons of Israel said to him, "We shall go up by the highway, and **if I and my livestock do drink any of your water, then I will pay its price.** Let me only pass through on my feet, nothing else."

Numbers 20:19

"**You shall buy food from them** with money so that you may eat, and you shall also purchase water from them with money so that you may drink."

Deuteronomy 2:6

He said to the closest relative, "**Naomi,** who has come back from the land of Moab, has to sell the piece of land which belonged to our brother Elimelech. So I thought to inform you, saying, '**Buy it before those who are sitting here,** and before the elders of my people. If you will redeem it, redeem it; but if not, tell me that I may know; for there is no one but you to redeem it, and I am after you.'" And he said, "I will redeem it." Then Boaz said, "On the day you buy the field from the hand of Naomi, you must also acquire Ruth the Moabitess, the widow of the deceased, in order to raise up the name of the deceased on his inheritance."

Ruth 4:3–5

The king said to Araunah, "**No, but I will surely buy it from you for a price, for I will not offer burnt offerings to the Lord my God which cost me nothing.**" So David bought the threshing floor and the oxen for fifty shekels of silver.

2 Samuel 24:24

A chariot was imported from Egypt for 600 shekels of silver, and a horse for 150; and by the same means they exported them to all the kings of the Hittites and to the kings of the Arameans.

1 Kings 10:29

They hired for themselves 32,000 chariots, and the king of Maacah and his people, who came and camped before Medeba. And the sons of Ammon gathered together from their cities and came to battle.

1 Chronicles 19:7

King David said to Ornan, "No, **but I will surely buy it for the full price; for I will not take what is yours for the Lord,** or offer a burnt offering which costs me nothing."

1 Chronicles 21:24

They imported chariots from Egypt for 600 shekels of silver apiece, and horses for 150 apiece, and by the same means they exported them to all the kings of the Hittites and the kings of Aram.

2 Chronicles 1:17

They in turn gave it to the carpenters and to the builders to buy quarried stone and timber for couplings and to make beams for the houses which the kings of Judah had let go to ruin.

2 Chronicles 34:11

As for the peoples of the land who bring wares or any grain on the sabbath day to sell, **we will not buy from them on the sabbath or a holy day,** and we will forego the crops the seventh year and the exaction of every debt. We also placed ourselves under obligation to contribute yearly one third of a shekel for the service of the house of our God.

Nehemiah 10:31–32

Behold, Hanamel the son of Shallum your uncle is coming to you, saying, "**Buy for yourself my field which is at Anathoth,** for you have the right of redemption to buy it." Then Hanamel my uncle's son came to me in the court of the guard according to the word of the Lord, and said to me, "Buy my field, please, that is at Anathoth, which is in the land of Benjamin; for you have the right of possession and the redemption is yours; buy it for yourself." Then I knew that this was the word of the Lord. **And I bought the field which was at Anathoth** from Hanamel my uncle's son, and I weighed out the silver for him, seventeen shekels of silver. And I signed and sealed the deed, and called in witnesses, and weighed out the silver on the scales. Then I took the deeds of purchase, both the sealed copy containing the terms and conditions, and the open copy; and I gave the deed of purchase to Baruch the son of Neriah, the son of Mahseiah, in the sight of Hanamel my uncle's son, and in the sight of the witnesses who signed the deed of purchase, before all the Jews who were sitting in the court of the guard. And I commanded Baruch in their presence, saying, "Thus says the Lord of hosts, the God of Israel, 'Take these deeds, this sealed deed of purchase, and this open deed, and put them in an earthenware jar, that they may last a long time.'"

Jeremiah 32:7–14

"Thou hast said to me, O Lord God, '**Buy for yourself the field with money,** and call in witnesses—although the city is given into the hand of the Chaldeans.'"

Jeremiah 32:25

"**Men shall buy fields for money,** sign and seal deeds, and call in witnesses in the land of Benjamin, in the environs of Jerusalem, in the cities of Judah, in the cities of the hill country, in the cities of the lowland, and in the cities of the Negev; for I will restore their fortunes," declares the Lord.

Jeremiah 32:44

"The time has come, the day has arrived. **Let not the buyer rejoice nor the seller mourn;** for wrath is against all their multitude. Indeed, the seller will not regain what he sold as long as they both live, for the vision regarding all their multitude will not be averted; nor will any of them maintain his life by his iniquity."

Ezekiel 7:12–13

"Tarshish was your customer because of the abundance of all kinds of wealth; with silver, iron, tin, and lead, they paid for your wares. Javan, Tubal, and Meshech, they were your traders; with the lives of men and vessels of bronze they paid for your merchandise. Those from Beth-togarmah gave horses and war horses and mules for your wares. The sons of Dedan were your traders. Many coastlands were your market; ivory tusks and ebony they brought as your payment. Aram was your customer because of the abundance of your goods; they paid for your wares with emeralds, purple, embroidered work, fine linen, coral, and rubies. Judah and the land of Israel, they were traders; with the wheat of Minnith, cakes, honey, oil, and balm they paid for your merchandise. Damascus was your customer because of the abundance of your goods, because of the abundance of all kinds of wealth, because of the wine of Helbon and white wool. Vedan and Javan paid for your wares from Uzal; wrought iron, cassia, and sweet cane were among your merchandise. Dedan traded with you in saddlecloths for riding. Arabia and all the princes of Kedar, they were your customers for lambs, rams, and goats; for these they were your customers."

Ezekiel 27:12–21

"By the abundance of your trade you were internally filled with violence, and you sinned; therefore I have cast you as profane from the mountain of God. And I have destroyed you, O covering cherub, from the midst of the stones of fire."

Ezekiel 28:16

"I bought her for myself for fifteen shekels of silver and a homer and a half of barley."

Hosea 3:2

Jonah rose up to flee Tarshish from the presence of the Lord. So he went down to Joppa, found a ship which was going to Tarshish, **paid the fare,** and went down into it to go with them to Tarshish from the presence of the Lord.

Jonah 1:3

"Those who buy them slay them and go unpunished, and each of those who sell them says, 'Blessed be the Lord, for I have become rich!' And their own shepherds have no pity on them."

Zechariah 11:5

"The kingdom of heaven is like a treasure hidden in the field, which a man found and hid; and from joy over it he goes and sells all that he has, and buys that field. Again, **the kingdom of heaven is like a merchant seeking fine pearls,** and upon finding one pearl of great value, he went and sold all that he had, and bought it."

Matthew 13:44–46

When it was evening, the disciples came to Him, saying, "The place is desolate, and the time is already past; **so send the multitudes away,** that they may go into the villages and buy food for themselves."

Matthew 14:15

"The prudent answered, saying, '**No, there will not be enough for us and you too;** go instead to the dealers and buy some for yourselves.' And while they were going away to make the purchase, the bridegroom came, and those who were ready went in with him to the wedding feast; and the door was shut."

Matthew 25:9–10

He answered and said to them, "**You give them something to eat!**" And they said to Him, "Shall we go and spend two hundred denarii on bread and give them something to eat?"

Mark 6:37

He said to them, "**You give them something to eat!**" And they said, "We have no more than five loaves and two fish, unless perhaps we go and buy food for all these people."

Luke 9:13

Jesus therefore lifting up His eyes, and seeing that a great multitude was coming to Him, said to Philip, "**Where are we to buy bread, that these may eat?**" And this He was saying to test him; for He himself knew what He was intending to do. Philip answered Him, "Two hundred denarii worth of bread is not sufficient for them, for everyone to receive a little."

John 6:5–7

Some were supposing, because **Judas had the money box,** that Jesus was saying to him, "Buy the things we have need of for the feast"; or else, that he should give something to the poor.

John 13:29

The commander answered, "**I acquired this citizenship with a large sum of money.**" And Paul said, "But I was actually born a citizen."

Acts 22:28

He stayed two full years in his own rented quarters, and was welcoming all who came to him.

Acts 28:30

You have been bought with a price: therefore glorify God in your body.

1 Corinthians 6:20

You were bought with a price; do not become slaves of men.

1 Corinthians 7:23

He provides that **no one should be able to buy or to sell,** except the one who has the mark, either the name of the beast or the number of his name.

Revelation 13:17

"The merchants of the earth weep and mourn over her, because **no one buys their cargoes any more.**"

Revelation 18:11

GET-RICH-QUICK SCHEMES

A get-rich-quick scheme is developed to entrap the weak and especially the poor. After all, what does a wealthy man need with a get-rich-quick scheme? These schemes usually offer excessive gain for the apparent risk and usually involve areas about which we know little or nothing, require quick decisions, and were recommended by a friend.

It's amazing how susceptible Christians are to get-rich-quick schemes and how logical they seem at first. Every year, thousands of Christian families risk and lose money they cannot afford to lose while seeking that "big deal." This can be avoided but not on the basis of human wisdom. We cannot get caught up in our own desires and fail to yield control to God's wisdom.

To avoid financial traps, we should establish our standards by God's Word: seek God's plan for our lives, stick with what we know, seek good counsel, and wait on God's peace before acting.

Rest in the Lord and **wait patiently for Him**; do not fret because of him who prospers in his way, because of the man who carries out wicked schemes.

Psalm 37:7

Trust in the Lord with all your heart, and do not lean on your own understanding.

Proverbs 3:5

It is the blessing of the Lord that makes rich, and He adds no sorrow to it.

Proverbs 10:22

The way of a fool is right in his own eyes, but a wise man is he who listens to counsel.

Proverbs 12:15

A man of great anger shall bear the penalty, for if you rescue him, you will only have to do it again.

Proverbs 19:19

The plans of the diligent lead surely to advantage, but **everyone who is hasty comes surely to poverty.**

Proverbs 21:5

Do not weary yourself to gain wealth, cease from your consideration of it. When you set your eyes on it, it is gone. For wealth certainly makes itself wings, like an eagle that flies toward the heavens.

Proverbs 23:4–5

By wisdom a house is built, and by understanding it is established; and **by knowledge the rooms are filled with all precious and pleasant riches.**

Proverbs 24:3–4

Do not boast about tomorrow, for you do not know what a day may bring forth.

Proverbs 27:1

The prudent man sees evil and hides himself, the **naive proceed and pay the penalty.**

Proverbs 27:12

A faithful man will abound with blessings, but he who makes haste to be rich will not go unpunished.

Proverbs 28:20

A man with an evil eye hastens after wealth, and does not know that want will come upon him.

Proverbs 28:22

She considers a field and buys it; from her earnings she plants a vineyard. She makes linen garments and sells them, and supplies belts to the tradesmen.

Proverbs 31:16, 24

Those who want to get rich fall into temptation and a snare and many foolish and harmful desires which plunge men into ruin and destruction. For **the love of money is a root of all sorts of evil,** and some by longing for it have wandered away from the faith, and pierced themselves with many a pang.

1 Timothy 6:9–10

LOSS

When you invest money and get no return on it, you suffer loss. That generally happens as a result of ignoring the wisdom on finances taught in God's Word. One good principle to follow: Never invest money you can't afford to lose.

Also, there are many kinds of gambling, most of which result in monetary loss, as well as loss of fellowship with family and with the Lord.

When **those riches were lost** through a bad investment and he had fathered a son, then there was nothing to support him.

Ecclesiastes 5:14

If any man's work is burned up, **he shall suffer loss.** Let no man deceive himself. If any man among you thinks that he is wise in this age, let him become foolish that he may become wise.

1 Corinthians 3:15, 18

Whether, then, you eat or drink or whatever you do, do all to the glory of God. Give no offense either to Jews or to Greeks or to the church of God; just as I also please all men in all things, **not seeking my own profit, but the profit of the many,** that they may be saved.

1 Corinthians 10:31–33

For many walk, of whom I often told you, and now tell you even weeping, that they are enemies of the cross of Christ, whose end is destruction, **whose god is their appetite, and whose glory is in their shame,** who set their minds on earthly things.

Philippians 3:18–19

MULTIPLICATION

There's nothing wrong with the multiplication of your assets. In fact, we're told in the parable of talents that one man who had five talents multiplied them to ten; the one with two talents multiplied his to four; and the third, who had one talent, only maintained what his master had given him. His master called him a worthless and a wicked steward.

However, it isn't just the multiplication of assets that God is after; it is the multiplication of those assets for the benefit of God's kingdom.

Cast your bread on the surface of the waters, for you will find it after many days.

Ecclesiastes 11:1

"**It is just like a man about to go on a journey, who called his own slaves, and entrusted his possessions** to them. And to one he gave five talents, to another, two, and to another, one, each according to his own ability; and he went on his journey. Immediately the one who had received the five talents went and traded with them, and gained five more talents. In the same manner the one who had received the two talents gained two more. But he who received the one talent went away and dug in the ground, and hid his master's money. Now after a long time the master of those slaves came and settled accounts with them. And the one who had received the five talents came up and brought five more talents, saying, 'Master, you entrusted five talents to me; see, I have gained five more talents.' His master said to him, 'Well done, good and faithful slave; you were faithful with a few things, I will put you in charge of many things; enter into the joy of your master.' The one also who had received the two talents came up and said, 'Master, you entrusted to me two talents; see, I have gained two more talents.' His master said to him, 'Well done, good and faithful slave; you were faithful with a few things, I will put you in charge of many things; enter into the joy of your master.' And the one also who had received the one talent came up and said, 'Master, I knew you to be a hard man, reaping where you did not sow, and gathering where you scattered no seed. And I was afraid, and went away and hid your talent in the ground; see, you have what is yours.' But his master answered and said to him, 'You wicked, lazy slave, you knew that I reap where I did not sow, and gather where I scattered no seed. Then you ought to have put my money in the bank, and on my arrival I would have received my money back with interest. Therefore take away the talent from him, and give it to the one who has the ten talents.' For to everyone who has shall more be given, and he shall have an abundance; but from the one who does not have, even what he does have shall be taken away. And cast out the worthless slave into the outer darkness; in that place there shall be weeping and gnashing of teeth.''

Matthew 25:14–30

PROFIT

Too many times Christians believe that there's something inherently wrong with profit. In reality, there is not. A profit is the by-product of selling something that someone else needs and reaping a small reward as a result of it.

Hasty profits are discouraged by God's Word, and excessive profits are condemned according to God's Word, but a reasonable profit is the result of providing the product or service that other people need or want.

Joseph gathered all the money that was found in the land of Egypt and in the land of Canaan for the grain which they bought, and Joseph brought the money into Pharaoh's house. And when the money was all spent in the land of Egypt and in the land of Canaan, all the Egyptians came to Joseph and said, "Give us food, for why should we die in your presence? For our money is gone." Then Joseph said, "Give up your livestock, and I will give you food for your livestock, since your money is gone." **So they brought their livestock to Joseph,** and Joseph gave them food in exchange for the horses and the flocks and the herds and the donkeys; and he fed them with food in exchange for all their livestock that year.

Genesis 47:14–17

She considers a field and buys it; from her earnings she plants a vineyard.

Proverbs 31:16

Two are better than one because they have a good return for their labor.

Ecclesiastes 4:9

"It just like a man about to go on a journey, who called his own slaves, and entrusted his possessions to them. And to one he gave five talents, to another, two, and to another, one, each according to his own ability; and he went on his journey. Immediately the one who had received the five talents went and traded with them, and gained five more talents. In the same manner the one who had received the two talents gained two more. But he who received the one talent went away and dug in the ground, and hid his master's money. Now after a long time the master of those slaves came and settled accounts with them. And the one who had received the five talents came up and brought five more talents, saying, 'Master, you entrusted five talents to me; see, I have gained five more talents.' His master said to him, '**Well done, good and faithful slave; you were faithful with a few things, I will put you in charge of many things; enter into the joy of your master.**' The one also who had received the two talents came up and said, 'Master, you entrusted to me two talents; see, I have gained two more talents.' His master said to him, 'Well done, good and faithful slave; you were faithful with a few things, I will put you in charge of many things; enter into the joy of your master.' And the one also who had received the one talent came up and said, 'Master, I knew you to be a hard man, reaping where you did not sow, and gathering where you scattered no seed. And I was afraid, and went away and hid your talent in the ground; see, you have what is yours.' But his master answered and said to him, 'You wicked, lazy slave, you knew that I reap where I did not sow, and gather where I scattered no seed. Then you ought to have put my money in the bank, and on my arrival I would have received my money back with interest. Therefore take away the talent from him, and give it to the one who has the ten talents.' For to everyone who has shall more be given, and he shall have an abundance; but from the one who does not have, even what he does have shall be taken away. And cast out the worthless slave into the outer darkness; in that place there shall be weeping and gnashing of teeth.''

Matthew 25:14–30

"The one who did not know it, and committed deeds worthy of a flogging, will receive but few. And **from everyone who has been given much shall much be required;** and to whom they entrusted much, of him they will ask all the more."

Luke 12:48

"He called ten of his slaves, and gave them ten minas, and said to them, 'Do business with this until I come back.' But his citizens hated him, and sent a delegation after him, saying, 'We do not want this man to reign over us.' And it came about that when he returned, after receiving the kingdom, he ordered that these slaves, to whom he had given the money, be called to him in order that he might know what business they had done. And the first appeared, saying, 'Master, your mina has made ten minas more.' And he said to him, '**Well done, good slave, because you have been faithful in a very little thing, be in authority over ten cities.'** And the second came, saying, 'Your mina, master, has made five minas.' And he said to him also, 'And you are to be over five cities.' And another came, saying, 'Master, behold your mina, which I kept put away in a handkerchief; for I was afraid of you, because you are an exacting man; you take up what you did not lay down, and reap what you did not sow.' He said to him, 'By your own words I will judge you, you worthless slave. Did you know that I am an exacting man, taking up what I did not lay down, and reaping what I did not sow? Then why did you not put the money in the bank, and having come, I would have collected it with interest?' And he said to the bystanders, 'Take the mina away from him, and give it to the one who has the ten minas.' And they said to him, 'Master, he has ten minas already.' I tell you, that to everyone who has shall more be given, but from the one who does not have, even what he does have shall be taken away."

Luke 19:13–26

All those who had believed were together, and had all things in common; and they began selling their property and possessions, and were sharing them with all, as anyone might have need.

Acts 2:44–45

Joseph, a Levite of Cyprian birth, who was also called **Barnabas** by the apostles (which translated means, Son of Encouragement), and **who owned a tract of land**, sold it and brought the money and laid it at the apostles' feet.

Acts 4:36–37

Come now, you who say, "Today or tomorrow, we shall go to such and such a city, and spend a year there and engage in business and make a profit." Yet you do not know what your life will be like tomorrow. You are just a vapor that appears for a little while and then vanishes away.

James 4:13–14

SAVINGS

It is not unspiritual to save; nor does it represent a lack of faith. This is one principle that God's people need to learn and practice more. To put money into savings means to have the ability to store money for the purchase of a future need. Too often we use credit —the reverse of savings. When you use credit you buy a product and then try to pay the purchase price later. Unfortunately, the price also incurs an interest charge, which makes that payment even more difficult.

A far better concept taught in God's word is to sacrifice in the short-term to attain long-term goals. It is important to budget some savings. Otherwise, the use of credit becomes a lifelong necessity and debt a way of life. Savings allows you to purchase with cash and shop for the best buys.

Another long-term goal for savings is to finance retirement. God will allow some accumulation in prospect of advancing years, but He will not allow hoarding. That transfers dependence from God to money. A savings plan has a specific purpose for the money being stored.

Go to the ant, O sluggard, observe her ways and be wise, which, having no chief, officer or ruler, prepares her food in the summer, and gathers her provision in the harvest.

Proverbs 6:6–8

There is precious treasure and oil in the dwelling of the wise, but **a foolish man swallows it up.**

Proverbs 21:20

Divide your portion to seven, or even to eight, for you do not know what misfortune may occur on the earth.

Ecclesiastes 11:2

SELLING

There are many references to selling in God's Word. Buying and selling is a normal function for God's people. The requirement that God lays down in His Word for sellers of products is that they (1) sell at a fair price; (2) give an honest report on that product; and (3) be willing to stand behind it.

J.C. Penney epitomized this philosophy in his store when he said "The customer is always right." And he also instituted a policy that if a product was defective in any way it could be returned to his store for an exchange or for a refund without question.

Meanwhile, **the Midianites sold him in Egypt to Potiphar,** Pharaoh's officer, the captain of the bodyguard.

Genesis 37:36

When the famine was spread over all the face of the earth, then **Joseph opened all the storehouses, and sold to the Egyptians;** and the famine was severe in the land of Egypt. And the people of all the earth came to Egypt to buy grain from Joseph, because the famine was severe in all the earth.

Genesis 41:56–57

"**If a man sells his daughter** as a female slave, she is not to go free as the male slaves do. If she is displeasing in the eyes of her master . . . he shall let her be redeemed. He does not have authority to sell her to a foreign people because of his unfairness to her. And if he designates her for his son, he shall deal with her according to the custom of daughters. If he takes to himself another woman, he may not reduce her food, her clothing, or her conjugal rights. And if he will not do these three things for her, then **she shall go out for nothing, without payment of money.**"

Exodus 21:7–11

"**The land,** moreover, **shall not be sold permanently,** for the land is Mine; for you are but aliens and sojourners with Me. Thus for every piece of your property, you are to provide for the redemption of the land. **If a fellow countryman of yours becomes so poor he has to sell a part of his property, then his nearest kinsman is to come and buy back what his relative has sold.**"

Leviticus 25:23–25

"They are My servants whom I brought out from the land of Egypt; they are not to be sold in a slave sale."

Leviticus 25:42

"If the means of a stranger or of a sojourner with you becomes sufficient, and a countryman of yours becomes so poor with regard to him as to sell himself to a stranger who is sojourning with you, or to the descendants of a stranger's family, then he shall have redemption right after he has been sold. One of his brothers may redeem him, or his uncle, or his uncle's son, may redeem him, or one of his blood relatives from his family may redeem him; or if he prospers, he may redeem himself. He then with his purchaser shall calculate from the year when he sold himself to him up to the year of jubilee; and the price of his sale shall correspond to the number of years. It is like the days of a hired man that he shall be with him."

Leviticus 25:47–50

"**You will sell me food for money so that I may eat,** and give me water for money so that I may drink, only let me pass through on foot."

Deuteronomy 2:28

"You shall not eat anything which dies of itself. You may give it to the alien who is in your town, so that he may eat it, or you may sell it to a foreigner, for you are a holy people to the Lord your God. You shall not boil a kid in its mother's milk."

Deuteronomy 14:21

354

"It shall be, if you are not pleased with her, then you shall let her go wherever she wishes; but **you shall certainly not sell her for money,** you shall not mistreat her, because you have humbled her."

Deuteronomy 21:14

"If a man is caught **kidnapping** any of his countrymen of the sons of Israel, and he deals with him violently, or **sells him,** then that thief shall die; so you shall purge the evil from among you."

Deuteronomy 24:7

"The Lord will bring you back to Egypt in ships, by the way about which I spoke to you, 'You will never see it again!' And there **you shall offer yourselves for sale to your enemies** as male and female slaves, but there will be no buyer."

Deuteronomy 28:68

There was a great famine in Samaria; and behold, they besieged it, until **a donkey's head was sold for eighty shekels of silver,** and a fourth of a kab of dove's dung for five shekels of silver.

2 Kings 6:25

David said to Ornan, "**Give me the site of this threshing floor,** that I may build on it an altar to the Lord; for the full price you shall give it to me, that the plague may be restrained from the people."

1 Chronicles 21:22

Thou dost sell Thy people cheaply, and hast not profited by their sale.

Psalm 44:12

He who withholds grain, the people will curse him, but blessing will be on the head of him who sells it.

Proverbs 11:26

She makes linen garments and sells them, and supplies belts to the tradesmen.

Proverbs 31:24

"The time has come, the day has arrived. **Let not the buyer rejoice nor the seller mourn;** for wrath is against all their multitude. Indeed, the seller will not regain what he sold as long as they both live, for the vision regarding all their multitude will not be averted; nor will any of them maintain his life by his iniquity."

Ezekiel 7:12–13

"Since you have taken My silver and My gold, brought My precious treasures to your temples, and sold the sons of Judah and Jerusalem to the Greeks in order to remove them far from their territory, behold, I am going to arouse them from the place where you have sold them, and return your recompense on your head. Also **I will sell your sons and your daughters into the hand of the sons of Judah,** and they will sell them to the Sabeans, to a distant nations," for the Lord has spoken.

Joel 3:5–8

"Those who buy them slay them and go unpunished, and each of those who sell them says, 'Blessed be the Lord, for I have become rich!' And their own shepherds have no pity on them."

Zechariah 11:5

Jesus said to him, "**If you wish to be complete, go and sell your possessions** and give to the poor, and you shall have treasure in heaven; and come, follow Me."

Matthew 19:21

Jesus entered the temple and cast out all those who were buying and selling in the temple, and overturned the tables of the moneychangers and the seats of those who were selling doves. And He said to them, "It is written, 'My

356

house shall be called a house of prayer'; but you are making it a robbers' den."

Matthew 21:12–13

"This perfume might have been sold for a high price and the money given to the poor."

Matthew 26:9

They came to Jerusalem. And He entered the temple and began **to cast out those who were buying and selling** in the temple, and overturned the tables of the moneychangers and the seats of those who were selling doves.

Mark 11:15

"This perfume might have been sold for over three hundred denarii, and the money given to the poor." And they were scolding her.

Mark 14:5

"**Are not five sparrows sold for two cents?** And yet not one of them is forgotten before God."

Luke 12:6

He entered the temple and **began to cast out those who were selling,** saying to them, "It is written, '**And My house shall be a house of prayer,**' but you have made it a robbers' den."

Luke 19:45–46

He found in the temple those who were selling oxen and sheep and doves, and the moneychangers seated. And He made a scourge of cords, and **drove them all out of the temple,** with the sheep and the oxen; and He poured out the coins of the moneychangers, and overturned their tables; and to those who were selling the doves He said, "Take these things away; stop making My Father's house a house of merchandise."

John 2:14–16

A certain man named Ananias, with his wife Sapphira, sold a piece of property, and kept back some of the price for himself, with his wife's full knowledge, and bringing a portion of it, he laid it at the apostles' feet. But Peter said, "Ananias, why has Satan filled your heart to lie to the Holy Spirit, and to keep back some of the price of the land? While it remained unsold, did it not remain your own? And after it was sold, was it not under your control? Why is it that you have conceived this deed in your heart? You have not lied to men, but to God." And as he heard these words, Ananias fell down and breathed his last; and great fear came upon all who heard of it. And the young men arose and covered him up, and after carrying him out, they buried him. Now there elapsed an interval of about three hours, and his wife came in, not knowing what had happened. And Peter responded to her, "Tell me whether you sold the land for such and such a price?" And she said, "Yes, that was the price." Then Peter said to her, "Why is it that you have agreed together to put the Spirit of the Lord to the test? Behold, the feet of those who have buried your husband are at the door, and they shall carry you out as well." And she fell immediately at his feet, and breathed her last; and the young men came in and found her dead, and they carried her out and buried her beside her husband.

Acts 5:1–10

I heard as it were a voice in the center of the four living creatures saying, **"A quart of wheat for a denarius, and three quarts of barley for a denarius;** and do not harm the oil and the wine."

Revelation 6:6

WORK AND WAGES

This section involves labor and compensation. Perhaps nothing in America is more distorted than the topic of work and wages. Too often when young people come out of college they expect guaranteed employment and a ready-made position. Unfortunately, the world doesn't work that way. Ever since Adam and Eve were cast out of the Garden of Eden, it has been our lot to work.

Hopefully, if we know God's plan for our lives and we know what God has equipped us to do, our work also can be very satisfying. Not only can it provide the financial means to sustain our families, but it also can help in our spiritual growth in the Lord. The prerequisites to this are to know God's plan for our lives and to use the talents He has equipped us with.

There are many Scripture passages dealing with paying employees. God demands fairness in paying employees, as He does in everything else a Christian does. Christian employers have a responsibility to meet the minimum needs of their employees.

DILIGENCE

In the workplace, nothing is more important in a valued employee than to be diligent. Diligence is a work ethic; it means that you do the task set before you to the best of your ability in a timely fashion. Diligence encompasses honesty, purpose, energy, excellence, and working heartily.

Being diligent in financial matters requires the same honesty, purpose, and resolve as in the workplace—especially now that the world has become so complex. We must watch over even the smallest of expenditures.

"Of the gold, the silver and the bronze and the iron, there is no limit. **Arise and work, and may the Lord be with you.**"

1 Chronicles 22:16

He who gathers in summer is a son who acts wisely, but he who sleeps in harvest is a son who acts shamefully.

Proverbs 10:5

He who tills his land will have plenty of bread, but **he who pursues vain things lacks sense.**

Proverbs 12:11

The hand of the diligent will rule, but the slack hand will be put to forced labor.

Proverbs 12:24

The prudent sees the evil and hides himself, but the naive go on, and are punished for it.

Proverbs 22:3

He who tends the fig tree will eat its fruit; and he who cares for his master will be honored.

Proverbs 27:18

He who tills his land will have plenty of food, but he who follows empty pursuits will have poverty in plenty.

Proverbs 28:19

Whatever your hand finds to do, verily do it with all your might; for there is no activity or planning or wisdom in Sheol where you are going.

Ecclesiastes 9:10

Sow your seed in the morning, and do not be idle in the evening, for you do not know whether morning or evening sowing will succeed, or whether both of them alike will be good.

Ecclesiastes 11:6

It seemed good to Darius to appoint 120 satraps over the kingdom, that they should be in charge of the whole kingdom, and over them three commissioners (of whom Daniel was one), that these satraps might be accountable to them, and that the king might not suffer loss. Then this Daniel began distinguishing himself among the commissioners and satraps because **he possessed an extraordinary spirit, and the king planned to appoint him over the entire kingdom.**

Daniel 6:1–3

The Lord said, "Who then is the faithful and sensible steward, whom his master will put in charge of his servants, to give them their rations at the proper time?"

Luke 12:42

"Truly I say to you, that **he will put him in charge of all his possessions.**"

Luke 12:44

"I have coveted no one's silver or gold or clothes. You yourselves know that **these hands ministered to my own needs** and to the men who were with me. In everything I showed you that **by working hard** in this manner you must help the weak and remember the words of the Lord Jesus, that He Himself said, "It is more blessed to give than to receive."'

Acts 20:33–35

Whether, then, you eat or drink or whatever you do, **do all to the glory of God.**

1 Corinthians 10:31

Let us not lose heart in doing good, for in due time we shall reap if we do not grow weary.

Galatians 6:9

Whatever you do in word or deed, **do all in the name of the Lord Jesus,** giving thanks through Him to God the Father.

Colossians 3:17

Whatever you do, **do your work heartily,** as for the Lord rather than for men.

Colossians 3:23

Nor did we eat anyone's bread without paying for it, but with labor and hardship we kept working night and day so that we might not be a burden to any of you; not because we do not have the right to do this, but in order to offer ourselves as a model for you, that you might follow our example. For even when we were with you, we used to give you this order: **if anyone will not work, neither let him eat.**

2 Thessalonians 3:8–10

Whoever speaks, let him speak, as it were, the utterances of God; whoever serves, let him do so as by the strength which God supplies; **so that in all things God may be glorified** through Jesus Christ, to whom belongs the glory and dominion forever and ever. Amen.

1 Peter 4:11

For this very reason also, **applying all diligence, in your faith supply moral excellence,** and in your moral excellence, knowledge; and in your knowledge, self-control, and in your self-control, perseverance, and in your perseverance, godliness; and in your godliness, brotherly kindness, and in your brotherly kindness, love. For if these qualities are yours and are increasing, they render you neither useless or unfruitful in the true knowledge of our Lord Jesus Christ.

2 Peter 1:5–8

"I know your deeds, and your love and faith and service and perseverance, and that your deeds of late are greater than the first."

Revelation 2:19

EMPLOYEE/EMPLOYER

Quite often Christians are confused about the relationship between employees and employers. The relationship of an employer to an employee is one of authority. It is not a partnership; therefore, the relationship is not governed by the principles dealing with partnerships. God tells us that, without qualification, we are to honor the authorities placed above us.

On the other hand, employers are to treat employees fairly, whether dealing with working conditions or wages. Christians have a responsibility to obey the concepts and principles taught in God's Word and apply them—whether employee or employer.

Abram said to Lot, **"Please let there be no strife between you and me,** nor between my herdsmen and your herdsmen, for we are brothers."

Genesis 13:8

"Like a man hired year by year he shall be with him; he shall not rule over him with severity in your sight."

Leviticus 25:53

QUALITY

God's Word requires believers to make quality products and make them available at a fair price. Quality really means putting the best possible effort into whatever we are doing—whether it be a product or a service—because, by doing so, it reflects our value system.

There's nothing more honoring to God than quality service or a quality product from a professing Christian. And there's probably nothing more dishonoring to God than poor service or a poor quality product from a professing Christian.

Do you see a man skilled in his work? He will stand before kings; he will not stand before obscure men.

Proverbs 22:29

So that you may approve the things that are excellent, **in order to be sincere and blameless until the day of Christ;** having been filled with the fruit of righteousness which comes through Jesus Christ, to the glory and praise of God.

Philippians 1:10

Keep your **behavior excellent** among the Gentiles, so that in the things in which they slander you as evildoers, they may on account of your good deeds, as they observe them, glorify God in the day of visitation.

1 Peter 2:12

RESTITUTION

The most important relationship you have is between you and God. God's Word states that if you've cheated someone or deceived someone, you are to make restitution. To make restitution simply means to right a wrong and to restore. If you will establish an absolute standard that you'll retain no personal benefit as a result of deception, it will precondition your response to any temptation. This is especially true if you adopt the same restitution policy Zaccheus did—to repay 400 percent. It then becomes economically unprofitable to cheat or to deceive because you know that, ultimately, even more must be repaid.

"[He] who kidnaps a man, whether he sells him or he is found in his possession, shall surely be put to death."

Exodus 21:16

"If he gets up and walks around outside on his staff, then he who struck him shall go unpunished; **he shall only pay for his loss of time**, and shall take care of him until he is completely healed."

Exodus 21:19

"If, however, **he survives a day or two, no vengeance shall be taken;** for he is his property. And if men struggle with each other and strike a woman with child so that **she has a miscarriage,** yet there is no further injury, **he shall surely be fined as the woman's husband may demand of him**; and he shall pay as the judges decide."

Exodus 21:21–22

"If a ransom is demanded of him, then he shall give for the redemption of his life whatever is demanded of him."

Exodus 21:30

"If the ox gores a male or female slave, the owner shall give his or her master thirty shekels of silver, and the ox shall be stoned."

Exodus 21:32

"If a man steals an ox or a sheep, and slaughters it or sells it, he shall pay five oxen for the ox and four sheep for the sheep."

Exodus 22:1

"He shall surely make restitution; if he owns nothing, then he shall be sold for his theft. If what he stole is actually found alive in his possession, whether an ox or a donkey or a sheep, he shall **pay double."**

Exodus 22:3–4

"If a man lets a field or vineyard be grazed bare and lets his animal loose so that it grazes in another man's field, he shall make restitution from the best of his own field and the best of his own vineyard. **If a fire breaks out and spreads to thorn bushes,** so that stacked grain or the standing grain or the field itself is consumed, he who started the fire shall surely make restitution. **If a man gives his neighbor money or goods to keep for him,** and it is stolen from the man's house, if the thief is caught, he shall pay double. If the thief is not caught, then the owner of the house shall appear before the judges, to determine whether he laid his hands on his neighbor's property. **For every breach of trust,** whether it is for ox, for donkey, for sheep, for clothing, or for any lost thing about which one says, 'This is it,' the case of both parties shall come before the judges; he whom the judges condemn **shall pay double** to his neighbor."

Exodus 22:5–9

"If it is actually stolen from him, he shall make restitution to its owner. If it is all torn to pieces, let him bring it as evidence; he shall not make restitution for what has been torn to pieces. **And if a man borrows anything from his neighbor,** and it is injured or dies while its owner is not

368

with it, **he shall make full restitution.** If its owner is with it, he shall not make restitution; if it is hired, it came for its hire."

Exodus 22:12–15

"If her father absolutely refuses to give her to him, **he shall pay money equal to the dowry for virgins.**"

Exodus 22:17

"If a person acts unfaithfully and sins unintentionally against the Lord's holy things, then he shall bring his guilt offering to the Lord: a ram without defect from the flock, according to your valuation in silver by shekels, in terms of the shekel of the sanctuary, **for a guilt offering.**"

Leviticus 5:15

The Lord spoke to Moses, saying, "When a person sins and acts unfaithfully against the Lord, and deceives his companion **in regard to a deposit or a security entrusted to him, or through robbery,** or if he has extorted from his companion, or has found what was lost and lied about it and sworn falsely, so that he sins in regard to any one of the things a man may do; then it shall be, when he sins and becomes guilty, that he shall restore what he took by robbery, or what he got by extortion, or the deposit which was entrusted to him, or the lost thing which he found, or anything about which he swore falsely; **he shall make restitution for it in full, and add to it one-fifth more.** He shall give it to the one to whom it belongs on the day he presents his guilt offering."

Leviticus 6:1–5

"He shall confess his sins which he has committed, and he **shall make restitution in full** for his wrong, and add to it one-fifth of it, and give it to him whom he has wronged."

Numbers 5:7

"**They shall fine him a hundred shekels of silver** and give it to the girl's father, because he publicly defamed a virgin of

369

Israel. And she shall remain his wife; he cannot divorce her all his days."

Deuteronomy 22:19

"The man who lay with her shall give to the girl's father fifty shekels of silver, and she shall become his wife because he has violated her; he cannot divorce her all his days."

Deuteronomy 22:29

Joshua and all Israel with him, took Achan the son of Zerah, the silver, the mantle, the bar of gold, his sons, his daughters, his oxen, his donkeys, his sheep, his tent and all that belonged to him; and they brought them up to the valley of Achor. And Joshua said, "Why have you troubled us? The Lord will trouble you this day." And all Israel stoned them with stones; and they burned them with fire after they had stoned them with stones.

Joshua 7:24–25

"Here I am; bear witness against me before the Lord and His anointed. Whose ox have I taken, or whose donkey have I taken, or **whom have I defrauded? Whom have I oppressed,** or from whose hand have I taken a bribe to blind my eyes with it? **I will restore it to you.**"

1 Samuel 12:3

"A traveler came to the rich man, and he was unwilling to take from his own flock or his own herd, to prepare for the wayfarer who had come to him; **rather he took the poor man's ewe lamb and prepared it for the man who had come to him.**" Then David's anger burned greatly against the man, and he said to Nathan, "As the Lord lives, surely the man who has done this deserves to die. And he **must make restitution for the lamb fourfold,** because he did this thing and had no compassion."

2 Samuel 12:4–6

The Gibeonites said to him, "We have no concern of silver or gold with Saul or his house, nor is it for us to put any man to death in Israel." And he said, "I will do for you whatever you say."

2 Samuel 21:4

As the king passed by, he cried to the king and said, "Your servant went out into the midst of the battle; and behold, a man turned aside and brought a man to me and said, 'Guard this man; if for any reason he is missing, then your life shall be for his life, or else you shall pay a talent of silver.'"

1 Kings 20:39

"If therefore you are presenting your offering at the altar, and there remember that your brother has something against you, **leave your offering there before the altar,** and go your way; **first be reconciled** to your brother, and then come and present your offering. **Make friends quickly with your opponent at law** while you are with him on the way, in order that your opponent may not deliver you to the judge, and the judge to the officer, and you be thrown into prison. Truly I say to you, you shall not come out of there, until you have paid up the last cent."

Matthew 5:23–26

Zaccheus stopped and said to the Lord, "Behold, Lord, **half of my possessions I will give to the poor,** and if I have defrauded anyone of anything, I will give back four times as much." And Jesus said to him, "Today salvation has come to this house, because he, too, is a son of Abraham."

Luke 19:8–9

RETIREMENT

Retirement is something most of us have come to accept as an attainable goal after our working careers. In fact, since the advent of Social Security in the thirties, it has become an assumed right. Health care and extended life cycles have driven up the cost of retirement. People live longer, collect more benefits, and utilize more expensive life support systems. The demand for more taxes to support retirees places ever-increasing burdens on those who have not yet attained their "golden years." Consequently, the liabilities of retirement to society now far outweigh the assets.

The fear of doing without in the future causes many Christians to rob God's work of the very funds He has provided. God's Word does not prohibit, but rather encourages, saving for retirement. The keys to good planning for the future are found in the timeless wisdom of God's Word. Saving for retirement is another financial decision that can be made on the basis of God's principles.

"This is what applies to the Levites: from twenty-five years old and upward they shall enter to perform service in the work of the tent of meeting. But at the age of fifty years **they shall retire** from service in the work and not work any more."

Numbers 8:24–25

Trust in the Lord with all your heart, and do not lean on your own understanding. In all your ways acknowledge Him, and **He will make your paths straight.**

Proverbs 3:5–6

Go to the ant, O sluggard, observe her ways and be wise, which, having no chief, officer or ruler, prepares her food in the summer, and **gathers her provision** in the harvest.

Proverbs 6:6–8

By wisdom a house is built, and by understanding it is established; and **by knowledge the rooms are filled with all precious and pleasant riches.**

Proverbs 24:3–4

"A little sleep, a little slumber, a little folding of the hands to rest," then your poverty will come as a robber, and your want like an armed man.

Proverbs 24:33–34

"Do not be anxious then, saying 'What shall we eat?" or 'What shall we drink?' or 'With what shall we clothe ourselves?' For all these things the Gentiles eagerly seek; for your heavenly Father knows that you need all these things. But seek first His kingdom and His righteousness; and all these things shall be added to you. Therefore **do not be anxious for tomorrow;** for tomorrow will care for itself."

Matthew 6:31–34

Whether Paul or Apollos or Cephas or the world or life or death or things present or things to come; **all things belong to you, and you belong to Christ;** and Christ belongs to God.

1 Corinthians 3:22–23

Without faith it is impossible to please Him, for he who comes to God must believe that He is, and that **He is a rewarder of those who seek Him.**

Hebrews 11:6

He Himself has said, "I will never desert you, nor will I ever forsake you," so that we may confidently say, "**The Lord is my helper, I will not be afraid.**"

Hebrews 13:5–6

SLOTHFULNESS

When people are willing to just "get by," they are doing less than their best. Slothful employees do not perform to the extent of the abilities God has instilled within them. One by-product of being slothful is being a negative witness for the Lord Jesus Christ. In fact, a slothful Christian is one of the worst witnesses for the Lord.

Slothfulness is not limited to the workplace. Not being slothful includes keeping your home well, keeping your checkbook balanced, and living on a budget. All these show diligence—the opposite of slothfulness.

How long will you lie down, O sluggard? When will you arise from your sleep? "A little sleep, a little slumber, a little folding of the hands to rest"—and your poverty will come in like a vagabond, and your need like an armed man.

Proverbs 6:9–11

Poor is he who works with a negligent hand, but the hand of the diligent makes rich.

Proverbs 10:4

A slothful man does not roast his prey, but the precious possession of a man is diligence.

Proverbs 12:27

The soul of the sluggard craves and gets nothing, but the soul of the diligent is made fat.

Proverbs 13:4

Where no oxen are, the manger is clean, but much increase comes by the strength of the ox.

Proverbs 14:4

The way of the sluggard is as a hedge of thorns, but the path of the upright is a highway.

Proverbs 15:19

He also who is slack in his work is brother to him who destroys.

Proverbs 18:9

Laziness casts into a deep sleep, and an idle man will suffer hunger.

Proverbs 19:15

The sluggard buries his hand in the dish, and will not even bring it back to his mouth.

Proverbs 19:24

The sluggard does not plow after the autumn, so he begs during the harvest and has nothing.

Proverbs 20:4

Do not love sleep, lest you become poor; open your eyes and you will be satisfied with food.

Proverbs 20:13

The desire of the sluggard puts him to death, for his hands refuse to work; all day long he is craving, while the righteous gives and does not hold back.

Proverbs 21:25–26

The sluggard says, "There is a lion outside; I shall be slain in the streets."

Proverbs 22:13

The heavy drinker and the glutton will come to poverty.

Proverbs 23:21

If you are slack in the day of distress, your strength is limited.

Proverbs 24:10

I passed by the field of the sluggard, and by the vineyard of the man lacking sense; and behold, it was completely overgrown with thistles, its surface was covered with nettles, and its stone wall was broken down. When I saw, I reflected upon it; I looked, and received instruction. "A little sleep, a little slumber, a little folding of the hands to rest," then your poverty will come as a robber, and your want like an armed man.

Proverbs 24:30–34

The sluggard says, "There is a lion in the road! A lion is in the open square!" As the door turns on its hinges, **so does the sluggard** on his bed. **The sluggard buries his hand** in the dish; he is weary of bringing it to his mouth again. **The sluggard is wiser in his own eyes** than seven men who can give a discreet answer.

Proverbs 26:13–16

Even when we were with you, we used to give you this order; **if anyone will not work, neither let him eat.**

2 Thessalonians 3:10

WAGES

God's Word sets down many standards for how wages are to be earned and how they are to be paid. In the book of James, the Lord's brother warned against withholding pay from the laborers, whose outcry will reach the Lord. On the other hand, the Lord admonishes employees to give a fair day of work for a fair wage, without being concerned whether someone else is making more.

Remember the parable Christ gave us about the workers in the field: One was hired early in the morning for a certain wage and the other was hired late in the afternoon for the same wage. The first worker felt cheated because he had worked longer without greater compensation. The employer asked, "Was it not my money? Did I not have a right to do with that money whatever I desired? Did I give you less than I promised?"

Laban said to Jacob, "Because you are my relative, **should you therefore serve me for nothing? Tell me, what shall your wages be?**"

Genesis 29:15

In the days of wheat harvest Reuben went and found mandrakes in the field, and brought them to his mother Leah. Then Rachel said to Leah, "Please give me some of your son's mandrakes." But she said to her, "Is it a small matter for you to take my husband? And would you take my son's mandrakes also?"

Genesis 30:14–15

Leah said, "**God has given me my wages,** because I gave my maid to my husband." So she named him Issachar.

Genesis 30:18

"Give me my wives and my children for whom I have served you, and let me depart; for you yourself know my service which I have rendered you."

Genesis 30:26

He continued, **"Name me your wages,** and I will give it." But he said to him, "You yourself know how I have served you and how your cattle have fared with me. For you had little before I came, and it has increased to a multitude; and the Lord has blessed you wherever I turned. But now, when shall I provide for my own household also?" So he said, "What shall I give you?" And Jacob said, "You shall not give me anything. If you will do this one thing for me, I will again pasture and keep your flock: let me pass through your entire flock today, removing from there every speckled and spotted sheep, and every black one among the lambs, and the spotted and speckled among the goats, and such shall be my wages. So **my honesty will answer for me later, when you come concerning my wages.** Every one that is not speckled and spotted among the goats and black among the lambs, if found with me, will be considered stolen."

Genesis 30:28–32

"Yet **your father has cheated me and changed my wages ten times;** however, God did not allow him to hurt me. If he spoke thus, **'The speckled shall be your wages,'** then all the flock brought forth speckled; and if he spoke thus, **'The striped shall be your wages,'** then all the flock brought forth striped."

Genesis 31:7–8

"You changed my wages ten times, . . . God has seen my affliction and the toil of my hands, so He rendered judgment last night."

Genesis 31:41–42

Pharaoh's daughter said to her, **"Take this child** away and nurse him for me and **I shall give you your wages."** So the woman took the child and nursed him.

Exodus 2:9

"**You shall not oppress your neighbor,** nor rob him. The wages of a hired man are not to remain with you all night until morning."

Leviticus 19:13

"**All of you shall have the sabbath products of the land for food;** yourself, and your male and female slaves, and your hired man and your foreign resident, those who live as aliens with you."

Leviticus 25:6

"**If a countryman** of yours becomes so poor with regard to you that he **sells himself to you, you shall not subject him to a slave's service.** He shall be with you as a hired man, as if he were a sojourner; he shall serve with you until the year of jubilee."

Leviticus 25:39–40

"**You shall not oppress a hired servant who is poor and needy,** whether he is one of your countrymen or one of your aliens who is in your land in your towns. **You shall give him his wages** on his day before the sun sets, for he is poor and sets his heart on it; so that he may not cry against you to the Lord and it become sin in you."

Deuteronomy 24:14–15

Yet Gideon said to them, "**I would request of you, that each of you give me an earring from his spoil.**" (For they had gold earrings, because they were Ishmaelites.) And they said, "We will surely give them." So they spread out a garment, and every one of them threw an earring there from his spoil. And the weight of the gold earrings that he requested was 1,700 shekels of gold, besides the crescent ornaments and the pendants and the purple robes which were on the kings of Midian, and besides the neck bands that were on their camels' necks.

Judges 8:24–26

Micah then said to him, "**Dwell with me** and be a father and a priest to me, **and I will give you ten pieces of silver a**

Wages

year, a suit of clothes, and your maintenance." So the Levite went in.

Judges 17:10

"May the Lord reward your work, and **your wages be full from the Lord,** the God of Israel, under whose wings you have come to seek refuge."

Ruth 2:12

Then David said, "You must not do so, my brothers, with what the Lord has given us, who has kept us and delivered into our hand the band that came against us. And who will listen to you in this matter? For as his share is who goes down to the battle, **so shall his share be who stays by the baggage;** they shall share alike."

1 Samuel 30:23–24

"Now therefore, command that they cut for me cedars from Lebanon, and my servants will be with your servants; and **I will give you wages for your servants according to all that you say,** for you know that there is no one among us who knows how to cut timber like the Sidonians."

1 Kings 5:6

"Let them deliver it into the hand of the workmen who have the oversight of the house of the Lord, and **let them give it to the workmen who are in the house of the Lord to repair the damages of the house,** to the carpenters and the builders and the masons and for buying timber and hewn stone to repair the house. Only no accounting shall be made with them for the money delivered into their hands, for they deal faithfully." Then Hilkiah the high priest said to Shaphan the scribe, "I have found the book of the law in the house of the Lord." And Hilkiah gave the book to Shaphan who read it. And Shaphan the scribe came to the king and brought back word to the king and said, "Your servants have emptied out the money that was found in the house, and have delivered it into the hand of the workmen who have the oversight of the house of the Lord."

2 Kings 22:5–9

When the sons of Ammon saw that they had made themselves odious to David, Hanun and the **sons of Ammon sent 1,000 talents of silver to hire for themselves chariots and horsemen from Mesopotamia,** from Aram-maacah, and from Zobah. So they hired for themselves 32,000 chariots, and the king of Maacah and his people, who came and camped before Medeba. And the sons of Ammon gathered together from their cities and came to battle.

1 Chronicles 19:6–7

He hired also 100,000 valiant warriors out of Israel for one hundred talents of silver. But a man of God came to him saying, "O king, do not let the army of Israel go with you, for the Lord is not with Israel nor with any of the sons of Ephraim. But if you do go, do it, be strong for the battle; yet God will bring you down before the enemy, for God has the power to help and to bring down." And Amaziah said to the man of God, "But **what shall we do for the hundred talents which I have given to the troops of Israel?**" And the man of God answered, "The Lord has much more to give you than this."

2 Chronicles 25:6–9

They gave money to the masons and carpenters, and food, drink, and oil to the Sidonians and to the Tyrians, to bring cedar wood from Lebanon to the sea at Joppa, according to the permission they had from Cyrus king of Persia.

Ezra 3:7

For all this **I did not demand the governor's food allowance,** because the servitude was heavy on this people.

Nehemiah 5:18

All Israel in the days of Zerubbabel and Nehemiah gave the portions due the singers and the gatekeepers as each day required, and **set apart the consecrated portion for the Levites,** and the Levites set apart the consecrated portion for the sons of Aaron.

Nehemiah 12:47

"As a slave who pants for the shade, and **as a hired man who eagerly waits for his wages . . ."**

Job 7:2

The wages of the righteous is life, the income of the wicked, punishment.

Proverbs 10:16

"Woe to him who builds his house without righteousness and his upper rooms without justice, who uses his neighbor's services without pay and **does not give him his wages."**

Jeremiah 22:13

For his allowance, **a regular allowance was given him** by the king of Babylon, a daily portion all the days of his life until the day of his death.

Jeremiah 52:34

Son of man, Nebuchadnezzar king of Babylon made his army labor hard against Tyre; every head was made bald, and every shoulder was rubbed bare. But he and his army had no wages from Tyre for the labor that he had performed against it. Therefore, thus says the Lord God, "Behold, **I shall give the land of Egypt to Nebuchadnezzar** king of Babylon. And **he will carry off her wealth,** and capture her spoil and seize her plunder; and it will be wages for his army."

Ezekiel 29:18–19

I said to them, "If it is good in your sight, give me my wages; but if not never mind!" So **they weighed out thirty shekels of silver as my wages.** Then the Lord said to me, "Throw it to the potter, that magnificent price at which I was valued by them." So I took the thirty shekels of silver and threw them to the potter in the house of the Lord.

Zechariah 11:12–13

"I will draw near to you for judgment; and I will be a swift witness against the sorcerers and against the adulterers and against those who swear falsely, and **against those who oppress the wage earner in his ways,** the widow and the orphan, and those who turn aside the alien, and do not fear Me," says the Lord of hosts.

Malachi 3:5

"Do not acquire gold, or silver, or copper for your money belts, or a bag for your journey, or even two tunics, or sandals, or a staff; for **the worker is worthy of his support.**"

Matthew 10:9–10

Some soldiers were questioning him, saying, "And what about us, what shall we do?" And he said to them, "**Do not take money from anyone by force,** or accuse anyone falsely, and be content with your wages."

Luke 3:14

"Stay in that house, eating and drinking what they give you; for **the laborer is worthy of his wages.** Do not keep moving from house to house."

Luke 10:7

The wages of sin is death, but the free gift of God is eternal life in Christ Jesus our Lord.

Romans 6:23

Who at any time serves as a soldier at his own expense? Who plants a vineyard, and does not eat the fruit of it? Or who tends a flock and does not use the milk of the flock?

1 Corinthians 9:7

It is written in the Law of Moses, "**You shall not muzzle the ox while he is threshing.**" God is not concerned about oxen, is He? Or is He speaking altogether for our sake? Yes, for our sake it was written, because the plowman ought to plow in hope, and the thresher to thresh **in hope of sharing the crops.** If we sowed spiritual things in you, is it too much if we should reap material things from you?

1 Corinthians 9:9–11

The Lord directed those who proclaim the gospel to get their living from the gospel.

1 Corinthians 9:14

Or did I commit a sin in humbling myself that you might be exalted, because I preached the gospel of God to you without charge? **I robbed other churches, taking wages from them to serve you;** and when I was present with you and was in need, I was not a burden to anyone; for when the brethren came from Macedonia, they fully supplied my need, and in everything I kept myself from being a burden to you, and will continue to do so.

2 Corinthians 11:7–9

The Scripture says, "**You shall not muzzle the ox while he is threshing,**" and "The laborer is worthy of his wages."

1 Timothy 5:18

Behold, the pay of the laborers who mowed your fields, and which has been withheld by you, cries out against you; and the outcry of those who did the harvesting has reached the ears of the Lord of Sabaoth.

James 5:4

They bear witness to your love before the church; and **you will do well to send them on their way in a manner worthy of God.** For they went out for the sake of the Name, accepting nothing from the Gentiles.

3 John 6–7

WORK

There's a balance needed in work. It is not unusual for a person building a business to work 80-hour weeks, and in some cases 100. It's true that a 40-hour work week will rarely, if ever, build a successful business, but 100 hours of work reflects a gross imbalance of priorities. No one can maintain the correct balance between work, family, and God if he or she is working more than 60 hours per week. There may be periods when excess working hours are necessary, but usually relationships suffer during these times. If you cannot apply the right priority to your time, ask God to give you the wisdom to maintain the correct priorities or remove the temptation by shutting down the business.

All work we do should be as unto the Lord so that when people see us they literally see Christ through us. That can be a very positive witness for the Lord or it can be a very negative witness. What God expects from His people is common sense, diligence, and excellence in their work.

The Lord God took the man and put him into **the garden of Eden to cultivate it** and keep it.

Genesis 2:15

It came about **on the seventh day that some of the people went out to gather, but they found none.** Then the Lord said to Moses, "How long do you refuse to keep My commandments and My instructions?"

Exodus 16:27–28

"Six days you shall labor and do all your work."

Exodus 20:9

"**If a priest buys a slave** as his property with his money, that one may eat of it, and those who are born in his house may eat of his food."

Leviticus 22:11

"**For six days work may be done;** but on the seventh day there is a sabbath of complete rest, a holy convocation. You shall not do any work; it is a sabbath to the Lord in all your dwellings."

Leviticus 23:3

"You shall thus consecrate the fiftieth year and proclaim it a release through the land to all its inhabitants. **It shall be a jubilee for you, and each of you shall return to his own property, and each of you shall return to his family.**"

Leviticus 25:10

King Solomon levied forced laborers from all Israel; and the forced laborers numbered 30,000 men. And he sent them to Lebanon, 10,000 a month in relays; they were in Lebanon a month and two months at home. And Adoniram was over the forced laborers. Now Solomon had 70,000 transporters, and 80,000 hewers of stone in the mountains.

1 Kings 5:13–15

Moreover, from the day that I was appointed to be their governor in the land of Judah, from the twentieth year to the thirty-second year of King Artaxerxes, for twelve years, neither I nor my kinsmen have eaten the governor's food allowance. But the former governors who were before me laid burdens on the people and took from them bread and wine besides forty shekels of silver; even their servants domineered the people. But I did not do so because of the fear of God. And I also **applied myself to the work on this wall;** we did not buy any land, and all my servants were gathered there for the work.

Nehemiah 5:14–16

"Is not man forced to labor on earth, and are not his days like the days of a hired man?"

Job 7:1

A worker's appetite works for him, for his hunger urges him on.

Proverbs 16:26

Every man who eats and drinks sees good in all his labor— it is the gift of God.

Ecclesiastes 3:13

Here is what I have seen to be good and fitting: to eat, to drink and **enjoy oneself in all one's labor** in which he toils under the sun during the few years of his life which God has given him; for this is his reward. Furthermore, as **for every man to whom God has given riches and wealth, He has also empowered him to eat from them** and receive his reward and rejoice in his labor; this is the gift of God.

Ecclesiastes 5:18–19

So I said, "**Wisdom is better than strength.**" But the wisdom of the poor man is despised and his words are not heeded.

Ecclesiastes 9:16

"Let your light shine before men in such a way that they may see your good works, and glorify your Father who is in heaven."

Matthew 5:16

He said to them, "What man shall there be among you, who shall have one sheep, and if it falls into a pit on the Sabbath, will he not take hold of it, and lift it out?

Matthew 12:11

Simon Peter said to them, "I am going fishing." They said to him, "We will also come with you." They went out, and got into the boat; and that night they caught nothing.

John 21:3

A certain woman named Lydia, from the city of Thyatira, a seller of purple fabrics, a worshiper of God, was listening; and the Lord opened her heart to respond to things spoken by Paul.

Acts 16:14

Because he was of the same trade, he stayed with them and they were working; for by their trade they were tent-makers.

Acts 18:3

Let him who steals steal no longer; but rather **let him labor, performing with his own hands what is good,** in order that he may have something to share with him who has need.

Ephesians 4:28

Whatever you do, **do your work heartily,** as for the Lord rather than for men.

Colossians 3:23

Make it your ambition to lead a quiet life and attend to your own business and work with your hands, just as we commended you; so that you may behave properly toward outsiders and **not be in any need.**

1 Thessalonians 4:11–12

You yourselves know how you ought to follow our example, because we did not act in an undisciplined manner among you, **nor did we eat anyone's bread without paying for it,** but with labor and hardship we kept working night and day so that we might not be a burden to any of you.

2 Thessalonians 3:7–8

Even when we were with you, we used to give you this order: **if anyone will not work, neither let him eat.**

2 Thessalonians 3:10

No soldier in active service **entangles himself in the affairs of everyday life,** so that he may please the one who enlisted him as a soldier.

2 Timothy 2:4

The hard-working farmer ought to be the first to receive his share of the crops.

2 Timothy 2:6

YOKE

In the Old Testament there are two distinct types of yokes presented. One is a collar used on slaves to show their total subjugation. The second is a harness used to link two working animals together, usually oxen. Once connected by the yoke, the slaves or oxen were no longer two who could choose to go their own way; rather, they became one working unit bound together for the purpose of accomplishing a task.

This analogy can be applied to marriage or to business partners. In either situation, two have bound themselves together and each is individually and jointly reliable for each action of the marriage or the business. God admonishes us not to be yoked together with unbelievers, because we have different value systems. People with opposite goals and values will not be compatible. Differing values will ultimately create conflicts.

Do not be bound together with unbelievers; for what partnership have righteousness and lawlessness, or what fellowship has light with darkness? Or what harmony has Christ with Belial, or what has a believer in common with an unbeliever?

2 Corinthians 6:14–15

PART TWO

SCRIPTURE INDEX

Christian
Financial
Concepts

Teaching God's Principles of Handling Money

Larry Burkett, founder and president of Christian Financial Concepts, is the best-selling author of more than a dozen books on business and personal finances. He also hosts two radio programs broadcast on hundreds of stations worldwide.

Larry holds degrees in marketing and finance, and for several years served as a manager in the space program at Cape Canaveral, Florida. He also has been vice president of an electronics manufacturing firm. Larry's education, business experience, and solid understanding of God's Word enable him to give practical, Bible-based financial counsel to families, churches, and businesses.

Founded in 1976, Christian Financial Concepts is a nonprofit, nondenominational ministry dedicated to helping God's people gain a clear understanding of how to manage their money according to scriptural principles. While practical assistance is provided on many levels, the purpose of CFC is simply *to bring glory to God by freeing His people from financial bondage so they may serve Him to their utmost.*

One major avenue of ministry involves the training of volunteers in budget and debt counseling and linking them with financially troubled families and individuals through a nationwide referral network. CFC also provides financial management seminars and workshops for churches and other groups. (Formats available include audio, video, video with moderator, and live instruction.) A full line of printed and audio-visual materials related to money management is available through CFC's materials department (1-800-722-1976).

For further information about the ministry of Christian Financial Concepts, write to:

Christian Financial Concepts
P.O. Box 2377
Gainesville, Georgia 30503-2377